# THE STORY OF CANADA

# THE STORY OF CANADA

GEORGE W. BROWN, PH.D., F.R.S.C.
    Professor of History, University of Toronto

ELEANOR HARMAN, M.A..
    Associate Editor and Production Manager, University of Toronto Press

MARSH JEANNERET, B.A.
    Editor of Textbooks for the Publishers


DESIGNED AND EDITED BY THE AUTHORS. PICTURES AND MAPS BY
VIRGINIA BYERS, A.O.C.A. AND MARGARET SALISBURY, A.O.C.A.
ART EDITOR, SYLVIA BROWN


This edition published 2020
by Living Book Press

First published in 1950.

ISBN: 978-1-922348-10-4

All rights reserved. No part of this publication may be reproduced, stored in a retrieval system, or transmitted in any other form or means – electronic, mechanical, photocopying, recording or otherwise, without the prior permission of the copyright owner and the publisher or as provided by Australian law.

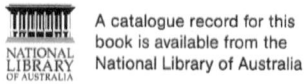

A catalogue record for this book is available from the National Library of Australia

TO THOSE CANADIANS

WHO BEST LOVED THE STORY OF CANADA

AMONG WHOM WAS

A LIEUTENANT IN THE

ROYAL CANADIAN CORPS OF SIGNALS

# FOREWORD

THIS book was begun in the classrooms which the authors have visited in each province of Canada, from British Columbia to Newfoundland. Frequently, teachers described with enthusiasm supplementary books—most of which were story-books—admitting their inadequacies, but pointing out how powerfully they impressed their contents upon the minds of boys and girls. The usual textbook narratives were, of course, intended to be read and remembered; stories were always read, and remembered.

Could a basic elementary history be written in story form and still maintain historical perspective throughout? The authors decided to try. The task has been a labour of love from beginning to end.

The decision to use stories complicated the problem of writing for two reasons. All the units had to be closely woven together into a clear historical pattern; and every story had to be a good story as well as good history. The historical outline, therefore, became a framework into which the stories were made to fit; this framework is shown in the table of contents. The stories themselves were tested in the classroom, where they were read by pupils and played from special gramophone recordings.

There are many kinds of stories, and many ways of telling them. A story can be told as a third-person narrative, or as an eye-witness account by a person who might have been on the scene or might even have participated in the action. It can also be related in a series of letters or entries in a diary, or even in dramatized form so that it may be re-enacted by its readers.

Almost any of the stories in this book might be rewritten in two or three ways. It is intended that pupils be encouraged to try such experiments of rewriting. Fictional characters and imaginative settings might be added, and the vividness of the history enhanced thereby. This has already been done with some of the stories, as teachers will easily recognize, but no real liberties have been taken with the original source materials on which the stories are based.

The topics have been selected carefully, in an attempt to picture impartially the people of Canada yesterday and to-day in all provinces of the nation. At the same time a serious attempt has been made to correlate the story of our own country with that of the United States, and to impart a sympathetic understanding of our relations with our neighbour.

The book is divided into thirty-seven units—approximately the number of weeks in the school year. The units vary in length according to the kind of presentation selected. Although the stories reflect the contemporary idiom as far as possible, the vocabulary has been restricted (for the greater part to the fifth-year level according to the Lorge scale), with a moderate and uniform increase in difficulty towards the end of the book.

Much of the customary constitutional terminology of a history textbook does not appear in this book. Instead, the authors have sought to develop important concepts through the stories, providing labels only where labels seemed really helpful, and only after the idea had been made sufficiently clear. The official names of some Acts of Parliament and peace treaties, the multiplication of which can confuse and discourage young students, have also been avoided. However, in order that such topics may be readily located by teachers, they have been included in the index, to be found by those who look for them.

The arrangement of the text is chronological, and events have been related to contemporary history whenever this seemed likely to orient the pupil better than mere dates.

Material for the pictures has been obtained from contemporary drawings, portraits, photographs, and prints; from historical reconstructions; and from personal observation by the authors at historic places. The authors are greatly indebted to the Public Archives of Canada, to the governments of all the provinces, and to many industrial organizations, for assistance in securing prints and photostats to guide the artists in preparing the illustrations and maps.

The very warm thanks of the authors go also to the teachers, and to the pupils, who experimented with much of the material in this volume.

A special note of thanks is due the Directors of the Copp Clark Co. Limited, who asked the authors to help them produce a story history of Canada "that will always open at a picture", and who have agreed to every suggestion technical improvement during the several years of preparation.

G.W.B.<br>
E.H.<br>
M.J.

# CONTENTS

*The Story Of New France*

| | | |
|---|---|---|
| 1. | The White Man Comes To Canada | 2 |
| | How The Cabots Found The Cod-Banks | 5 |
| | The Second Voyage | 9 |
| | Jacques Cartier Finds The St. Lawrence Gateway | 12 |
| | The Discovery Of Hudson Bay | 18 |
| 2. | The First "Canadians" | 22 |
| | The Indians Of Canada | 23 |
| | Natives Of The North--The Eskimos | 38 |
| 3. | The Coming of the French | 43 |
| | The Bay Of Fundy | 44 |
| | The Founding Of Quebec | 48 |
| | Making Enemies For New France | 50 |
| | Champlain Explores Ontario | 52 |
| 4. | "For the Glory of God" | 56 |
| | The Black Robes | 58 |
| | The Story of Montreal. | 61 |
| | The Fate of The Huron Missions | 64 |
| | How Daulac Saved The Colony | 65 |
| 5. | The French in Arcadia | 69 |
| | The Heroine Of Acadia | 71 |
| | Changing Hands In Acadia | 73 |

| 6. | Canada Under the Old Regime | 75 |
|---|---|---|
| | The May-Pole | 77 |
| | "Black-Market" In Furs | 82 |
| | The Great Intendant | 84 |
| | A Visit To Quebec, 1666 | 87 |
| 7. | The Coming of the "Adventurers" | 93 |
| | The Story Of Radisson And Groseilliers | 95 |
| | The Founding Of The Great Company | 97 |
| | Iberville The Conqueror | 101 |
| 8. | The Fighting Governor | 108 |
| | "By The Mouths Of My Cannon!" | 109 |
| 9. | To the Heart of the Continent | 113 |
| | La Salle On The Upper Lakes | 116 |
| | Down The Mississippi | 119 |
| | The Discovery Of The Great Plains | 122 |
| | The Story Of The La Vérendryes | 124 |

## The Story of British Canada

| 10. | The British In North America | 129 |
|---|---|---|
| | The Thirteen Colonies | 129 |
| | The Founding Of Halifax, 1749 | 133 |
| | Three Letters From Acadia | 139 |
| 11. | The Seven Years' War | 146 |
| | The Story Of A British Defeat | 146 |
| | Wolfe And Montcalm | 151 |
| 12. | After the British Victory | 157 |
| | The Second Battle Of The Plains | 157 |
| | The War Chief Of The Ottawas | 161 |

| | | |
|---|---|---|
| 13. | The American Revolution | 165 |
| | The Invasion Of Canada | 168 |
| | The Father Of His Country | 173 |
| 14. | "His Majesty's Loyal Subjects" | 175 |
| | The Loyalists In The Maritimes | 176 |
| | The Loyalists In Canada | 179 |
| | "The Diary Of Mrs. Simcoe" | 181 |
| 15. | Furs of Empire | 186 |
| | To The North-West | 189 |
| 16. | To the West Coast | 196 |
| | Overland To The Pacific | 200 |
| | Across The Rockies | 205 |
| 17. | The War of 1812-1814 | 208 |
| | The Story Of A Shawnee Chief | 211 |
| | "At Queenston Heights" | 214 |
| | An Even Struggle | 217 |
| 18. | The Red River Colony | 221 |
| | The Story of Lord Selkirk | 222 |
| | The End Of Fur Trade Rivalry | 227 |
| 19. | Settlers from Overseas | 228 |
| | Steerage Diary, 1832 | 230 |
| | Upper Canada, 1832 | 238 |
| 20. | Ruling Our Law-Makers | 242 |
| | The Little Rebel | 244 |
| | The Struggle In Lower Canada | 250 |
| | Nova Scotia's Great Leader | 253 |
| | The Cry For Reform | 257 |
| 21. | "Government by the People" | 258 |
| | A Famous Report | 260 |
| | "Cabinet" Government | 262 |
| | Lord Elgin's Decision | 264 |

| | | |
|---|---|---|
| 22. | The Story Of British Columbia | 269 |
| | On The Cariboo Road | 272 |
| 23. | Life Across the Colonies a Century Ago | 278 |
| | Spring Journey, 1844 | 279 |
| | The Coming Change | 286 |
| | Provincial Fair, 1852 | 287 |

## *The Growth of a Nation*

| | | |
|---|---|---|
| 24. | Building a Dominion | 298 |
| | "Let Us Be United" | 299 |
| | John A. Macdonald And Confederation | 302 |
| | The Law That Made A Nation | 305 |
| 25. | "Dominion from Sea to Sea" | 308 |
| | Two New Provinces | 314 |
| 26. | "Scarlet and Gold" | 315 |
| | The North-West Rebellion | 318 |
| | Steel Of Empire | 321 |
| | The Mounted Police To-Day | 326 |
| 27. | The Growth of the West | 328 |
| | Western Pioneer | 331 |
| | Alberta And Saskatchewan Become Provinces | 337 |
| 28. | "Growing Up" | 338 |
| | Queen Victoria's Diamond Jubilee | 339 |
| | The "Golden Age" | 342 |
| | Canada In World War I | 344 |
| 29. | Canada Comes of Age | 347 |
| | How Canada Helped Win World War II | 352 |

| | | |
|---|---|---|
| 30. | "Cornerstone of Empire" | 357 |
| | The Voice Of Newfoundland | 358 |
| | The Story Of Newfoundland | 366 |
| 31. | The Story of Travel in Canada | 372 |
| | Waterways To Settlement | 372 |
| | Digging The Canals | 376 |
| | The Coming Of The Steamboat | 377 |
| | From Indian Trail To Super-Highway | 380 |
| | New Roads To Confederation | 381 |

## *Living Across Canada*

| | | |
|---|---|---|
| 32. | Food for the World | 383 |
| | "Our Daily Bread" | 387 |
| | "Wheat Begins To Move" | 390 |
| 33. | Harvest of the Waters | 395 |
| | Newfoundland Sealing | 398 |
| | "Salmon Is King" | 398 |
| | Fresh-Water Fishing | 400 |
| 34. | The New Fur Trade | 401 |
| | Fur Trapping In Canada To-Day | 402 |
| | Fur Farming In Canada To-Day | 404 |
| 35. | Buried Treasure | 407 |
| | The New North | 413 |
| 36. | Turning Trees into Dollars | 415 |
| 37. | Wheels of Industry | 422 |
| | Canada Buys And Sells | 423 |
| INDEX | | 425 |

THE story of our young country is a thrilling adventure from beginning to end. Of course, every story can be told in many ways, and there are many kinds of adventure stories in this book. Some are told by those who saw them happen, some are told by the very people to whom they happened. Still others are told as if they were taking place in front of us. Often, we shall read what the Indians or explorers or leaders were saying; we shall be able to "act out" these stories again ourselves.

Although this is a story-history, it cannot tell all the splendid stories of Canada's past. The authors hope that it will make boys and girls hungry for still more stories, especially those about their home communities. For no part of Canada is without its own stories, although many of these tales have yet to be put into books.

We hope, too, that some boy or girl who reads this book will one day make the stiff climb from Sous-le-Fort to the ramparts and, looking down, see just what Pierre saw in the year 1666. We hope that another will stand with Guy on the citadel above Halifax and pick out the lines of the old town-site below. We hope that still another will revisit Fort Victoria with Governor Douglas or sail downstream with Alexander Mackenzie or hear the cannon roar from Queenston Heights.

If these things can happen, this story is not yet finished.
*The Authors*

## THE WHITE MAN COMES TO CANADA

A thousand years ago, the people of Europe knew very little about the rest of the world. Their wisest geographers would have been amazed by what any boy or girl to-day could teach them about the map of the world. They still believed that the earth was flat. Although their maps showed unexplored lands stretching south and east of Europe, the dangerous waters of the Atlantic Ocean still marked the western boundary of the world they knew.

Yet the shores of North America were visited by white men from Europe at about this time in history—almost a thousand years ago.

These first newcomers were Norsemen—bold sea-rovers from the coasts of Norway who already had planted colonies in Iceland and Greenland. Their large, open-decked vessels, each driven by a single large sail and rowed by as many as fifty warriors, were the most sea-worthy craft that had yet been invented. The farmers and villagers who lived along the shores of Europe had long before learned to fear the savage Norse landing parties which might sweep in at any moment to lay waste to settlements near the coasts. At last, during one of their early voyages from Iceland to Greenland, some of these hardy Norse seafarers were blown within sight of North America itself. This happened shortly before A.D. 1000.

The Norse colonists in Greenland were excited to hear that one of their ships had found a forest-covered land to the southwest, for there was no timber at all in the cold, bleak land in which they had made their homes. It was not long before they sent further expeditions to explore the strange coasts. We are told that one party of these Norse explorers came ashore at a place where wild fruit was growing in abundance. They called the new country "Vineland", and decided that some of their people should be sent to it to build another colony. It is quite likely that they had reached an eastern part of Canada, later to become one of the beautiful Maritime provinces.

The story of the Norse settlements in North America was not written down until many years later, and by that time the homes the Norsemen had built in Canada no longer existed.

For this reason, we cannot be sure exactly where Vineland was, or why the colonies did not last. It is said, however, that many boat-loads of lumber were shipped from Vineland to Greenland, and if this is so, Canada's export business began a long time ago! If the Norsemen had carried home rich cargoes of gold and silver, or even if they had brought rich loads of furs and fish to the market-places of Europe, we may be sure that the race to explore the New World would have begun right away. They had found a land filled with untold riches; but they did not know this and so the story of the Norsemen did not spread rapidly in Europe. Several more centuries passed before the secrets of the New World began to unfold, and even then they were only learned slowly, one by one.

## HOW THE CABOTS FOUND THE COD-BANKS

Henry Tudor, King of England, smoothed out the map which Master John Cabot had spread before him. The English admirals crowded closer as His Majesty studied it again. John Cabot had just finished describing an amazing voyage of discovery that he had recently completed in the little ship *Mathew*, and now he stood anxiously waiting to hear what King Henry would say.

The map which so interested the King had been drawn by John Cabot since his return to Bristol. It showed the northern part of the Atlantic Ocean. To be sure, it did not look much like the maps of the North Atlantic which we find in our atlases today. But this was the year 1497, and a vast amount of exploring had still to be done before anyone could draw a true map of the world. To Henry VII and his courtiers, however, the important thing about John Cabot's new map was that it showed lands lying west of England in the Atlantic Ocean—lands that had never been mapped before!

King Henry recognized, of course, the Danish island of Iceland, because his Bristol merchants had been carrying on a brisk trade with its people for many years. It was these merchants of Bristol who had fitted out the little vessel *Mathew* for John Cabot's voyage into the West the spring before. If Cabot's story were true, it seemed that they had risked their money wisely. King Henry had not been so hopeful at that time himself. But now he could not help smiling as he recalled that one-fifth of all profits made by trading with China and Japan were to be paid to the Crown. And John Cabot insisted that it was the land of the Great Khan that he had reached by sailing across the Atlantic Ocean!

"How many days out of Bristol to these parts did you say, Master John?" demanded King Henry, as he pointed to the left-hand edge of the map.

"Fifty days, Your Majesty," replied the master-pilot. "But the voyage, it will be shorter, since we know now where to go." John Cabot did not speak perfect English, for he had been born in Italy and had come to live in England only recently. But he did understand the art of sailing, as he had spent most of his forty years at sea.

"You met no one at all?" asked the King.

"As I have explained, Your Majesty, we did not carry sufficient provisions to stay longer off the new coasts. If that had been possible, I doubtless should have reached the winter palace of the Great Khan himself, which Marco Polo, the Venetian, saw two hundred years ago."

"Then what saw you of value, if anything?" demanded King Henry. "I care not, Master John, for emptying the royal treasury now to map the lonely coasts you have described."

"—The waters, Your Majesty! Those seas are full of fish, which are not only to be caught in nets, but even in baskets if stones are tied to them first to sink them into the water. We

"AT MECCA I SAW MANY CARAVANS FROM INDIA"

can take so many fish that this kingdom will no longer need to trade with Iceland. The dried fish they call the stock-fish, which we now bring from Iceland, is much like the cod that are so plentiful off the new land."

"We already have greater fisheries off our own coasts, Master John, than can be found anywhere else in the world."

"Until this summer, that was true, Your Majesty. But these waters I have visited were so full of fish that sometimes they slowed the motion of our vessel!"

King Henry frowned, as if to say he did not believe.

"You feel certain, Master John, that by sailing west as you have done, you have reached China itself?" asked King Henry.

"Your Majesty," answered Cabot, "I myself crossed the Holy Land to Arabia many years ago, while trading in the Eastern Mediterranean. At Mecca, the Holy City of the Arabs, I saw many caravans laden with spices, silks, and rich ornaments, arriving from India. I asked many careful questions about where these things were made, and the people of Mecca told me they

did not know. But some of the traders there told me that they came from a great, great distance beyond India itself. When I think how far east I then was from this happy kingdom of yours, Your Majesty, I do not find it hard to believe that those spices and silks had been brought overland more than half way around the world. If they came from China, then China must be much closer to us in the West than in the East. This is why I know that I have reached the shores of Asia on the other side of the Atlantic Ocean, Your Majesty."

"You are sure these are not the lands claimed by Columbus for my Spanish cousin, King Ferdinand?" went on King Henry.

"Fear not, Your Majesty," replied Cabot. "The shores I have visited this summer have never before been charted. That is why I claimed them in your name. The English flag is certainly the first Christian banner ever to fly over the new land, and I raised it there myself."

King Henry was satisfied. "How many ships did you say would be needed for your voyage next spring, Master John?" he asked.

"If the merchants this time will let me have six vessels," replied John Cabot enthusiastically, "they will be weighed down to the water's edge with the riches of the Orient when I return!"

King Henry's eyes sparkled, but he paused to think. At last he replied.

"The traders will have to pay for the ships and provisions, of course. But we shall give orders that what you ask must be granted, Master John, and you will have your choice of any vessels lying in our ports."

## THE SECOND VOYAGE

For the whole of the winter which followed, John Cabot was the hero of London. Everyone was sure that Asia had been reached and none was more sure than John Cabot himself. People called him "the Great Admiral", and were quick to believe him when he promised great riches to those who were chosen to go with him the next spring.

Of course, everyone was doomed to disappointment.

Like Columbus five years earlier, John Cabot thought that he had travelled all the way to the Far East by sailing west. Although people were willing to believe that the earth must be round, no one in those days knew how large it really is. If Cabot could have known that he had travelled only one-fifth of the distance to China on his first voyage, he might have guessed that he had discovered an entirely new continent.

Early in May, 1498, the little English fleet set sail from Bristol. This time John Cabot took his son, Sebastian, with him. The merchants, who paid for the expedition, ordered the vessels laden with "cloth, laces, and other trifles" to trade with the people of China.

By midsummer, the vessels were in sight of a rocky, northern coast and their way was blocked by icebergs. Surely this is not the land that Marco Polo visited, thought John Cabot. Turning south, the little fleet skirted the eastern shores of what is now Canada until they were sailing along the Atlantic coast of the present-day United States of America.

We do not know exactly how this second voyage of John Cabot to North America ended, but it is not hard to guess. It is likely that the ships made their way back to England, one by one, their sailors and passengers filled with feelings of bitter disappointment. Perhaps they still believed that they had visited some part of Asia, for the idea that a vast new continent lay across the North Atlantic took root only slowly in the years that followed.

But even if King Henry VII and the merchants of Bristol who paid for these first expeditions believed that John Cabot had failed, we know to-day how important his voyages really were. We cannot be certain of the exact place where Cabot landed, but the flag of England flew over Canadian soil only five years after the discovery of the New World by Columbus.

A VISIT TO "NEW-FOUND-LAND," ABOUT 1740

Although many years passed before Englishmen crossed the Atlantic Ocean to make their homes in the lands that John Cabot had discovered, one part of the story he had told about his travels brought quick results. For the fishermen of England, and of the other countries of western Europe as well, were quite willing to brave the dangers of the Atlantic crossing to cast their nets in the rich waters that Cabot had described. Soon after 1497, the year of John Cabot's first voyage, fishing-fleets were setting out every spring to spend the summer over the great fishing banks that lie off the eastern coast of Nova Scotia, south of Newfoundland.

Until the time of John Cabot, the vast expanse of the North Atlantic had been a barrier that stood between the Old World and the New. Now the mysteries of this once unending ocean had been explained. It was the forest-covered coasts that lay close by the new fishing grounds which now held secrets for further adventurers. Were these the shores of Asia? Were they islands that lay between Europe and Asia? The only way to find out was to begin explorations inland. That was to be the next step.

## JACQUES CARTIER FINDS THE ST. LAWRENCE GATEWAY

Five years before John Cabot's first voyage, Christopher Columbus had startled Europe by proving that strange lands, inhabited by strange peoples, lay at the western edge of the Atlantic Ocean. Although Columbus believed that these lands were part of Asia, John Cabot and the other explorers who followed him to the New World were of course unable to find the land of the Great Khan. However, the adventurers of Spain and Portugal who invaded the lands about the Caribbean quickly realized that riches were to be had there after all. Before long, the South Atlantic sea-lanes flashed white with the sails of Spanish galleons—many of them weighed down with gold and silver taken from the Indians of Mexico and Peru.

Even before John Cabot first crossed the Atlantic, the Spaniards and Portuguese laid claim to the whole of the New World. However, they did not try to extend their empires far beyond the Caribbean lands, which contained such treasures of gold and silver. It was not very long, therefore, until the kings of

other European countries began to say to themselves: "Perhaps the new lands *do* prevent us from sending our merchant fleets straight west to the rich lands of China and Japan. But even if this New World has no silks and spices, it is possible that the Spaniards and Portuguese have not yet seized *all* the wealth of the New World."

Certainly we know what one ruler in Europe had to say—Francis the First, King of France:

"So!" he jeered, "my cousins in

Spain and Portugal are trying to divide the whole New World between themselves! I should very much like to see the clause in our father Adam's will which leaves America to them." King Francis was keenly anxious to learn more about the mysterious lands that lay across the Atlantic.

Early in 1534, therefore, two little French vessels set sail from St. Malo, a seaport on the English Channel. They were under the command of Jacques Cartier, an experienced sea-captain, whose name was to become one of the best-known in Canadian history.

Jacques Cartier's ships were each of about sixty tons—only one-quarter the size of the famous Nova Scotian fishing schooner, Bluenose. However, we do not admire Cartier so much for his daring in crossing the Atlantic; the Atlantic crossing was already being made every year by the fishing fleets from Europe, about which we have already read. And it is even likely that Cartier himself had already visited the coasts of the New World. We

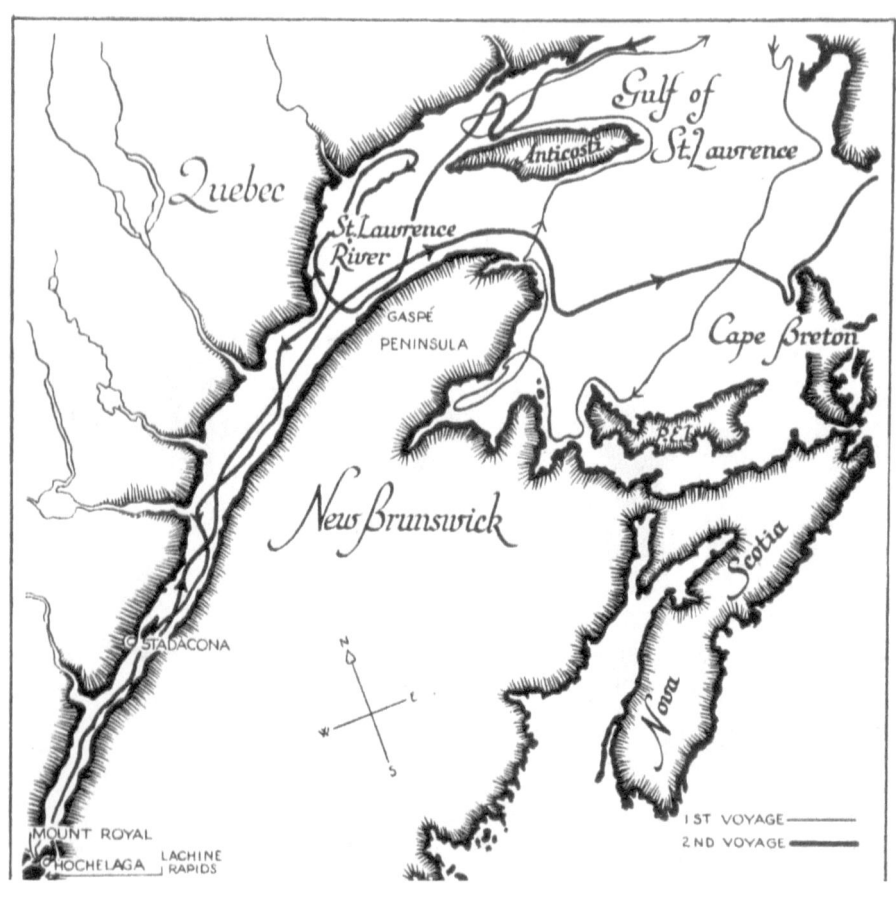

*Cartier's Voyages in 1534 and 1535*

admire Cartier, rather, for the skill and thoroughness he showed in exploring the St. Lawrence waterway, the key to the continent.

On this famous voyage of 1534, Cartier passed through the Strait of Belle Isle, between Newfoundland and Labrador, and explored the Gulf of St. Lawrence. Not until he neared the island of Anticosti, however, did he guess that he might be in the mouth of a great new river flowing out of North America. He did not have time to explore upstream that year, but he did land on the shore of Gaspe and claim the country in the name of the King of France.

The following year, 1535, Cartier set out again. Although his little fleet of three vessels spent almost seven weeks on the North Atlantic, he reached the Gulf at last and began to sail upstream. It was the first time, so far as we know, that any explorer had ever been on the great St. Lawrence River, as Cartier had named it.

Cartier found an Indian village called Stadacona nestled at the foot of the great rock, where Quebec City now stands. The Indians there did not want him to go farther upstream, but the French explorer was determined to sail as far inland as possible. Almost two hundred miles farther up the St. Lawrence, he reached a large island in the middle of the river. On it he found another Indian village, called Hochelaga.

The Indians of Hochelaga led Cartier to the top of a steep mountain on the island. From it he could see many miles farther up the St. Lawrence. Not far away the river's course was broken by foaming rapids, and Cartier knew that he had sailed as far upstream as he could go. Cartier was a sailor, and he had no desire to explore farther than his ships would carry him. The mountain on which he stood he called Mont Real, or "Mount Royal".

From Hochelaga, Cartier returned downstream to Stadacona to spend the winter. Little did he realize how bitter a Canadian winter could be. Before spring came, many of his men fell sick with scurvy, a disease caused by the lack of fresh fruit and vegetables. "With such infection did this sickness spread in our three ships," wrote Cartier, "that about the middle of February, of a hundred and ten persons that we were, there were not ten well, so that one could not help the other, a most horrible and pitiful case." Many of the men died. Often they were buried only under the snow because the others were too weak to dig graves.

By great good fortune, Cartier learned of an Indian remedy made from tree bark. When it was tried out on the sick men, it worked wonders. "It wrought so well," said Cartier, "that if all the physicians of Montpelier and Louvain had been there with all the drugs of Alexandria, they would not have done as much in one year as that tree did in six days, for it did so happen that as many as used it by the grace of God recovered their health!"

The little band of Frenchmen was glad to set sail again for France the following spring. With them they took many valuable furs that the Indians had traded to them during their stay on the St. Lawrence. Indeed, they took more than furs. Before setting sail, Cartier invited the Indian chiefs aboard his ship. Of those who came, several were not allowed to return to shore. Instead, they were kidnapped and taken to France. Unfortunately, they were never to see Canada again, for they all died in the strange land of the white man.

In 1541, the King of France sent Jacques Cartier to Canada once more. He was to be followed shortly by another French leader, the Sieur de Roberval, who had been told to take colonists to the new country and to build a settlement there.

This time Cartier spent the winter on the St. Lawrence, a little upstream from Stadacona. The Indians were now unfriendly, and when spring arrived with no word from Roberval and his party, Cartier broke camp and set sail down the St. Lawrence for France. Off the coast of Newfoundland, he met the little fleet carrying the colonists under Roberval, who ordered Cartier to accompany them back to the St. Lawrence. Cartier was anxious

to get home, however, and that night under cover of darkness he gave orders to raise the anchor, and set sail back to France.

Roberval continued up the St. Lawrence, and tried to build his settlement where Cartier had spent the winter. But when the snow came, Roberval's colonists began to fall sick with scurvy just as had Cartier's men six years earlier. By spring, over fifty of them had died. Before a second winter could come upon them, Roberval ordered his colonists to the ships, and they all set sail again for France.

To build a settlement in Canada seemed almost impossible; not until almost sixty years had passed did France make another attempt. But Jacques Cartier had already travelled up the great St. Lawrence for over a thousand miles. He had found the route to the heart of the continent. By his feats, Jacques Cartier had well earned the title which history has given him—Discoverer of Canada.

## THE DISCOVERY OF HUDSON BAY

In the month of April, 1610, the little sailing ship *Discovery* set out from England towards the New World. Her captain, Henry Hudson, was already famous as an explorer. The year before, he had discovered and explored the river on the east coast of North America which to-day bears his name.

Now Hudson was trying to reach the Far East by sailing west, as so many others had tried to do since the time of Columbus. He had already decided that there was no passage through the New World south of the Gulf of St. Lawrence. But he was determined to explore the northern limits of the mysterious new continent which barred the way to the Orient. Perhaps he could find a way around its northern tip, just as Magellan—exactly ninety years earlier—had found a route around its southern end.

Hudson crossed the Atlantic by way of Iceland and Greenland and finally sailed into the channel north of the Province of Quebec which is now known as Hudson Strait. Here for many days his ship made little progress because of ice-floes, which sometimes threatened to crush it. But at last the little Discovery was able to turn south, and before long she sailed out upon a great body of open water. Hudson, quite naturally, thought that he had travelled around the northern end of North America, and that he must now be on the Pacific Ocean.

Imagine Hudson's disappointment when, after sailing almost due south for hundreds of miles, the Discovery was brought to a stop at the southernmost end of James Bay! The ship now coasted back and forth along the shore, but it was soon realized that this was a "blind alley" and that no further progress south was possible.

Hudson had spent the whole summer in his explorations, and winter was fast approaching. Instead of trying to return

to England the same year, he now had his men haul up the *Discovery* on the shore of James Bay, and prepared to spend the winter in the New World.

Before long, they were completely frozen in.

Even people who get on well with one another are likely to quarrel sometimes, especially if they are forced to spend a great deal of time alone together. Hudson's men had not felt kindly towards their leader to begin with, and fights and arguments went on all winter long. To make matters worse, the food supplies began to run low. Some fish and game were secured from time to time, but it soon was clear that there were not enough supplies to feed them all until they could reach England.

They had to wait until June of the next year before they could again launch the *Discovery*. Even then, they soon found themselves caught in drift ice, and were unable to continue on their way back to England. Their food was now almost all gone, and day by day the men grew more quarrelsome.

We are told that one Sunday morning the crew mutinied against their leader. What happened was very sad. Hudson, his son, the ship's carpenter, and the sick members of the crew were forced into a small life-boat, and cast adrift in the midst of the vast inland sea which they had discovered. They were never heard of again.

As the *Discovery* was passing through Hudson Strait on her way home, a landing was made to look for game before beginning the long voyage across the North Atlantic. The sailors who went ashore met some Eskimos, and a fight broke out. In the battle, a number of the Englishmen were killed, including the leader of the mutineers. A handful escaped to the *Discovery*, and after a voyage filled with all the terrors and hardships which they deserved, eight of the crew finally reached Ireland. It is said that the mutineers who got home were brought to trial for what they had done, but we do not know for certain what punishment they received.

It was still hoped in England that the Bay which Hudson had discovered might lead to the Pacific Ocean. In the year following the return of the mutineers, therefore, another expedition was sent out. Its leader was Thomas Button, who was later to be made a knight for his work as an explorer. One of Button's two vessels was the *Discovery*, the same ship in which Hudson had sailed in 1610.

Button's expedition reached Hudson Bay safely, and spent the summer exploring the western coast of the great inland sea. It was soon realized that the Bay was land-locked on all sides, and when Button's party reached the mouth of the Nelson River that autumn he decided to spend the winter on the shore near by.

Not since the days of the Norsemen had white men tried to winter so far north in the New World, and it was a bitter experience. Many of them died of scurvy before the coming of spring. Before the ice broke up along the coast, which Button had named New Wales, a wooden cross was raised which carried a message claiming the land in the name of the king of

THE FIRST BRITISH CLAIM TO MANITOBA, 1613

England. It is interesting to think that what is now one of the Prairie Provinces—Manitoba—was visited by Englishmen so early in our history!

Leaving his other ship in the New World, Button returned to England in the *Discovery*. This brave little vessel was used in still another voyage the following year, but it, too, was unsuccessful. Englishmen were quickly realizing that it was useless to try to reach the Pacific through the northern straits. Of course, a north-west passage to the Pacific really does exist, for Canada is bounded on the north by the Arctic Ocean. But it was not until the present century that a ship succeeded in passing northward around Canada and Alaska all the way from the Atlantic to the Pacific. This famous voyage was made by a Norwegian, Roald Amundsen, in the year 1904. It has been repeated by others only a very few times.

It was because so little was known three hundred years ago about the geography of North America that sailors from Europe were willing to search for the north-west passage to the Pacific Ocean. But when we think that it was this search that brought such famous explorers to our shores as Cabot, Cartier, Hudson, and Button, we can see how it helped to make our country better known to the people of the Old World.

# THE FIRST "CANADIANS"

THE people of Europe who lived in Jacques Cartier's time had long known how to dig ores from the earth and how to separate the metals they contained. They knew how to mould metal tools and weapons, vessels, and ornaments. Ever since Biblical days, man had kept herds of cattle and sheep and used horses to help him do heavy work and to carry him from place to place. He had long since learned to plough his fields and fertilize the soil in order to produce better crops.

Perhaps these all seem like simple inventions.

But at that time, less than five centuries ago, there were over two hundred thousand people living in what is now the Dominion of Canada who knew nothing of any of these important discoveries! These were the Indians and the Eskimos, and they were still living in the Stone Age.

Wherever the early white explorers travelled in southern Canada, they met Indian tribes. The Eskimos lived along the northern fringe of our country, and because they seldom travelled far inland, they had little to do with the white man until recent years.

When did the Indians and Eskimos come to our continent, and where did they come from? Historians have found both these questions difficult to answer. It is thought likely that they crossed from Asia to North America at some time in the distant past by way of Behring Strait, the narrow body of water between Alaska and Siberia. They must have come many, many centuries ago, because by the time the first explorers arrived from Europe there were great differences among the Indian tribes who lived in various parts of the New World.

## THE INDIANS OF CANADA

Just as the peoples of Europe differed from one another, so the Indians of the New World could be divided into many different groups. Over fifty separate languages were spoken among the Indian tribes of Canada alone. Although some tribes roamed through large areas of the country, for the most part each had its own hunting and fishing grounds and lived pretty much to itself.

We must not suppose, however, that the Indians all had strong governments like those of France and England. Most Indian tribes were broken up into small bands, which seldom met together. But as a rule, all the bands in any one tribe dwelt in the same part of Canada, and made their living in the same way. Some Canadian tribes lived chiefly by hunting, some by fishing, some by both. In addition, there were a few very important tribes that depended on farming for most of their food supply.

All the hunting- and fishing-tribes except those of the Pacific coast lived in scattered camps, or "villages". These were moved from place to place whenever game became scarce. The Indian of the western plains, for example, watched the movements of the vast herds of buffalo from day to day as anxiously as the prairie farmer to-day watches changes in the weather. These Indians of the prairies, who did no farming, little knew that some day the land of the buffalo would become one of the greatest wheat belts of the modern world.

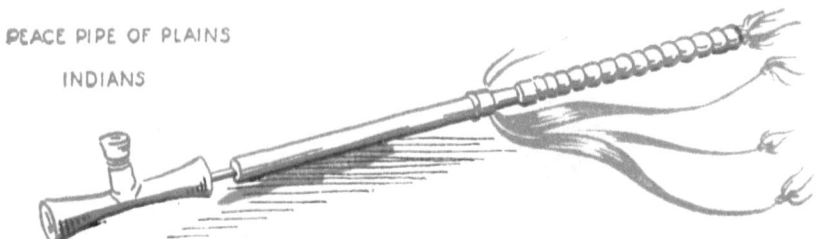
PEACE PIPE OF PLAINS INDIANS

The buffalo-hunting Plains tribes lived in light *tipis* which could be quickly folded for carrying whenever the word to "break camp" was given. These homes were made of buffalo skins stretched over a framework of poles, which came together near the top and made the tipi look something like an ice-cream cone turned upside down. The ends of the poles reached into the air above the peak like straight, bare branches. From two of the poles, skin flaps hung down to protect the smoke-hole at the top of the tipi. By moving the bottoms of these two poles so that flaps, or "ears", pointed away from the wind, the smoke from the open fire within the tipi was sucked out.

As they moved across the flat prairies on the track of the buffalo herds, the Plains Indians found little use for canoes—the most important means of transportation of the Indians in every other part of what is now Canada. Since horses were unknown in the New World until after the white man brought them from Europe, the prairie tribes had to travel on foot. However, they made use of the only animals they kept—their dogs. To make it possible for the small, wiry creatures they owned to carry useful loads, the Plains Indians invented the *travois*. A dog could drag a much heavier load on a travois than it could carry on its back.

About two hundred years ago, the first packs of wild horses began to appear on the western plains. These had descended from

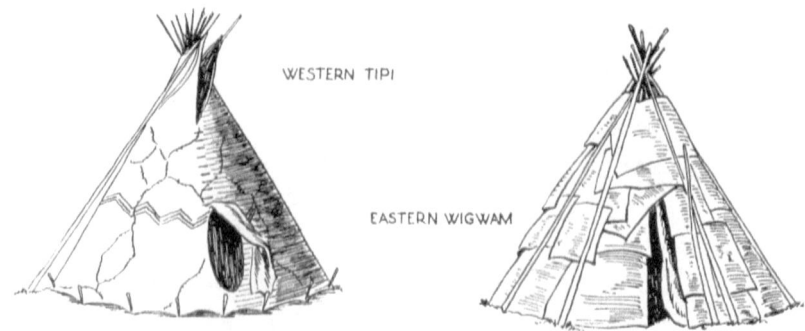

DOG TRAVOIS    HORSE TRAVOIS

horses that escaped from the Spanish explorers in the South. The Plains Indians quickly learned to use this new animal. Instead of having to creep up stealthily on the grazing buffalo, they could now ride into the herd and slaughter great numbers. Moreover, the horse could drag a much larger travois than the dog. To the Indians of the Canadian West, the horse was one of the white man's greatest gifts.

Throughout the eastern woodlands, which stretched from present-day Ontario to the Atlantic coast, lived tribes that depended on the wild life of the forest for their food. Like the Plains Indians, these eastern tribes moved their "villages", or camps, whenever game became hard to find.

The winter *wigwams* of the hunting-and-fishing tribes of eastern Canada looked much like the tipis of the Plains Indians, although they were often covered by birch bark or rushes instead of animal hides. The earth floor around the open fire inside each wigwam was usually kept dry by a layer of evergreen needles. The smoke escaped between the poles, which were left uncovered near the top of the tent. Unlike the western tipis, the wigwams of the eastern tribes had no "ears" to help draw out the smoke.

In summer, the eastern Indians also built cabins. These were often large enough to hold, several families. The tribes in Northern Ontario sometimes planted the poles of the framework in the ground, and bent the tops together. This made a house shaped like a bee-hive, which held a dozen persons.

Some of these hunting-and-fishing Indians of eastern Canada did a little farming as well. But only in the most southern part of the country were there tribes that depended on farm crops as well as meat and fish for most of their food supply. Every fall, the bark chests in the villages of the Hurons bulged wide with maize grown in the forest clearings roundabout. Beans and pumpkins helped to swell the harvest that the women of the tribe gathered each autumn.

These Huron villages lay between Georgian Bay and Lake Ontario, in what is now Southern Ontario. The Hurons were a branch of the Iroquois family, which was made up of a number of tribes living south and east of Lake Ontario and the upper St. Lawrence River. The Hurons and Iroquois, however, were bitter enemies, and during the summer months their war-parties ranged through each other's lands almost constantly.

Since both Iroquois and Hurons were farming Indians, their villages were moved only when the soil became too poor to raise good crops. This happened about every twelve or fifteen years, since the Indians knew little of the art of fertilizing the soil to keep it rich. Because they moved less often, both the Hurons and the Iroquois built homes that were larger and more permanent than those of any other tribe of eastern Canada. As many as two dozen families—over a hundred persons—could live together in their great bark-covered lodges, or "long-houses",

IROQUOIS CORN AND CORN GRINDER

as they were called. Here is an early explorer's description of the interior of one of these dwellings:

"Their long-houses are covered with bark, about fifty or sixty yards long and twelve yards wide, with a passage-way ten or twelve feet broad down the middle from one end to the other. Along each side runs a bench four feet above the ground, where the people sleep in summer to avoid the fleas. In winter they sleep close to the fire on mats, underneath the benches where it is warmer; and they fill the hut with a supply of dry wood to burn at that time of year. A space is left at one end of the cabin for storing their maize, which they place in large bark barrels in the middle of the floor. Boards overhead preserve their clothing, food, and other things from the mice."

Around each Huron and Iroquois village lay the fields in which women of the tribe spent the summers planting, weeding, and harvesting the crops. Cattle and sheep were unknown, and the work in the fields was done without the help of any of the machinery that can be found on the smallest Canadian farm to-day. Instead of using the plough, which had been known in Europe since the days of the early Egyptians, the Indians used simple wooden digging-sticks and hoes. Wherever possible, crops were planted in the natural openings in the woods, since clearing away the forest was always a difficult task for the Indians. With their crude stone tools, it often took one man more than a week to cut down a single large tree. Even when the forest was burned away, the crops had to be planted and harvested among the roots and stumps that remained.

INDIAN WAR-CLUB, OFTEN CALLED A TOMAHAWK

HAIDA VILLAGE

Along Canada's Pacific coast dwelt a group of Indians whose way of life was much different from that of the tribes of the plains and forests east of the Rocky Mountains. Then as now, the great shoals of salmon that come up the coastal rivers once each year were such an important source of food that fishing became one of the chief industries of the natives of that part of the country. Because their food supply was brought by Nature to their very doors, the Pacific coast tribes did not have to move their villages as did other Canadian Indians. The first white explorers found them living in large dwellings, built of cedar planks, quite unlike the light tipis and bark lodges of eastern Canada. Some of these dwellings were several hundred feet long, and fifty or sixty feet wide. To build such homes, the Indians of the West Coast cut down the huge cedar trees and split them into planks, with no better tools than adzes and chisels made of stone and shell, and wedges of wood and horn!

Some of the Pacific coast tribes divided themselves into "noblemen" and "commoners", and even kept large numbers of slaves captured from neighbouring Indians. These slaves were forced to do the heavy work around the village. They helped to paddle the huge war canoes, and hunted and fished for their masters. As in the days of the Roman emperors, a nobleman's wealth could be judged by the number of slaves he owned. The Pacific coast tribes had never heard of democracy!

In addition to salmon, the Indians of the British Columbia coast caught quantities of halibut and oolakan, or "candle-fish". Sea-otters, porpoises, and seals provided them with meat. A mixture of oolakan grease and berries was thought a great delicacy by some of the tribes. The Nootka Indians, who dwelt on the western side of Vancouver Island, had even learned how to harpoon whales. The other tribes secured whale-meat and whale-oil only when one of these huge animals was left stranded by the tide.

It is a mistake to think that the Indians of Canada were an ignorant people just because they did not have the same inventions and ways of life as the white men. The Indians understood how to make a living with what there was in the New World much better than did the early settlers from Europe. For many years, the colonists who came to this country depended on their home-lands for the tools and machinery they needed to carry on. If they had not been able to bring with them their seeds, livestock, and fire-arms, they would soon have been quite helpless.

All the Indians' tools and weapons were made from stone, bone, or wood. Some of the tribes

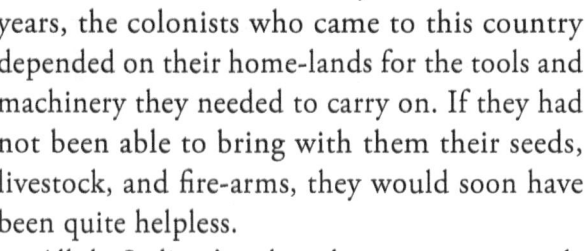

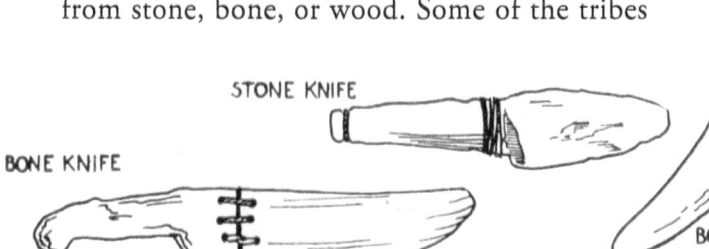

knew a little about pounding soft copper into the shape of knives. But they knew nothing about melting it and mixing it with harder metals to make knives and axes like those the white man brought them as barter. The Indians' stone tools, which were almost useless for cutting and sawing large trees, made it impossible for them to build log cabins like those of the early white colonists. Nor had they learned the use of mortar with brick or stone. But because none of the Indians east of the Rockies, not even the Iroquois, built permanent villages, such methods of building would not have suited them anyway. The Pacific coast tribes, as we shall remember, did build large houses of planks split from the cedar trees that grew in that part of the country.

The Indians' greatest invention was the birch-bark canoe. Since the eastern part of our country was covered with dense forests,

no method of land transportation would have made it possible for the white man to explore inland. Horses, for example, could not be used for travel until roads were built, and roads were not built until there were settlements that needed them. Only the great Canadian river systems offered ready-made highways through the forest-clad wilderness.

The Indian birch-bark canoe was light; it could be used in very shallow water, and it was quickly mended when broken. The finest of these canoes were made by the Algonkin Indians, who lived in the eastern woodlands of Canada, north of the Iroquois tribes. The Iroquois, who had few birch trees in their part of the country, sometimes covered their canoes with elm bark. Sometimes, too, they hollowed out logs into what were known as "dug-outs".

It took an Indian and his squaw about two weeks to build a birch-bark canoe large

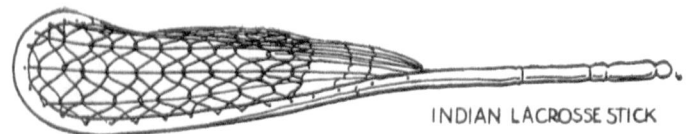
INDIAN LACROSSE STICK

enough to hold two or three persons. Of course, canoes many times this size were often made. These could be paddled by crews of as many as twenty or thirty Indians.

The cedar dug-outs made by the tribes of the Pacific coast differed greatly from the bark canoes of the rest of the country. Some of these were "ocean-going" vessels, large enough to carry fifty Indians each. Although they never ventured far beyond sight of land, they were often used for coastal voyages of several hundred miles.

Snow-shoes and toboggans made it possible for the Indians to travel and to carry their goods in winter. These inventions, too, were quickly copied by the first white settlers. In early days, there was no better means of travel and transportation in a land which was covered with heavy drifts of snow during several months each year.

It is easy to see that if there had been no Indians in Canada when the first white men arrived, our country would have been opened up much more slowly than it was. The rich furs that were shipped to Europe during the early days of our history were nearly all gathered by Indians. Wherever they travelled, the first white explorers used the Indians as guides. The wheat from Europe planted by the first settlers did not grow in Canada as well as the maize, beans, and pumpkins of the Iroquois. The

INDIAN SNOWSHOE

first white farmers, therefore, grew these Indian crops in their forest clearings.

The rivalry between the early white fur traders often increased the rivalry between the Indian tribes. No longer did they hunt and trap only to satisfy their own needs for food and clothing—now they were working against each other to satisfy the fashions of a continent on the other side of the ocean! In return for the furs they brought out of their forests, the Indians soon began to accept worse things than steel-edged knives and hatchets. Worst of all was the strong drink of the white man. The Indians often would trade everything they owned for this "fire-water". In the words of one of the earliest settlers, "when they set about drinking, their wives remove from the wigwams the guns, axes, spears, and every other weapon. After taking everything with which they can hurt themselves, the women go into the woods, afar off, where they hide with all their children. After that the Indians have a fine time, beating, injuring, and killing one another. Their wives do not return until the next day. At that time the fighting can be done only

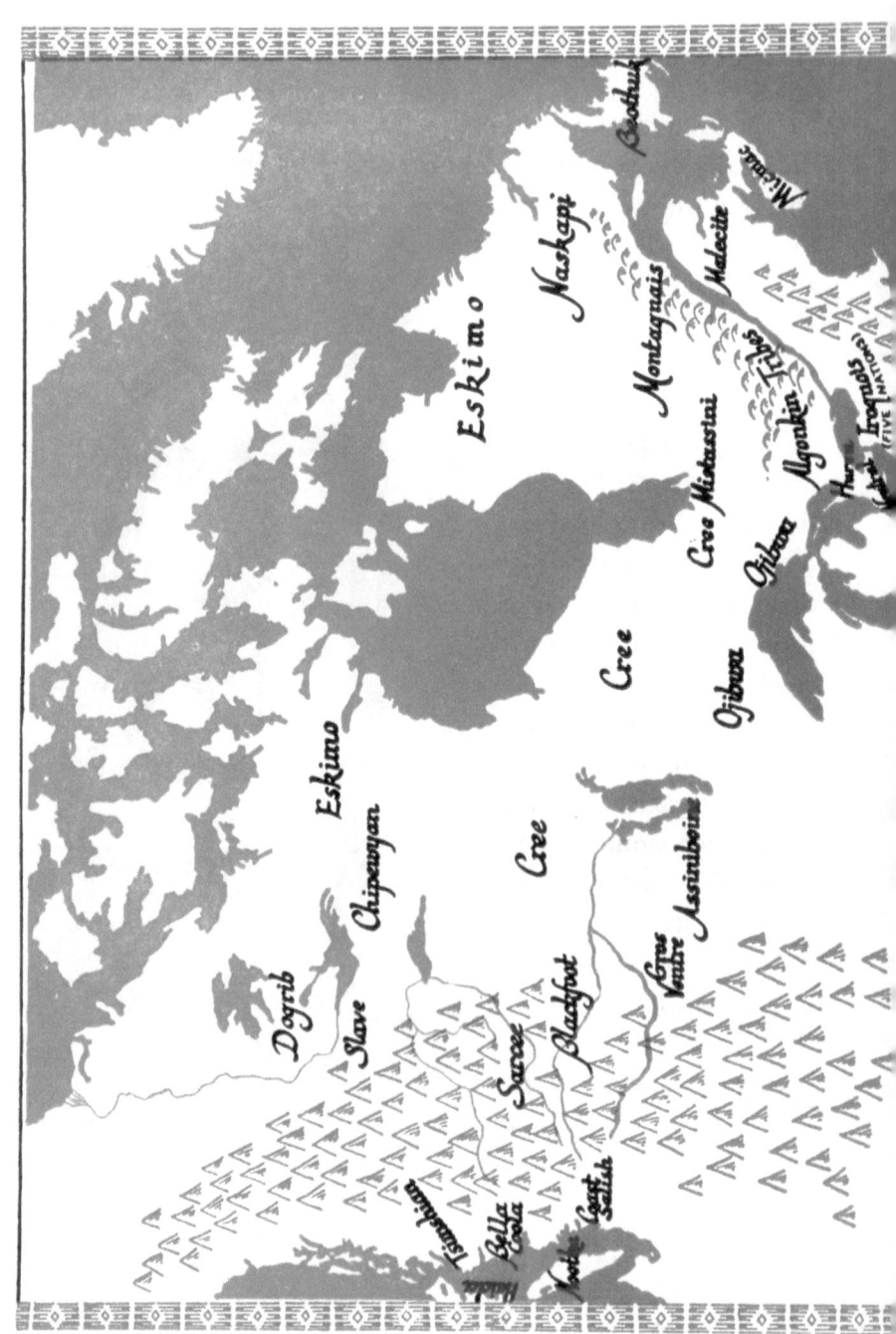

with the poles of their wigwams, which they pull to pieces for this purpose."

Not all the white men, however, were willing to let the Indians carry on so foolishly. For even during the early days of settlement, missionaries came among the natives to teach them Christianity, to help them heal their sick, and to show them why they should live in peace with each other and with their white brothers from Europe.

There are over fifty times as many people living in Canada to-day as when the first white man arrived. That is because a country can support many more farmers and factory-workers than it can people who live by hunting and fishing. A band of natives might go hungry for days before a single deer or buffalo was brought home by its hunters. A journey half the length of the St. Lawrence River might be made by another hunting party in search of game for the village. Compare such a way of life with that of the modern farmer, who may have a herd of thirty cattle safely stabled in his barn to supply milk as well as meat, both for his family and for sale in the city. A modern threshing-machine or automobile can be made in our factories more quickly than an Indian could chip a piece of flint into the shape of an arrow-head, or build a birch-bark canoe.

What has happened to the descendants of the two hundred thousand Indians who once lived in Canada? Unfortunately, their numbers dropped rapidly as the white man came among them, bringing his new way of life and destroying the old. As the forests were cut down, the wild life moved ever farther west and north. The Indian could no longer live as he had, and because he found it difficult to learn the white man's ways, his numbers gradually began to shrink. Many bands were almost wiped out by diseases the white man brought with him from Europe—smallpox, tuberculosis, typhoid fever, and measles.

ALGONKIN

To-day, however, the number of Indians is once more increasing, slowly but gradually. Over one hundred thousand live in Canada at the present time. "Reserves" of land have been set aside for these Indians in many parts of the Dominion. There are many special laws to protect the Indians on the reservations. They are allowed to trap, hunt, and fish at times of the year when white men are forbidden to do so. In many cases, they are paid cash grants each year. They are given assistance in farming, and their education is looked after by the Dominion government. On the other hand, they are not allowed to buy whisky, and a white man who sells them "fire-water" may be heavily fined.

MALECITE

IROQUOIS

Many Canadians whose ancestors were Indian do not now live on reservations. They have become farmers or city-dwellers with the full rights of citizenship enjoyed by other Canadians. The men and women who helped open our country to fur trade and settlement were often the descendants of Indian and white parents, and carried the blood of both the Old World and the New in their veins. When we think that many of our modern Canadian place-names—"Winnipeg", "Saskatoon", "Toronto", and even "Canada" itself—come from Indian words, we realize how important the Indians are in the story of the country in which we live.

IROQUOIS WAR CANOE

## NATIVES OF THE NORTH--THE ESKIMOS

Across the northern fringe of Canada, all the way from Alaska to Labrador, dwell little groups of people whose way of life is certainly the hardest of any in the Dominion. The Indians were the first to call them "Eskimos", which meant "eaters of raw meat". The name suits them very well, for even to-day a great part of the Eskimos' food is raw seal meat. In the summer, however, the Eskimos often journey some distance inland to hunt caribou and musk-oxen, since the skins of these animals make very warm clothing. But because winter is much longer than summer in the Far North, the Eskimos have to depend on seal and walrus meat during the greater part of every year.

The Eskimos' method of hunting seals is interesting. Although seals spend a great deal of the time under water, they have to come to the surface to breathe. Because the surface of the Arctic Ocean is frozen over during most of the winter, each seal keeps several "breathing holes" open through the ice to which it can return from time to time. These breathing holes are usually covered by a foot or more of snow. But the Eskimo—often with the aid of his dogs—finds them in the icy wastes without much difficulty. Then his long wait begins. With his spear aimed into the little opening in the ice above the breathing hole, he may stand motionless for many hours. During all this time he must not make a sound, since seals have a keen sense of hearing. Seal hunting, "Eskimo fashion", requires a great deal of patience!

Eskimos built two kinds of boats, the umiak and the kayak. The umiak was much like a large row-boat, but was made of skins stretched over a framework of bone. The kayak is smaller, and just as clever an invention as the birch-bark canoe of the Indian. Like the umiak, the kayak is made of skins stretched

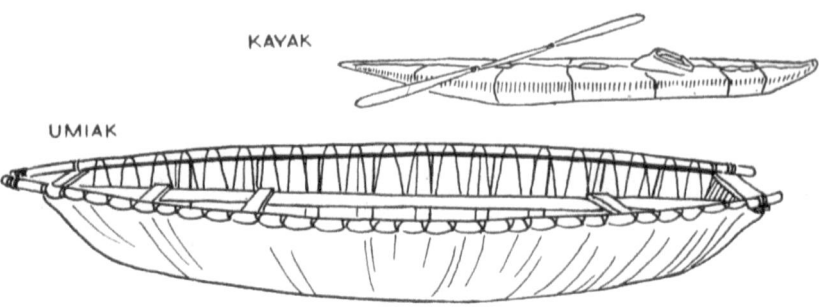

kayak over a bone framework. It is meant for a single passenger, however, who guides it along with a double-bladed paddle. The top of the kayak is made watertight by a layer of skins. These skins can be drawn tightly about the waist of the person paddling it, and the craft can be turned upside down and righted again without filling with water.

In summer, the Eskimos live in tents. Until recent years, these were made of caribou or seal skin; they are now usually made of canvas. Log huts were often built, for winter use, from the driftwood which floated north down the rivers. Sometimes, when driftwood was scarce, whale bones were used instead. These log huts were covered with roofs made of sod or skins.

The snow hut, or "igloo", is the cleverest dwelling of all. It is made of blocks of snow, carefully carved from a snow bank, and fitted together to make a solid dome. When the air inside is warmed by a seal-oil lamp, a layer of ice forms which makes

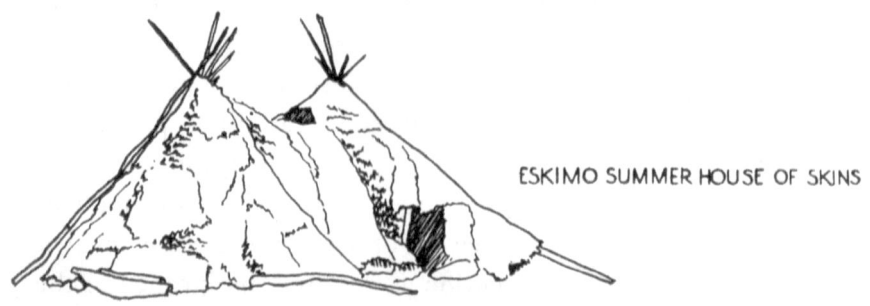

BUILDING A SNOW HUT

the igloo so strong that it will even support the weight of a man. Two Eskimos, working together, can build an igloo in two or three hours. Indeed, the Eskimos in some parts of Canada build igloos only when stopping off overnight during a winter journey.

Because of the harsh climate in which they live, the Eskimos had still fewer materials at hand for making tools and weapons than had the Indians. However, they made good use of everything they did have. From the antlers of the caribou, the bones of the whale, and the ivory tusks of the walrus, they were able to make arrows, harpoons, needles, thimbles, and a host of other articles they needed. The heavy clothing required during most of the year was usually made of caribou fur, while their boots were made of seal skin.

Although the Eskimos' dwellings are the same to-day as in the past, the coming of the white man changed many of the

ESKIMO WOODEN FIRE-DRILL

MOUTHPIECE

ESKIMO BONE BOW-DRILL

details in their lives. They have learned to depend on the rifle in hunting, and on the kerosene stove for heating the white man's tea (of which the Eskimos have become very fond). They often dress in woollen clothing instead of caribou skins as in days gone by. Instead of spending his winters hunting seals for food for himself and his family, the Eskimo now hunts the arctic white fox, which is of use only as an article of trade at the white man's stores. In return, he secures groceries, including flour, sugar, and tea.

In many ways, these changes brought by the white man have been unfortunate for the Eskimos. The white man's food is not nearly as healthful for the Eskimos as their old diet of seal meat. They have suffered from sicknesses which the white man brought, and even such a mild disease as measles has killed great numbers of Eskimos. The white man's woollen garments are not nearly as well suited to Eskimo life as the skins of the caribou, which used to be so plentiful.

When the white man first came, it is thought there were about 22,500 Eskimos living along the northern shores of Canada. Since that time, their number has dropped to about 8000. However, the Canadian government has already taken steps to improve the lot of the Eskimos. Reindeer have been brought in from Alaska to take the place of the dwindling herds of caribou. More doctors and nurses are being sent into the Arctic. If these steps succeed, it is likely that the Eskimos will continue to live on the northern shores of our Dominion for many years to come, finding a living for themselves in a region too bleak and bitter for white men.

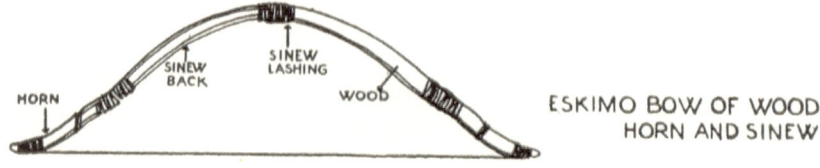

ESKIMO BOW OF WOOD HORN AND SINEW

## THE COMING OF THE FRENCH

AFTER Roberval left Canada in 1542, the kings of France seemed to forget about the lands Jacques Cartier had claimed for them. Almost sixty years went by before the French tried again to start a colony in our country.

It was thought, of course, that Canada had no valuable minerals. The only riches which the natives of Canada had for the white men were furs. The European fishermen who visited the shores of North America each summer were glad to trade in furs as well as fish. Because they found the fur trade so profitable, they sometimes went as far up the St. Lawrence as the island of Montreal to meet the Indians. But they did not build homes in Canada, and by the time the snows covered the frozen St. Lawrence Valley each winter, they had all returned to their home ports on the other side of the Atlantic.

By the end of the 1500's, however, Spain and Portugal had built empires in the New World which the court of France would

SIR HUMPHREY GILBERT RENEWS ENGLAND'S CLAIM TO NEWFOUNDLAND, 1583

have dearly loved to match. Besides this, France's weak claim to the unsettled country in the north had been threatened by another rival. Queen Elizabeth of England had sent five shiploads of colonists to the New World under Sir Humphrey Gilbert.

Although Gilbert claimed Newfoundland in the name of the English queen, his expedition met with disaster and he himself was lost when his ship went down at sea. The time had come, however, for France to make good her claim to the strange lands in the West.

## THE BAY OF FUNDY

We have seen that while the new king of France, Henry IV, was now ready to start building an empire in North America, the French "visitors" to Canada were interested only in fishing and fur-trading. They did not wish to make their homes in the country, and certainly they were not anxious that other Frenchmen should settle in the lands from which the furs came.

If Henry IV was going to make his dream of a French colony in Canada come true, he would have to make the task of founding it worth while to the men he placed in charge. How could this be done? Henry was shrewd enough to find an answer. He decided to start a fur-trading company, which would have the right to trade in furs all to itself—but on one condition. This condition was that the company should take colonists to the country and build a settlement there. Because this company had the sole right to trade in furs, it was said to have a *monopoly*. A monopoly of the fur trade in Canada was worth a great deal, and the leaders to whom it was granted were only too willing to agree to take a certain number of settlers to the country during each year.

Unfortunately, the system never did work very well. From time to time, the king had to take the monopoly away from one leader and give it to another. Usually, too, the holder of the monopoly was more interested in making money from the fur trade than in keeping his part of the bargain, which was to bring settlers to the country. There were exceptions, however.

In 1604, an expedition was sent to the New World under the leadership of the Sieur de Monts, who had been granted the fur-trading monopoly. De Monts took with him two ship-loads of settlers to make homes in the new country. He took, as geographer for the expedition, a man whose name was to become the best known in early Canadian history—Samuel de Champlain.

De Monts landed his colonists on an island at the mouth of the St. Croix River, which now divides the Province of New Brunswick from the State of Maine. But the St. Croix settlement was not a success. In spite of careful preparations for winter, the colonists ran short of food and fresh water long before spring came. The dread disease of scurvy, too, began to strike them down, and they searched in vain for the tree bark which had

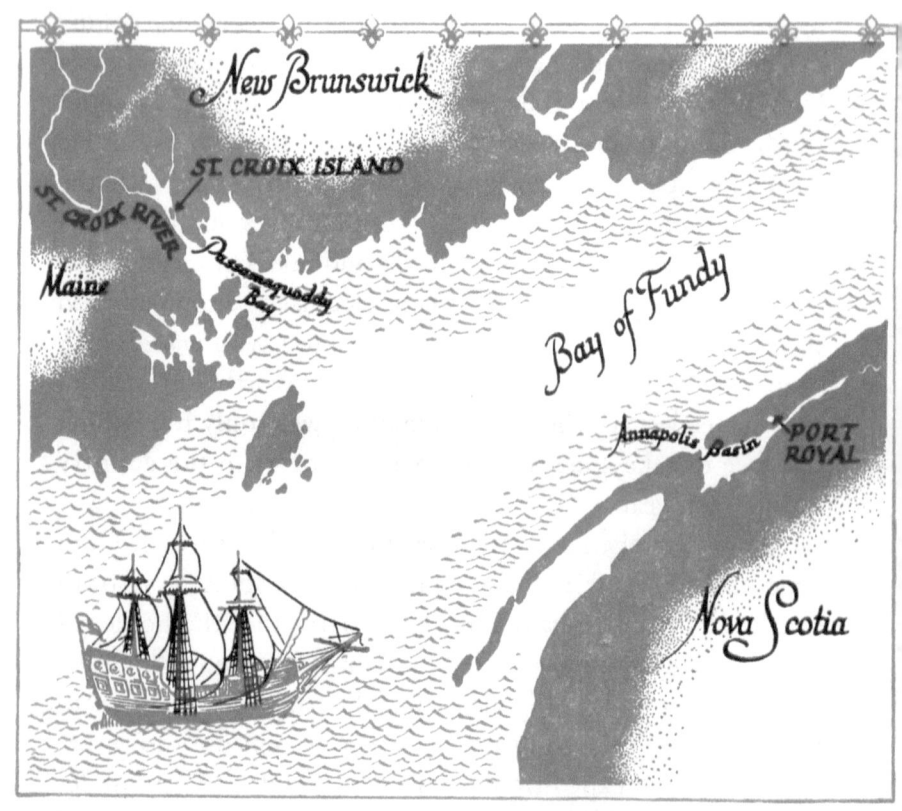

*The First French Settlement on the Bay of Fundy*

saved the lives of many of Cartier's men seventy years earlier. There was no fresh water on the island. It was so cold that their cider froze solid and had to be measured out by the pound.

After scouring the coast of New England for a better location, de Monts moved his colony across the Bay of Fundy in 1605 to the shore of the Annapolis Basin in Nova Scotia. He had already granted the land to one of his officers, Baron de Poutrincourt. The new settlement was named Port Royal, and in spite of the severe winters, it lasted for two years. The settlers were well fed and entertained, for during the long winter months Champlain kept them busy by beginning what he called "The Order of Good Cheer".

"Each day," wrote Champlain, "a different member of the party had the duty of taking care that we were all well provided for." So the time passed pleasantly enough. Champlain himself saw to the burning of the grass and the sowing of crops of wheat. He planted gardens near the fort, where he hoed away with his companions late into the summer evenings.

At the same time, another of the Port Royal settlers was busying himself writing the first Canadian history book. This was Marc Lescarbot, a young French lawyer and poet, many of whose writings have been preserved to the present day. The second winter spent at Port Royal turned out to be mild, and Lescarbot wrote: "I remember that on the fourteenth of January, on a Sunday afternoon, we amused ourselves with singing and music on the river, and that in the same month we went to see the wheat-fields two leagues from the fort, and dined merrily in the sunshine."

PORT ROYAL — 1606

All the plans of the little band of settlers at Port Royal were soon to be upset. One day in the spring of 1607, news came from the Indians that the first sail of the year had been sighted off the mouth of the Annapolis Basin. Poutrincourt and his men rushed down to the water to welcome it, but deep was their disappointment when they heard the news it brought from France. The monopoly of the fur trade held by the Sieur de Monts had been cancelled by the king, and without the profits of the fur trade the settlement could not support itself. There was nothing for Poutrincourt to do but give orders to abandon the colony. In August, 1607, the last boat-load of settlers waved good-bye to the Indians who sorrowfully lined the shore, begging their white friends to return as speedily as possible to the Annapolis Basin.

## THE FOUNDING OF QUEBEC

When the Port Royal settlers arrived back in France, there was one among them who was determined to return to the New World. This was the young geographer, the Sieur de Champlain. He went straightway to his old leader, de Monts, hoping to persuade him to carry on with his plans to colonize Canada with Frenchmen. "I advised him," Champlain tells us, "to go and settle on the great River St. Lawrence, with which I was familiar through a voyage that I had made there. He spoke to His Majesty, who agreed and told him to go and settle the country."

De Monts did not go to the St. Lawrence now himself. He chose Champlain to go instead, and to take out settlers with him. At long last, France was completing the work begun by Jacques Cartier and Roberval over seventy years earlier!

In the summer of 1608, Champlain's lone ship, carrying barely two dozen colonists, threaded her way up the St. Lawrence past the Island of Orleans. A few miles farther upstream, "when I had reached the narrowest part of the river, which the natives call Quebec," wrote Champlain later, "I had a settlement built, and had the ground cleared, and had some garden plots made."

In choosing Quebec for the first French settlement on the St. Lawrence, Champlain had decided wisely. Furs could easily

"I HAD A SETTLEMENT BUILT..." CHAMPLAIN

be brought to it by the Indians living along the rivers and lakes to the west. More important, the great rock which rose behind the early settlement was a natural fortress that commanded the only highway into the interior—the St. Lawrence River.

Champlain had lived through a bitter Canadian winter at de Monts's colony at the mouth of the St. Croix four years earlier, but the first winter at Quebec proved even worse. Of twenty-eight settlers, only eight were still alive when spring came at last. But with the warmer weather help arrived from France, and the brave little colony carried on.

"THE IROQUOIS WERE MUCH SURPRISED"

## MAKING ENEMIES FOR NEW FRANCE

The summer of the year after he built the first homes at Quebec, Champlain set out on a strange journey into the unexplored wilds to the south. A few years earlier, some French fur traders had promised the Algonkin Indians of the St. Lawrence Valley that France would help them in their wars against the savage Confederacy of the Iroquois. Champlain was now reminded of this promise. Perhaps he was glad of the opportunity to explore the country. Perhaps he wished to show the Algonkins how powerful the French really were. Whatever his reasons, he agreed to go along with the war party, and to take a few of his men as well.

The expedition set sail up the St. Lawrence from Quebec. When they came to the mouth of the Richelieu River, just downstream from the Island of Montreal, they turned south and began to paddle up that river toward the land of the Iroquois. On their way up the Richelieu they came to a rapids, and here Champlain decided to send back all but two of the Frenchmen in his party. Champlain and his two companions then paddled on with the Indians, and before long they glided forth upon the waters of the large lake from which the Richelieu flows.

A few days later, they met a band of Iroquois warriors. The Iroquois were surprised to find the Algonkins so far inside their country, and made ready to attack. Of course, the Iroquois had never before seen any Frenchmen, and knew nothing about the white man's powerful weapons. Here is what Champlain himself had to say about the fight that followed:

"Our men put me at their head, where I marched until I was about thirty paces from the enemy. They at once saw me and halted, looking at me, and I at them. When I saw them making a move to shoot at us, I rested my gun against my cheek and aimed directly at one of the three chiefs. With this shot, two of them fell to the ground. When our men saw this very lucky shot, they began to make cries so loud that one could not have heard it thunder. Meanwhile the arrows flew from both sides. The Iroquois were much surprised that two men had been so quickly killed, although they wore armour woven from cotton thread and from wood.

"As I was loading again, one of my companions fired a shot from the woods, which astonished them again to such a degree that, seeing their chiefs dead, they lost courage, took to flight and abandoned the field, fleeing into the depths of the woods.

"This place, where this charge was made, I named Lake Champlain."

In taking sides in the Indian wars, Champlain had turned the powerful Iroquois into an enemy of the French. Perhaps this was unwise, but we must remember that the Algonkins

*Champlain's Journey Through Ontario*

had been his neighbours. They were the Indians upon whom the French depended for furs. Champlain had to decide which Indians he wanted as friends, and so he took the side of the Algonkins against the Iroquois.

### CHAMPLAIN EXPLORES ONTARIO

Champlain was not willing to rest idly in the new settlement he had founded at Quebec. Instead, he sailed back and forth between his colony and France, keeping the king and the fur merchants of Paris interested in the work he was doing in the New World. Indeed, he crossed the Atlantic Ocean at least twenty-five times during his lifetime. He also found time to make several long voyages through the unknown wilds upstream from Quebec, exploring the country and making friends with the Indians as far west as Georgian Bay on Lake Huron.

Since Champlain was not able to spend as much time as he would have liked exploring our vast country, he thought of a clever plan. This was to send adventurous young men from New France to live among the Indians. These young men learned the language of the Indians, and got to know the country beyond the frontiers of the colony. In return, Champlain had Indians come to Quebec to learn the Frenchmen's language and ways. This plan worked very well, and some of Champlain's "young men" later became famous Canadian explorers. Perhaps the best known of them all was Etienne Brule, who later travelled widely through Southern Ontario and even explored the north shore of Lake Huron as far as Lake Superior.

In 1615, however, Champlain decided to make an inland voyage of exploration himself. In that year he had brought out to New France four priests to begin France's missionary work among the Indians of Canada. One of these priests, father Le Caron, set out that summer up the St. Lawrence River. When he reached the Island of Montreal, he turned up the Ottawa River and crossed by way of Lake Nipissing and the French River to Georgian Bay. Champlain, accompanied by Brule, followed hard on the priest's heels. One day that fall he caught up with Father Le Caron in a Huron Indian village not far from the present town of Midland. From here, Champlain travelled about the surrounding country, visiting the other Huron villages and exploring the lakes and streams.

The Indians of Huronia—as the country south of Georgian Bay was called—were massing a war party to travel against their enemies the Iroquois, who lived in the country south-east of Lake Ontario. Champlain agreed to go with them. The Hurons led him eastward from Lake Simcoe to the Bay of Quinte on Lake Ontario. After paddling around the eastern end of this lake they landed on its south shore and struck inland in search of the Iroquois.

This time Champlain was not as lucky as he had been in the fight against the Iroquois at Lake Champlain six years earlier. The Iroquois warriors stood their ground, even against the fire-arms of the white man. Champlain himself was painfully wounded by their arrows. When it became clear that they were losing the battle, the Hurons retreated, carrying Champlain with them. By December they had reached Huronia once more, where Champlain was forced to spend the winter nursing his wounds. Next spring, however, he was able to set out for New France, where he arrived early in the summer.

This journey ended Champlain's explorations. But his work for New France was by no means over. A few years later, England and France went to war with each other. Before long, an English fleet appeared before Quebec and called on Champlain to surrender. Realizing that his little colony could not put up a successful fight, Champlain sorrowfully turned over Quebec to the English commanders, and was himself carried away to England as a prisoner. Little did he or his English captors know that peace had already been signed between France and England! Because this made the capture of Quebec unlawful, the English agreed to hand it back to France, and Champlain was able to return to his colony as governor.

Late in 1635, Champlain fell ill, and on Christmas Day of the same year he died at Quebec. But the work he had done lived on. During his lifetime he had helped to build the first French settlement in Nova Scotia. He had founded the colony of Quebec. He had explored the Iroquois country and most of Southern Ontario. He had made the Hurons and Algonkins close allies of the French, and he had given France complete control over the St. Lawrence River Valley. Truly, he had well earned the title which history has given him—"Founder of New France."

THE "DON DE DIEU", CHAMPLAIN'S VESSEL

## "FOR THE GLORY OF GOD"

MOST of the pioneers who began France's colony on the St. Lawrence came "on business". They hoped to make their fortunes in the New World, and were interested in the Indians who lived there only because of the furs they could get from them. However, there were some pioneers who wanted nothing for themselves, and wished only to help the natives. These were the Christian missionaries. Like the missionaries that our churches send to-day to distant parts of the world, those who came to New France not only told the story of the Gospel, but educated the natives, and healed their sick.

Besides the missionaries who went to live among the Indians, there were others who built churches, schools, and hospitals for the white settlers. Much of the early growth of the French colony on the St. Lawrence was the result of their labours. When the kings of France found that fortunes were not to be made in North America as easily as they had hoped, they became less willing to spend money on building up the colony. But the pioneer missionaries who were working among the Indians wrote letters and

sent reports back to France telling about their adventures. These reports, or *Relations* as they were called, described the terrible risks of their work, the extraordinary places they visited, and the strange ways of the Indians among whom they lived. It is no wonder that when these reports were published in France, people there read them eagerly. In this way the distant colony was kept in the public eye.

To-day, we still read with great interest the letters and reports of those missionaries of long ago. Much of our knowledge of Indian ways comes to us from them, and if it were not for their letters we should know much less about life in early Canada.

The very first mission in what is now the Dominion of Canada was begun at Port Royal in Nova Scotia in 1611. The next mission began in the St. Lawrence colony founded by Champlain. In 1615, seven years after Champlain landed with his settlers below the great rock which towers above the river at Quebec, three Recollet priests came to the settlement. One of them was Father Le Caron, who set out for Huronia at once. He was the first white man to see Lake Huron.

For ten years the Recollets laboured among the Indians. But the country was so large, the savages so many, and they themselves so few, that they looked to France for further help. So they invited the Jesuits to come to the colony and share the task. The Jesuit Order was then, as now, one of the most active teaching and missionary bodies in the Roman Catholic Church. In 1625, their first missionaries arrived in the settlements on the St. Lawrence.

"FOR THE GREATER GLORY..."

## THE BLACK ROBES

In a small Indian village on the shores of Lake Erie, the warriors of the tribe had gathered together in the long-house of the chief. They had come to hear the news brought by White Owl, a brave who had just returned from visiting the Hurons of Georgian Bay.

The Chief gave White Owl the signal to speak. The warrior looked about the circle of tribesmen, who stared gravely into the fire as they puffed slowly on their long pipes, and then he began:

"I have seen strange things, my brothers, wonders indeed, and I know not whether they are good or evil. There now dwell among our northern brothers three pale-faces. No,"—he held up a warning hand—"not like him of the iron breast and the weapon that spat fire and smoke, who helped us fight against the Iroquois many moons ago, but men wearing long skirts, like women. 'Black Robes' the Hurons call them.

"These Black Robes have a great house in the village of Ihonatiria. This house has three rooms, all full of wonders. When one wishes to go in, he pushes, and part of the wall moves! When one is inside, he can push the wall again and nobody else can come in! Each room has one or two of these openings. In the first room the Black Robes keep food and coverings; in the second they sleep and eat; in the third"—he paused—"they keep the god whom they worship! The sign of their god is a cross. A great cross is in front of the house, and they wear the same medicine about their necks. They have pictures of their god and his family on the walls of their house."

A murmur of surprise arose. "And did you go into this wonderful house?" asked the Chief.

"Yes, indeed," said White Owl. "Every day some visitors may go to see the Black Robes, to push the walls to and fro, and see their magic. They tell us about their Manitou, and about His Son, whom they call Jesus, and about the Heaven to which they will go when they die."

"Is it like the Happy Hunting Grounds?" asked the old chief.

"Oh, no, for in Heaven they do not hunt, nor make war, nor go to feasts. I told the Black Robes I did not think it would suit our people."

He went on. "The Black Robes are kind to the sick, and they give many presents to the children. But some do not trust the white man nor his medicines. They think his magic is not good for Indians. But it is great Magic! There is a glass which makes a fly as big as a grasshopper, or an ant as big as a cricket. Truly, I have seen!

"On the table is an animal called The Captain. He is not like any animal in the forests or the fields. Captain does not walk, but he is alive. He says 'tick, tock, tick, tock'. When it is time to put on the pot for dinner he says 'ting', and when

he says in his language, 'ting, ting, ting, ting' he means 'it is time to go home.'"

"I should like to see these wonders," said the Chief. "Perhaps, if we ask them, the Black Robes will come and stay with us."

It is very likely that the Chief did one day see the "magic" of the Jesuit missionaries, about which White Owl had told him. Many other Black Robes came to join the first three, to help them to teach and care for the Huron Indians. The Jesuit fathers had a difficult task, for the Indians often blamed them for their misfortunes—when small-pox struck the camps, or the rains did not come in a dry season. However, many of the Hurons came to love and trust the Black Robes.

The work of the missionaries went on, not only among the Hurons, but in other parts of New France. Even the Iroquois were visited. A brave missionary, Father Jogues, went among them and, though cruelly treated, returned to try to help them. In the end they murdered him.

The missionaries learned how to live among the Indians and share their rough food and crowded, smoky dwellings. They learned to travel in the Indian manner, by canoe, or trail; they wrote reports describing their journeys, and made maps of the routes.

Within the settlement of Quebec itself, the Jesuit Order built schools to educate French and Indian boys. In 1639, a group of Ursuline nuns landed in Quebec, and the first convent and hospital in New France was founded. Several of the institutions begun about this time arc still carrying on their work in the city of Quebec to-day.

Not only did the missionaries build churches, schools, and hospitals. On the Island of Montreal they built a new settlement which has since grown into Canada's largest city.

## THE STORY OF MONTREAL.

After the Jesuits had been working among the Indians for about fifteen or sixteen years, a group of people in France, who had been greatly stirred by the stories they read, decided they also should try to help the Indians. They made up their minds to build a new mission, which would mend the bodies and souls of the poor savages.

The best place for such a mission, it seemed to them, was the island which Cartier had named Mont Real and so they called themselves the Society of Our Lady of Montreal. At this island the Ottawa River flows into the St. Lawrence River. Up and down past the island, Indians paddled their canoes to and from the French settlements. Unfortunately, this was also the route which the fierce Iroquois took when they made war on the tribes farther west. And the Iroquois hated the French!

The new Society chose as leader of the mission the Sieur de Maisonneuve, a great soldier and a truly religious man. Jeanne Mance, another volunteer, was asked to look after the hospital they planned to build, and so she became Canada's first nurse. The Island of Montreal was granted to the Society by the King of France, and they decided to call the new settlement Ville-Marie (the city of Mary).

Maisonneuve, Jeanne Mance, and about forty other persons, sailed for Canada in 1641 in two small ships. When they landed at Quebec, they were met by the governor, who tried to discourage Maisonneuve from taking his companions on to the Island of Montreal. It was only thirty-three years since the founding of Quebec, and there were still not more than about three hundred people in all of New France. The governor thought that when there were so few people, they should all live together for safety. The Island of Montreal, 200 miles up the river, was right on the war-path of the Iroquois. But when the governor warned him of the dangers, Maisonneuve said he was determined to go on, even "if every tree were an Iroquois"!

After spending the winter at Quebec, Maisonneuve and his followers set out upstream. After ten days' travel they landed on the island. It was a beautiful spring day. The hearts of the little band were joyful at reaching their goal, and a service was held at once. The priest told them: "You are few, but your work is the work of God. His smile is upon you, and your children shall fill the land."

At the foot of the mountain the settlers built a fort with a strong palisade. At first the Iroquois did not know they were there, and the settlers were able to come and go in the forests without danger. But it was not long before the Iroquois discovered them. It was now unsafe for anyone to go out of the palisade. The Indians would hide in the forest, sometimes lying in wait for days.

The settlers grew very restless staying inside the fort, and complained that Maisonneuve was too cautious. He knew that his men were not used to Indian ways of fighting, and refused to let them go out as they wished. Once he did allow them to go into the forest to chase some Indians, but they were quickly

surrounded by a much larger force of savages. Three men were killed and others wounded, and Maisonneuve ordered a retreat. He himself held off the Indians with his pistols while his men withdrew. The Indians hoped to capture him, and their chief rushed towards him with his tomahawk. But Maisonneuve shot the warrior, and was able to reach the safety of the fort while the Indians stopped to carry away the body of their fallen chief.

For twenty-two years Maisonneuve governed Ville-Marie. To-day in Montreal, a fine statue of the founder of Canada's largest city stands on the spot where he held off the Iroquois single-handed in 1644.

FORT Ste MARIE

## THE FATE OF THE HURON MISSIONS

Before the white men came, the Iroquois and Hurons had been enemies, and this hatred increased greatly when the Indian nations became rivals in obtaining furs to sell to the white men. The Hurons traded with the French on the St. Lawrence, and the Iroquois with the Dutch on the Hudson River. From the Dutch the Iroquois obtained more guns and ammunition than the Hurons were able to secure from the French.

In the year Montreal was founded, the Iroquois made a terrible raid into Huron territory, destroying a large settlement of Hurons. For several years afterwards there were only small raids, but the threat of the Iroquois still hung over the Huron villages. Once one of the Black Robes baptized an Iroquois prisoner whom the Hurons were torturing to death. "Why did you baptize that Iroquois?" asked a Huron. "He will get to Heaven before we do, and when he sees us coming, he will drive us out."

By 1648, the Jesuits had built eleven or twelve mission stations in the country of the Hurons. Ste Marie, near present-day Midland, was the chief mission. Its buildings were large and well fortified. The missionaries planted corn, and kept fowls, pigs, and cattle. Though they lived very plainly, they were able to supply food to the Indians in time of famine, and to entertain them on feast-days. More and more Indians were being baptized.

Then the Iroquois struck. In the summer of 1648 an Iroquois war-party fell upon St. Joseph, an Indian village of two thousand people. The missionary, Father Daniel, was slaughtered, and many Indian men, women, and children with him. The following spring the Iroquois destroyed the villages of St. Ignace and St. Louis, and tortured to death two priests, Jean Brebeuf and Gabriel Lalemant.

One after another the Huron villages were now attacked, until the only mission which remained was Ste Marie. At last the Jesuit fathers decided that it was not safe to stay even there. They burned the mission, and took refuge on a small island in Georgian Bay. Here thousands of frightened Hurons came to escape their enemies. But there was not food on the island for so many people; numbers of them starved, and others went back to the mainland, where the Iroquois fell on them again. In the end, a few Hurons returned with the Black Robes to Quebec. Others went to live with friendly tribes near Lake Erie, but the great Huron nation had been destroyed forever.

## HOW DAULAC SAVED THE COLONY

Early in the spring of 1660, the Algonkin Indians, who were friends of the French, brought news to Quebec which struck terror into the hearts of the colonists. An Iroquois prisoner had told them that eight hundred of his tribesmen were in the forests below Montreal, and that four hundred more

were already coming down the Ottawa River to join them. The Iroquois plan was to attack the three main settlements in New France—Montreal, Three Rivers, and Quebec—and to drive the French from Canada forever.

The commander of the little French garrison at Montreal was a young man named Daulac. Daulac believed that if the French waited until the two Iroquois bands came together, the colonists would be unable to defend themselves against so many savages. Then he decided on a bold plan. Indeed, it is one of the bravest and most heroic plans known in Canadian history. He and sixteen other young Frenchmen decided to go forth and try to stop the four hundred Iroquois who were coming from the country around the Ottawa River. Daulac and his brave followers took an oath to fight to the death if necessary. Then they set out upstream to meet the Iroquois.

Beside the Long Sault Rapids, a little distance above Montreal, they found the ruins of an old fort. Here they decided to make their stand. In a little while they were joined by a few Huron and Algonkin Indians who had heard of Daulac's plan. These Indians had come to help their friends, the French.

They did not have to wait long for the enemy. A few days later a fleet of canoes appeared, filled with Iroquois warriors. The Frenchmen and their Indian allies barely had time to get inside the old fort before they were attacked.

At first the Iroquois were sure that the little band of Frenchmen could easily be beaten, and they were very much surprised when they found themselves driven back by the fire from the muskets inside the fort. When they drew away from the fort they left one of their chiefs dead behind them. Some of Daulac's men rushed out, hacked off the head of the chief, and placed it on the palisade. This made the Iroquois so furious that they decided to delay their plan to attack New France. Instead of going on downstream to meet their companions on the river below Montreal, they now sent a messenger to ask the other Iroquois to come and help them against Daulac! When they arrived, there were almost one thousand Indians at the Long Sault Rapids against about two dozen Frenchmen and Indians. But even so, the attacks failed, and Daulac and his brave followers continued to kill large numbers of the savages.

But now a horrible accident took place in the fort. Daulac had made a bomb which he tried to throw over the wall into the attacking Iroquois. Unfortunately it struck the top of the palisade and fell back among the defenders, where it exploded. Some of the Frenchmen were killed, and many others were wounded. Meanwhile the Iroquois tore a hole through the palisade and began to fire on those inside. Daulac sprang forward to stop them, but he was struck down and died almost instantly. The fight did not last much longer. True to the oath which they had taken in Montreal, the remaining Frenchmen fought on until they were all killed.

Although the Iroquois had won the fight, the brave defenders of the fort had succeeded in doing what they had planned. "If a handful of Frenchmen can fight like this," the Iroquois said to one another, "what hope have we of destroying all the colonies on the St. Lawrence?" For that year they thought no more of trying to attack New France, but went back to their homes south of the St. Lawrence.

## THE FRENCH IN ACADIA

MEMBERTOU, the great chief of the Micmac Indians, was sad at heart. His friends, the Frenchmen who had first settled at Port Royal six years earlier, were leaving Acadia for France. No more would Membertou sit, an honoured guest, at their table, feasting at the banquets provided by the Order of Good Cheer. No more would his tribesmen bring their furs to Port Royal to trade for the shiny knives and tools of the Frenchmen. True, his white friends promised to return—but Membertou was very old. He was the only living Indian who could remember the visit of Jacques Cartier to the Gulf of St. Lawrence seventy-five years ago. It was now the year 1611; Membertou might never see his French friends again.

"I shall return, Membertou," said Poutrincourt, leader of the French. "I shall come back just as soon as my king will allow me. In the meantime, I leave our homes in your care."

The old chief promised that the Micmacs would guard the French settlement. This they did so faithfully that when Poutrincourt returned the following year, not a stick or stone had been touched. Poutrincourt brought with him a number of colonists, and also several missionaries. By the end of the next winter, Membertou and many of his tribe had become Christians.

But the little colony did not thrive for long. Two years later, in 1613, Poutrincourt returned to France, leaving the colony in charge of his son. Then disaster struck. The English thought the French settlement in Acadia was a threat to their colonies farther south, and decided to destroy it. When the English ships arrived, the French were absent from the fort, working in the fields. The smoke rising from their fort was the first warning of the attack. Although the settlers had escaped the raiders, Port Royal soon lay in ruins. Left homeless, some of them went to live with the Indians; others made their way to Quebec, which Champlain had founded five years earlier.

In 1621, a Scottish nobleman, Sir William Alexander, thought of a scheme to make Acadia an English colony, and to make himself very rich. He persuaded the king of England to grant him all the land contained in what are now the provinces of Nova Scotia and New Brunswick. Sir William called the whole region "Nova Scotia", which is Latin for "New Scotland". He next offered to sell large grants of land to gentlemen of wealth who would promise to bring out settlers to Nova Scotia. The king agreed to give these gentlemen the title of "baronet", and this seems to have interested the purchasers more than the grants of land, for very few of them ever came to Nova Scotia, or brought any settlers to it.

NOVA SCOTIA FLAG — AUTHORIZED 1625

BADGE OF THE BARONETS OF NOVA SCOTIA

For a while it seemed that Acadia might become an English colony. But the whole scheme came to an end in 1632, when Acadia was returned to France by the same treaty that handed back Quebec, which Champlain had surrendered in 1629.

### THE HEROINE OF ACADIA

One of the few Frenchmen who remained in Acadia after the destruction of Port Royal was Charles de la Tour. He built a fort on Cape Sable, at the south-western tip of Nova Scotia. The English were unable to drive him away, and the king of France made him lieutenant-general of the whole of Acadia. La Tour's title did not mean very much at the time. Acadia was in the possession of the English, and it had been granted to Sir William Alexander by the English king!

In 1635, however, after Acadia had been returned to France, La Tour decided to move his trading-post to the mouth of the St. John River, where the city of Saint John, New Brunswick, stands to-day. Here he built a great log fort. To it he brought his young wife, who had come out from France to marry him.

The river St. John is a great water highway leading into the heart of New Brunswick. Up and down the river the Indians passed with their cargoes of furs and trade goods. The new French fort was kept busy with the fur trade, but it was buried in the wilderness, and Madame de la Tour must have been very lonely. There were many traders and soldiers in the fort, but no other white woman except her maid. Madame de la Tour had great courage, however, and was as good a pioneer as her husband.

Across the Bay of Fundy, Port Royal was once again a strong French settlement. Its new commander was a French nobleman, Charles d'Aulnay Charnisay. He and La Tour became bitter rivals.

La Tour and Charnisay both sought to rule Acadia. At first the king of France tried to divide the country between them. But this did not satisfy Charnisay, who wanted La Tour's fort at Saint John. He had powerful friends at the court of France, who persuaded the king that La Tour was disloyal. When Charnisay, with orders from the king, tried to arrest his rival, La Tour resisted fiercely. Charnisay blockaded the mouth of the St. John River with his ships, but La Tour hired men and ships from Boston, the English colony near by, to drive him off.

As the struggle continued, Madame de la Tour bravely supported her husband's cause. Once she went to France to plead for her husband with the French king. But the king would not hear her, and forbade her to leave France under penalty of death. She defied the royal command, and escaped to England, where she hired a ship to take her to join her husband in Acadia.

When the vessel arrived in the Bay of Fundy, it was stopped by Charnisay, who boarded it to search for Madame de la Tour. She was not discovered, for the captain had hidden her safely with the cargo in the hold. But the captain was now so terrified that he refused to sail to the fort on the St. John River, and landed at Boston instead. Madame de la Tour sued him in the courts of Massachusetts for breaking his bargain, and won a large sum of money. She now hired three ships and sailed for her husband's stronghold, where she arrived safely at last.

However, the La Tours were still threatened by their relentless enemy. Charles de la Tour decided to go to Boston again to seek help, and he left his wife in command of the fort. When Charnisay heard that La Tour had sailed, he attacked the fort. He learned, however, that his rival's wife was not only a brave woman but also a good soldier.

With her small force of defenders, Madame de la Tour held off Charnisay and all his men for more than two months. When at length she was forced to surrender, she did so only after Charnisay promised to grant life and liberty to her followers. But Charnisay broke his word, and forced one of the unfortunate prisoners to hang all his comrades. Madame de la Tour's heart was broken. Charnisay placed her in prison, but she did not remain there long. Her brave spirit could not endure defeat, and three weeks later she died.

### CHANGING HANDS IN ACADIA

Charnisay was triumphant. La Tour was a homeless wanderer; his brave wife was dead. But five years after La Tour's defeat, Charnisay himself died in an accident.

La Tour's friends now took up his cause again with the king of France. They succeeded so well that the former "rebel" was appointed governor of Acadia, and the long feud between the two families came to a strange ending when La Tour married Charnisay's widow!

La Tour's ability to survive defeat was soon tested once more. Nearly forty years after their first attack, a British force took Port Royal again. They also seized the fort on the St. John River. La Tour succeeded, however, in persuading the English to let him keep a part of Acadia, and the colony was divided between him and two Englishmen. Deciding that ruling in Acadia had too many ups and downs, La Tour sold his share to one of the Englishmen and retired. He did not live to see the next turn of the wheel, when, in 1667, the colony was again restored by Great Britain to France.

At this time there were fewer than four hundred and fifty white settlers living in the whole colony, and of these more than three hundred were at Port Royal. No more settlers were brought out, but in fifteen years the population nearly doubled, and it continued to grow slowly.

The French governors of Acadia took part in the struggle which went on for the next twenty years between the French and the English in the New World. They led the Indians in many raids against the New England settlements. In 1690, Port Royal was captured by a British fleet, and then, seven years later, it was returned to France for the third time!

Port Royal was not long left undisturbed. For only ten years the French ruled, and then the English struck again. Twice the French beat off the English attacks, but in 1710 such a powerful fleet came that Port Royal had to surrender once more. This was the last surrender. From that day to this the Atlantic provinces have been under the British flag. After the treaty signed in 1713, only the islands of Cape Breton and Ile St. Jean (Prince Edward Island) were left to France.

## CANADA UNDER THE OLD REGIME

DURING the centuries that followed the breaking up of the Roman Empire in Europe, the most powerful family in each district often gained control over large tracts of land. The peasants were usually willing to promise to fight for the lord on whose land they were living, and also to make payments of farm produce and livestock in return for the right to work the lands which they were allowed to hold.

When, later in history, the most powerful lord in the land rose to be king over a whole country, he was able to tell the other landlords that they could hold their lands only if they swore to be faithful to him. This was the system of land-holding which grew up in France during the thousand years that passed before the discovery of the New World. It was known as the *feudal* system.

When France began to build her colony on the St. Lawrence, the feudal system of land-holding was introduced to Canada as well. The farmers of New France were not given or sold lands by the king. Instead, tracts of land along the main rivers were granted to *seigneurs*, as the landlords were called. In return, these seigneurs had to promise to settle people on their estates, to clear the forests, and to obey and serve the king. This promise was made by the seigneur at the home of the governor in Quebec, at whose doorstep he had to kneel with bared head and with sword and spurs removed, as he repeated the oath of allegiance to the king.

Each seigneur, in turn, parcelled out most of his land to settlers. Usually these grants were of from fifty to one hundred acres each. The first task of a new settler, or *habitant*, as the farmers of New France called themselves, was to clear the trees from the land, for this was a condition of the seigneur's grant. There were other conditions, too, but they were easily fulfilled. Each habitant had to pay a small rent to the seigneur—usually only about ten cents a year! He had to supply his lord each fall with a small part of the produce of his land, perhaps a bushel of grain or half a dozen chickens.

In order that all might share the water-front, the farms were almost always laid out in long, narrow strips bordering at one end on the river. As these were divided among children as years went by, they became narrower and narrower. Although the feudal system in Canada disappeared just over a century ago, the long, ribbon-like farms are still a common sight in the Province of Quebec.

The holdings of a seigneur of New France seldom made him a rich man. But he was respected by all the habitants of the seigneury, and each fall his manor house became the scene of a merry gathering as his tenants gathered on St. Martin's Day to pay their annual dues.

There were other festivals, too, which the habitants were able to share with their seigneur.

## THE MAY-POLE

The sun was just rising over the distant Island of Orleans, when the country folk began to gather in the courtyard of the manor house. As they laughed and talked together, they could see carts lumbering up the road from the river, filled with neighbours on their way to join in the frolic.

Since almost every man carried a long musket over his shoulder, the crowd looked like a council of war. But the smiling faces of young and old, and their bright dresses, scarfs, and sashes, gave a holiday air to the gathering. For this was the first day of May, and everywhere across New France merry-making was getting under way.

Suddenly a cheer rose from the habitants, as the door of the manor house opened and the Sieur de la Tournaye stepped out to greet his people.

"Long live La Tournaye! Long live Seigneur de la Tournaye!"

The lord of the manor stood smiling, a handsome figure in his fine plumed hat and the shining leather knee boots which he wore only on special occasions.

"And what's this?" he shouted back cheerfully at the crowd just as if he hadn't the slightest idea what it was all about.

Three habitants now stepped forward and marched in single file up to the porch. Keeping at a respectful distance, their leader cried out so that all might hear:

"Sieur de la Tournaye! The habitants have gathered because to-day is the first of May, and we would have your permission to plant our may-pole at your door!"

"The may-pole? Why, indeed, we must have a may-pole," answered La Tournaye. "What a pleasant surprise! Pray, go ahead and make merry. Madame and I shall be pleased to join you."

Everybody cheered again, including a last group of stragglers just coming up the road. Now the young men ran quickly to bring the may-pole, and the Sieur and Madame de la Tournaye walked out into the centre of the courtyard, while the habitants gathered round. Shouting ceased, and for a brief moment all knelt silently to pray that God should save them from accidents during the day.

As the seigneur rose, the joyous clamour broke out again. What a fine may-pole it was—a stout fir-trunk, some forty feet in length, hewed out of the forest last year. It glistened white in the sun, for it had been stripped bare as a dag-post, except for a small cluster of foliage at the very top. To this bushy crown a short red pole was tied, and a wind-vane fixed to the top of that. Short wooden pegs had been hammered into the sides of the pole all the way up, every three feet or so.

A deep pit had been dug the night before, in which the men now set about planting the heavy pole. With much pulling and hauling, loud encouragement from the spectators, and wild thrashing of the lofty tuft, the may-pole rose waveringly into the air.

The women broke into a merry song, which was taken up by all who had breath for it. La Tournaye drew his sword, and waved it gaily to mark the time:

> *On the first of May, shall I dig away*
> *While the sky is clear above?*
> *Ah, no! Ah, no! I'm off to plant*
> *A may for my lady-love!*

Suddenly, as the may-pole seemed about to tumble over, it settled into its place in the pit, where it was soon firmly planted. Everyone cheered wildly.

The habitant leader again came forward. "Will our seigneur do us the honour of being the first to blacken the may?" As he spoke, he handed his musket to La Tournaye, and pointed towards the shining white pole.

At this, a slim young fellow pulled a wooden mallet through his belt and began to climb up the may-pole. He planted his feet with lightning speed on one wooden peg after another. When he reached the green cluster at the top, he grasped the wind-vane and spun it about, shouting to the folk below:

"Long live the king! Long live the Seigneur de la Tournaye!"

His shout was echoed from the ground, and he started down again, chopping away the wooden pegs with his mallet as he came.

La Tournaye raised the musket, and blazed away at the base of the may-pole. Everyone cheered him as the smoke rolled aside to reveal a great black smudge that reached half way around the trunk. They cheered even more loudly when Madame, from the other side, blackened it from the same level, making a neat collar of soot about five feet from the ground.

Now all the men blasted away furiously for a quarter of an hour, and lucky it was that the muskets were loaded with gunpowder only. The shining white tree-trunk turned to jet black: the day, the Sieur, and the may-pole, had all been thoroughly honoured!

Like all good celebrations, this one ended with refreshments. The habitants now followed the seigneur and his lady into the manor house for breakfast. The manor servants hurried the stragglers inside.

Even those habitants who had been at the May-Day breakfasts given by La Tournaye in previous years found themselves a little shy and confused as they stepped into the hall of the great stone manor. There were seats for everyone, and there were over fifty people present!

"Come in! Come in!" shouted La Tournaye from the head of the long table. "There's room for everyone!"

Not only was there room for everyone--there was food for everyone, too—every kind of food you could hope to find in New France! There were cold meats, pastries, cheeses, eggs, fish, and preserves. There were silver forks and spoons for all the guests, but of course no knives. The men of New France carried their own knives to a banquet such as this—heavy, wooden-handled pocket knives. It was too early in the year for green vegetables, but the pitchers filled with golden-brown maple syrup recalled the sugaring-off parties in the maple woods a few weeks earlier.

A huge cupboard reached almost to the ceiling along one wall of the low, spacious room. Most of the dishes with which it was usually loaded were now in use, although a row of silver goblets and willow-pattern dinner plates was arranged along its top shelf. Above a vast stone fire-place hung the coat-of-arms of La Tournaye. Beyond this, the furnishings of the room were simple

enough. For many of the noblemen of New France came to the colony only because they were too poor to live in style in France. And even those who were granted large seigneuries in Canada did not make much money from them.

The table was still piled high with food when the singing began again. It was La Tournaye himself who led the merrymakers, until he became so tired that he could hardly rise from his chair. Not until then did *papa* Bilodeau, the oldest habitant present, come to his feet and thank the seigneur for his hospitality to the people of La Tournaye, taking care to praise Madame de la Tournaye as well for her great kindness. His words brought loud applause, and a few minutes later the guests were crowding out through the doorway, followed by the smiling La Tournayes. Soon the courtyard, too, was empty once more, but not until a few parting shots had been fired against the blackened trunk of the unfortunate may-pole.

As the La Tournayes stood watching their habitants disappear down the road towards the river-front, the courtyard seemed very silent. A reddish bird fluttered to the ground near by. It was a robin.

"He was waiting for the noise to die down," said Madame de la Tournaye. "See, he's listening for more shooting!" The Seigneur smiled. Spring had come in New France.

### "BLACK-MARKET" IN FURS

In the early days of New France, the biggest business in the country was the fur trade. Of course, the fur traders were not interested in farming, and so the fur trade hindered settlement in New France instead of helping it. The king of France knew very well that unless his colonists could be made to clear away the forests and begin growing food for themselves, the colony

BUYING IN THE "BLACK MARKET"— *COUREURS DE BOIS*

would not "pay its keep", even though some merchants might grow rich from the fur trade.

In order to keep the settlers busy on their farms, the king decided to forbid all of them to trade for furs with the Indians. Then he placed the whole fur trade in the hands of a single company. As we read earlier, this sole right to the fur trade was known as a *monopoly*.

Any settler who disobeyed the king's orders by trading for furs with the Indians might be severely punished. At one time, anyone who was found guilty was sentenced to be hanged. But in spite of such dangers, many young habitants—and even some of the seigneurs themselves—could not resist the temptation to find adventure and to make "easy money" by breaking the law. So it was that a large number of them began to leave the farms of New France to go off into the forests to trap for furs and to trade with the Indians as they pleased. These outlaws came to be known as *coureurs de bois*, a French phrase meaning "runners of the woods".

Here is what one missionary had to say about the monopoly system, which had forced so many youths to become *coureurs de bois*: "It serves only to rob the country of all its young men. It unfits them for any trade, and makes them useless to themselves, their families, and the public. It carries them far away from churches, and removes them from all instruction. It sends them into places wild and far away, through a thousand perils by land and water, to carry on by shameful means a trade which would much better be carried on at Montreal." Very often, however, a *coureur de bois* would return to settle in a town or on a farm in New France after a year or two of roaming the woods.

Although nearly all the *coureurs de bois* were rough and lawless adventurers, they did much to help open up the country through which they travelled. Indeed, there was hardly a river or lake in all Southern Ontario—still an unsettled wilderness—which did not float the canoe of a *coureur de bois* sooner or later.

## THE GREAT INTENDANT

As we read about the French explorers and adventurers who travelled back and forth across most of eastern Canada, we might begin to suppose that the colony on the St. Lawrence was rapidly filling up with settlers from overseas. Actually the very opposite was true. Forty years after Champlain brought the first colonists to Quebec, there still were fewer than eight hundred men, women, and children in all New France.

Since many of these inhabitants had been born in the colony, we can see that the number of newcomers arriving each year from France was still very small. The French were trying to control an area many times larger than that held by the English colonists on the Atlantic sea-board. Even the English settlements already contained many more people than did Canada.

In 1665, there arrived at Quebec an officer of the king who

was to do much to encourage the growth of New France. This was Jean Talon, often spoken of as "the great intendant". As *intendant*, Talon was expected to look after such matters as taxes, police, and the law-courts. A clever and hard-working intendant could therefore become as powerful in the colony as the governor himself. Jean Talon was just such a man.

During the few years that Talon spent in Canada, he wrote report after report to the government of France telling what

TALON VISITS A FLOUR MILL

needed to be done to strengthen Canada. Before he left the colony, he was able to carry out many of the plans he made for the betterment of the new country.

Talon realized that the most pressing need of New France was settlers, and he set about obtaining them by every means he could think of. Soldiers leaving the army, who would ordinarily have returned to France, were encouraged to settle in the colony. For them Talon created new seigneuries along the Richelieu River, where the officers became seigneurs and granted holdings to new

habitants who a short while before were serving under them in the regiment. Talon showed his wisdom, too, in opening these seigneuries where he did. The Richelieu was the highway into the heart of the Iroquois country to the south, beyond which lay the English settlements. What better settlers to guard such a "back-door" to the colony than a regiment of fighting-men!

His repeated demands for more settlers from France began to bring results, too. On arriving in the colony, the newcomer might be sent to help habitants clear new farming land, or he might be required to serve a tradesman in one of the towns. In either event, he was paid a wage, and at the end of three years could become a settler on the land or open a trade or business of his own.

It was not enough to depend on disbanded troops and a handful of settlers each summer. To hasten the growth of the colony, it was necessary to increase the number of *families* in New France, so that the land would begin to fill up with people who had been born in the country. Because there were many more men than women in the colony, Talon now called on the government in France to send out young ladies who might make good wives for the settlers who had already arrived. Care was taken to send women suited to life in a rugged pioneer country, and on the whole the plan worked excellently. As quickly as they arrived, they found husbands and homes. "No sooner", it was said at the time, "have vessels arrived than the young men go to get wives. They are married by thirties at a time."

## A VISIT TO QUEBEC, 1666

As Pierre bumped up and down amid the vegetables in the back of his uncle's ox-cart, he could not help thinking that he was the luckiest boy in the whole colony—outside the capital, at least. Never before had he visited the city, where the marketplace was and where the government officers and shop-keepers lived. The habitants did not often leave the seigneuries—except, of course, on Fridays. That was market-day in New France. And now Pierre was going to market, too!

"Don't get wet back there!" cried Pierre's uncle, as the oxcart lurched down the bank of the St. Charles River. It was necessary to ford the St. Charles, which flows into the St. Lawrence just below Quebec, in order to reach the Lower Town from the seigneury of Beauport.

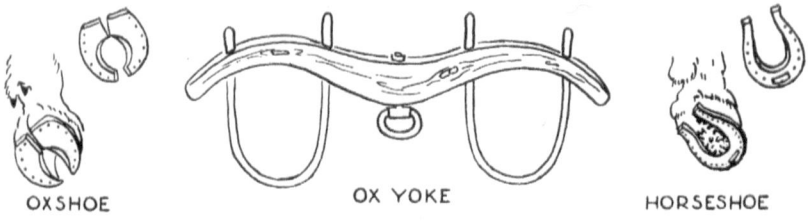

OXSHOE  OX YOKE  HORSESHOE

"Look, papa!" said Pierre, as they pulled slowly over the crest of the far bank a few minutes later. "Look at the houses. Where are the farms?"

Pierre's father smiled, for this was all new to his son. "That first house belongs to Roland the trader," he explained. "He left last week for Ville-Marie, where they are expecting a late shipment of furs from the Ottawa."

"And he had better hurry them down to Quebec, too," added Pierre's uncle. "The last ships will leave for France before the end of the month. October is too late to be looking for fur shipments in Ville-Marie, I say."

There were more houses now—low buildings with stone walls at the ends, for the most part. However, many had wooden fronts, and the roofs of all were covered with cedar shingles.

Pierre gazed up at the cliff which towered above everything along the water's edge. The stone palace of Bishop Laval, which served also as a college, a parish church, and a residence for priests, was almost directly overhead now. He knew the building well, for it could be seen clearly from their home on the seigneury of Beauport.

As they passed the foot of the road which wound up the side of the cliff from the Lower Town, Pierre wondered how an ox team could possibly draw a wagon up its steep slope. At the summit stood the Chateau St. Louis itself, built by the great Sieur de Champlain forty years before, during the early days of the settlement. Just below the Chateau, on the left side of the road from the Lower Town, Pierre could see the encampment of the Huron Indians, about which his father had often spoken. The Hurons had come there fifteen years ago, after being driven from their homes around Georgian Bay by the savage Iroquois warriors from the south.

"They were a pitiful band when they arrived," explained Pierre's uncle. "If it had not been for the Jesuit fathers, they surely would have starved, even in Quebec, during that first winter."

"Pierre could hardly remember that," smiled the lad's father. "After all, that all happened three years before he was born!"

It was only a few hundred feet more to the Champlain Market. A score of habitants were already bustling about. Pierre was so excited that he was not of much help while his father and uncle were getting ready to start the day's business.

"Papa, look at all the people!" Pierre exclaimed, as the marketplace filled up with farmers' carts laden with green things to sell.

"If everybody in Quebec comes to market to-day, Pierre," laughed his father, "there won't be many compared with market-day at home in France. Why, there are less than five hundred people in the whole city!"

"We won't be busy for a while," said Pierre's uncle. "Come along with me; we'll take a walk uphill. The gentlewomen do their own shopping in the market, and it's still too early for them."

A visit to the Upper Town! This would be something to tell about at Beauport, thought Pierre.

The little street along which they now walked contained several homes owned by traders and businessmen of the city. Pierre's uncle told him that the street was called Sous-le-Fort (*soo lfor*). In English, it would have been known as "Under-the-Fort", which was a good name because it ran up to the foot of the cliff, beneath Fort St. Louis, far above. Here it ended suddenly in a wooden stairway just as it does to-day.

"These are the Champlain Steps," explained Pierre's uncle, as he followed his nephew up them. "They save walking around to the foot of the hill. See," he added as they reached the top step, out of breath, "here we are half-way up already." Pierre looked about him. On the cliff straight ahead of them, around which the steep roadway wound on its way to the Upper Town, stood a beautiful home. "That is where our new intendant is going to keep house," said Pierre's uncle.

Pierre had heard about the new intendant, Jean Talon, who had arrived at Quebec only recently. "He seems to be a good man. In three weeks he has come to know most of us in the market by name. It is early to be saying, but he will soon be able to tell the government at Versailles a thing or two that is wrong in the colony."

It was a stiff climb to the top of the hill, but Pierre found the shops along the way so interesting that they had reached the level of Monsieur Talon's house before he knew it. "Step over here, Pierre," said the boy's uncle. "We can see everything at once from beside the intendant's garden."

When they reached the edge of the wall, Pierre understood what his uncle meant by saying that they could "see everything at once". The view below, above, all around them, was magnificent. The bright morning sun lighted the landscape so clearly that Pierre was sure that he could pick out their own farmhouse on the seigneury of Beauport, five miles away on the north shore of the St. Lawrence. In the distance beyond, all across the northern horizon, stretched the blue Laurentian Highlands.

The sights below interested Pierre most, for from Monsieur Talon's garden one could look straight down into the streets of the Lower Town, and out across the river to the heights on the other side. Three large sailing vessels were tied up to the docks not far from the Champlain Market. A fourth ship must have sailed while Pierre and his uncle were still in the Lower Town, for Pierre could now see it gliding quietly down the middle of the broad St. Lawrence, its white sails gleaming in the sunlight. He watched it until it tacked in the distance just before it reached the Island of Orleans, and disappeared behind Point Levy on its way downstream towards France.

Most of the people of Quebec lived on the shore below, between the foot of the cliff and the river's edge. There were not many houses, barely sixty in the whole city—just one for each year since Champlain had built his "habitation" in 1608.

Beside each one Pierre could see a huge pile of cord wood, ready for the coming winter.

"Look up there," said Pierre's uncle, pointing to the buildings beyond the Indian camp near by. "The great wooden Fort St. Louis is falling into ruin, as you can see. One would think His Majesty would be willing to spend money on it, when it stands guard over the whole of New France."

Pierre could see now, better than ever before, why the fortress gave its owners control of the whole St. Lawrence Valley. Any ship sailing upstream on the St. Lawrence had to pass within easy range of the guns on the heights near by. There was only one roadway up the cliff on this side of the city, and it could easily be defended against an enemy landing party. Pierre's uncle guessed the boy's thoughts.

"Yes," he said, nodding his head towards Fort St. Louis. "We may be in need of more people here in New France. But we do not have to worry about our safety, not if we stay living in the shadow of Fort St. Louis!"

"SKIN FOR SKIN"

COAT OF ARMS OF THE
HUDSON'S BAY COMPANY

## THE COMING OF THE "ADVENTURERS"

A hundred and seventy years had passed since John Cabot returned from his great voyage of 1497 to tell the English king about the lands he had found on the western side of the Atlantic Ocean. Now, in 1667, another English monarch listened to a tale of exploration no less wonderful about the mysterious country that lay beyond the English and French colonies in North America.

A good deal had been learned about the new continent since the time of John Cabot. The French had explored and settled Acadia and the St. Lawrence Valley, and already their voyageurs and missionaries were pressing westward through the country about the Great Lakes. The English, of course, had been busy in the New World, too. Only three years earlier, in 1664, an English fleet had forced the surrender of the Dutch colony at the mouth of the Hudson River. Now the whole Atlantic seaboard between the French in Acadia and the Spaniards in Florida was under the flag of His Majesty, King Charles II of England.

Like John Cabot, who had come from Venice, the two men who now described their adventures to King Charles were not English themselves. Strangely enough, they were French *coureurs de bois*, who only recently had been ranging through the distant wilds of the Lake Superior country, seeking furs to carry back

to the markets of New France. Their names were Radisson and Groseilliers (*gro-zay-yay*), and they had come to England with a bold plan to help King Charles II secure more of the fur trade in North America.

When Prince Rupert, the king's cousin, first heard the plan of the two *coureurs de bois*, he agreed that this was England's opportunity. He introduced Radisson and Groseilliers to the leading English merchants, and now had made possible a visit to Windsor Castle so that they might tell their story to King Charles himself.

## THE STORY OF RADISSON AND GROSEILLIERS

A few years earlier, a roving band of Iroquois warriors captured a young French settler near the town of Three Rivers. Instead of taking his life, they adopted him into their tribe and set about teaching him their language and their ways of living. This was sometimes done by the Iroquois when they brought home captives after their raids into the lands of other tribes. The Frenchman whose life they had spared was none other than Radisson himself, still a youth of only sixteen.

Young Radisson took well to life in the woods, but he longed to return to his family in New France. The first time that he tried to escape he was recaptured and savagely tortured. A little later he tried again, and this time he succeeded in reaching the Dutch settlements on the Hudson River. In all, Radisson had been away from New France for two years, and when he returned his friends found it hard to believe he was still alive.

In the meantime, his sister had married a *coureur de bois* named Groseilliers, who, like Radisson, had come to Canada from France as a young man. Radisson and Groseilliers became fast friends from the moment they met. A short while later they set out on the first of their many thrilling journeys through the wilds of the Upper Lakes, trading for furs and exploring the country as they travelled.

Because both Radisson and Groseilliers understood the ways and languages of the Indians, they were able to roam through great areas which had never before been explored. It is believed that they may have travelled as far as the Mississippi River. However, Radisson decided that the best beaver country lay north of the Great Lakes, and when the two adventurers returned to New France in 1660, no fewer than three hundred Indians in sixty canoes helped them bring back the furs they had gathered during two years in the wilds.

In Quebec they were given a royal welcome, for the whole colony of New France depended on the success of the fur trade. Radisson and Groseilliers had made many friends for the French among the Indian tribes they had visited. They had opened the way to the great North-West. From now on, parties of French voyageurs could travel to the rich beaver lands themselves, instead of waiting for the Indians to bring their furs down the lakes past the lurking bands of Iroquois.

RADISSON AND GROSEILLIERS ON THE UPPER LAKES

But when Radisson and Groseilliers made plans the next year to travel again into the rich northland, the governor demanded half the profits of their voyage. This angered the two traders, and they set out without his permission. Once again they found the natives willing to trade huge quantities of beaver. Radisson reports that he and one Indian alone shot over six hundred moose that spring. We are not sure how far they wandered that year before they turned north from Lake Superior and made a long journey overland—perhaps even as far as Hudson Bay!

By the end of August, the two adventurers were on their way back to New France with a fleet of three hundred and sixty canoes laden with furs. But this time the governor did not welcome them. Instead, they were so heavily fined for having set out without permission that they decided to leave New France. That was why they had offered their services to England.

For Radisson and Groseilliers brought back something more valuable than furs when they returned to New France for the last time from the great North-West. They knew now that the vast inland sea, which Henry Hudson had discovered over half a century earlier, reached down into the heart of that rich fur country. This meant that ships from Europe could meet and trade with the Indians far beyond the north-west borders of the French settlements. No longer would New France block the way to the beaver country lying north and west of the Great Lakes. They now asked King Charles II to help them lead an expedition into Hudson Bay by sea, and build English trading forts on its shores!

### THE FOUNDING OF THE GREAT COMPANY

King Charles thought well of the ambitious plan of the two French fur traders, and Prince Rupert, together with a number of other English noblemen and merchants, offered to pay the cost of an expedition to the "sea of the north". So it was that, in the spring of 1668, two sailing ships laden with such trade goods as hatchets, knives, looking-glasses, beads, and coloured cloth set sail from the Port of London and turned their prows towards Hudson Bay, which had not been visited by sailing ships for almost thirty-five years. The two fur traders separated from each other for the ocean passage, Radisson sailing on one vessel and Groseilliers on the other. Over a year was to pass before they saw each other again.

If we look at the map of Canada, we see that Hudson Bay is an ocean passage into the very heart of the Dominion. We shall learn later how this route has been used during recent years, and how new scientific discoveries may make it even more useful in the future. But Hudson Strait is blocked by drift ice during most of the year, and only during the last two months of summer could a passage through it be made with safety and certainty. So near is the north magnetic pole that the compasses on the early explorers' ships must have proved almost useless. Fogs, too, often cover the Strait, although the long daylight during the Arctic summers comes to the aid of sea-captains in these waters. Little wonder it is that so many years passed before much was learned about this important northern waterway. But these difficulties were not as great as they seemed. Ships have made the passage almost every year since the time of Radisson and Groseilliers, and with surprisingly few losses.

To Radisson's bitter disappointment, the vessel on which he sailed sprang a leak long before it reached the strait leading into the Bay, and had to return to England. What had happened to Groseilliers' party aboard the vessel *Nonsuch?* There was no way of finding out, and it was too late in the year for Radisson to make a fresh start. All winter long he waited impatiently in England, writing his diary and making plans to sail for the Bay the next year. When spring came he succeeded in securing another ship, and lost no time in setting forth again. But once more the ship in which he sailed was driven back. Imagine, however, Radisson's great joy when he reached port in England and beheld the sturdy little *Nonsuch* riding at anchor after a safe voyage back from Hudson Bay! Radisson could hardly wait to land and find his partner, Groseilliers. His delight knew no bounds when he learned that everything had gone according to plan with his friend's party. Groseilliers had led the *Nonsuch* to the mouth of the Rupert River, which flows into James Bay.

On its bank he had built a trading post, which was named Fort Charles in honour of the English king. At first the Indians were afraid to come near the white strangers, but Groseilliers persuaded them to bring their furs to the fort, where he offered them better prices than they had been receiving from New France. The expedition wintered safely at the fort, and the hold of the little *Nonsuch* was filled with a cargo of precious furs!

A beginning had been made, and Prince Rupert and his "merchant adventurers" who had paid for the expedition were highly pleased with the results. On May 2, 1670, King Charles granted a charter to "The Governor and Company of Adventurers of England Trading into Hudson's Bay". That company still exists, and we know it to-day as the Hudson's Bay Company. (Remember that the Bay is called *Hudson* Bay, and the Company the *Hudson's* Bay Company.)

The new company was given complete control of the fur trade "over all regions whose waters empty into Hudson Bay". King Charles did not know that he was handing over most of the Canadian West as far as the foothills of the Rockies, and large parts of Northern Ontario and Quebec. As one historian has said, "with a stroke of his pen King Charles made the Adventurers lords of nearly half a continent!"

During the years that followed, many more posts were built at the mouths of other rivers flowing into the Bay. It was not long before the French on the St. Lawrence realized that many of the furs of the north country were going to the English on Hudson Bay instead of to their posts in New France.

Radisson decided to return to the side of France for a time, but the English found him too clever an enemy and persuaded him to go to work for them once more. We may think harshly of Radisson for his lack of loyalty. But he and Groseilliers were dreamers who made their dreams come true. Had it not been for the work of these two *coureurs de bois*, the English would never have gained their foothold on Hudson Bay—the back door to the fur trade of Canada.

A struggle between the English and French for control of this northern fur trade was now almost certain. Before long, Hudson Bay echoed to the roar of cannon and musketry. But that is another story.

## IBERVILLE THE CONQUEROR

A few years passed before the merchants of New France realized that the Hudson's Bay Company was draining off a rich part of the northern fur trade. But the stories told them by their voyageurs who visited the Lake Superior country at last started talk in Montreal and Quebec of driving the English from the new posts on the Bay. "Fifty of our countrymen under good leadership," said one of the king's officers, "would make themselves masters of their chief fort, which is nothing better than a shanty with a palisade around it."

It was a seven-hundred-mile journey overland, however, from Montreal to the nearest Company fort on James Bay. Few arms and supplies could be carried across the rough portages which would have to be made on the way.

France and England were at peace with one another. Even so, the governor of New France decided to take action. In 1686, he sent an expedition from the colony to oppose the English on the shores of the "sea of the north". It was made up of about eighty men, and it took them three months of difficult travel to cross from the St. Lawrence to James Bay, where lay the nearest Company posts.

"...from the St. Lawrence to James Bay..."

It was still too early in the season for ships to pass through Hudson Strait into the Bay, and the English traders who had wintered in the forest along Hudson Bay and James Bay did not dream that they were in danger of attack. Certainly the Company's traders at Moose Factory, at the southern end of James Bay, were not expecting trouble as they went about their tasks during the middle of June that year. Little did they realize that their every movement was being closely watched by three Frenchmen in the woods near by, members of the war-party from New France!

One of these scouts was the Sieur d'Iberville, a young Canadian who was to become one of the most daring leaders in the whole history of New France. The story of his life is a story of adventure from beginning to end.

Late one night the French raiders struck. Iberville, with a handful of followers, climbed the palisade behind the fort. At the same time, the rest of the attackers burst through the main gate. The English traders were caught entirely by surprise, and in half an hour the Company's post was in French hands.

Before the season was over, the other two Company posts on James Bay fell to the raiders as well. The young Hudson's Bay Company had been dealt a serious blow. And all this had happened while France and England were supposed to be at peace with each other.

During the next two summers, the Company suffered further heavy losses as a result of visits by French raiding parties under the leadership of the Sieur d'Iberville. Their trading posts were no longer safe from attack, and even on the waters of the Bay their ships had to run the gauntlet to escape from daring sea-raiders led by Iberville. Soon Fort Nelson was the only armed post left to the English on the whole coast-line of the north, and the Company had lost over half a million dollars' worth of equipment and furs.

THE ENGLISH SURRENDER FORT NELSON, 1697

When the two powers went to war in 1689, the struggle on the Bay broke out afresh. The English recaptured Fort Albany; then Iberville came again and the English stronghold of Fort Nelson fell under his attack. Leaving a force to hold the post, Iberville returned to New France.

The war against the English kept Iberville busy on many fronts. He attacked the English settlements in Newfoundland, and laid them waste one by one. But he was needed everywhere at once, for the English were able to overpower Fort Nelson in his absence and win it back again. In the spring of 1697, a fleet of five warships was placed under Iberville's command, and he set out once again for Hudson Bay.

As Iberville sailed north towards Hudson Strait, he had no suspicion that an English fleet was approaching from the east, on its way to the Company's posts on the Bay. The English had no knowledge of the French ships either, but ice in the Strait blocked the way for both fleets. Soon they were within sight of one another and the race was on! Who would reach the English forts first—Iberville to attack them, or the English to bring aid?

At last Iberville's own ship broke its way into the Bay, but the rest of his fleet became separated, and Iberville was alone when he came in sight of Fort Nelson. Soon three sails appeared on the horizon. Thinking that they were his other ships, Iberville sailed to meet them to make plans to attack the fort. But just as he came within range of their guns, he realized that they were not his ships after all. The English ships had broken into the Bay first!

Although he was dangerously outnumbered, Iberville was a bold leader, and he decided to give battle immediately. As he sailed into the midst of the enemy, cannon balls pounded into his ship from both sides. Fortunately for Iberville, an approaching storm made the sea so rough that many of the shots missed his little vessel. It was a bitter fight, but at last the largest English ship was damaged so badly that it settled into the water and sank. In spite of the heavy pounding his own vessel had received, Iberville was then able to capture one of the other two Company ships, while the fire from his guns drove off the third. With one small vessel this great French captain had defeated three British warships.

As the roar of the cannon died down, the storm grew worse. A fierce gale was soon lashing across the decks of the two vessels Iberville now commanded. Their anchor chains would not hold, and they were driven before the storm towards the coast near by. Neither ship could escape, and before morning they had both been wrecked on the shore.

Iberville and most of the men reached land safely, but their brilliant victory seemed to have been turned into defeat. They

were alive, but without food or shelter. They had landed dangerously near Fort Nelson, which was held by the English. Iberville again showed how valiant a leader he was. He ordered his followers to make ready to attack the English fort!

At that moment, Iberville's luck changed again. Three of the ships he had left behind in Hudson Strait hove into sight. With these added forces, success was sure. The English inside the fort fought bravely, but they could not withstand the cannon brought ashore from the French ships. After refusing three demands from Iberville that they surrender, the governor of the fort at last gave orders to cease fire. Once more, Fort Nelson was in the hands of the French.

Iberville's days of adventure were far from over. The next year he sailed from France to the Gulf of Mexico, and planted a colony at the mouth of the Mississippi. He spent most of the rest of his life building the colony of Louisiana, in the land that the explorer La Salle had discovered fifteen years earlier. But his work on Hudson Bay was over. The English had almost been driven from the Bay as a result of the work of this daring leader from New France.

We might think that the French would have done as well in the fur trade on the Bay as the Company of Adventurers, now that all the English posts except Fort Albany had been captured. But the merchants of New France were not able to make the northern posts pay for themselves. This was because the English still controlled the sea-route into Hudson Bay. It was too expensive to carry supplies and furs to and from the Bay by the long overland route which was the only one the French could use. Besides, many Indians preferred to trade with the English at Fort Albany, and the rivalry between the traders of the two countries made both sides lose money.

France seemed to forget about the Hudson Bay country which Iberville had conquered. Years went by, and no ships were sent to the French posts on the Bay. At last, in 1713, France signed a treaty by which she agreed, among other things, to return the Hudson Bay lands to England.

Trade between the Hudson's Bay Company and the Indians of the north began to flourish once again. The dark days when French raiders might descend at any moment on the Company's posts were forgotten. No longer did the trading ships from England have to dread attack by French warships whenever they entered the Bay. Instead, England's overseas trade was increased in value and the foundations were laid for English exploration westward through the work of the Great Company.

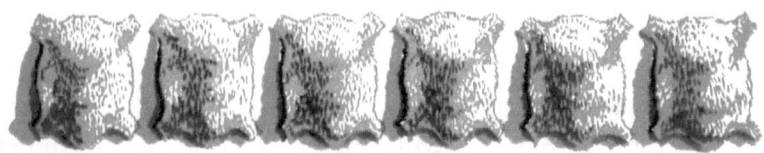

## THE FIGHTING GOVERNOR

THE people of New France were in gay humour over the news that came to them in the summer of 1689. Old Count Frontenac was coming out to be governor of the colony for a second time.

It was seven years since the fiery count had been called home to France because he quarrelled constantly with the intendant and with New France's first bishop, Laval. But the colonists had never forgotten how he had put fear into the hearts of their Indian enemies. Now the Iroquois had once again taken the war-path, and the lives of the settlers were again in danger. They felt cheered to think that the old leader was coming back to Canada.

The king of France had other reasons besides the Iroquois threat for sending out Frontenac as governor for a second term. For France had just gone to war with England. Iberville's raiders had already struck at the English on Hudson Bay. It was certain that there would now be trouble between New France and the English colonies to the south.

"I am sending you back to Canada," the king told Count Frontenac, "where I am sure you will serve me as well as you did before. I ask nothing more of you."

Frontenac decided to strike a blow at the English colonies as soon as he arrived in Canada. He did not even wait until the following summer, but sent his men south on snow-shoes during the middle of winter. Many Indian allies went with them, and village after village in the northern part of the English colonies was attacked and destroyed. Whole families of English settlers were wiped out, as the attackers left a trail of blood across the snows that blanketed the frontier towns.

These were cruel and savage raids, but we must remember that New France was attacked by the English colonists in the same way. It was sad to see white men acting like their Indian allies, but each side was trying to drive the other from the continent in order to gain the whole of the fur trade with the savages for itself.

New France did not have to wait long before the English colonists struck back—this time at the very heart of New France. In the next summer the people of Massachusetts sent a fleet of more than thirty vessels against Canada. These ships were under the command of Sir William Phips of Boston. In fact, the whole expedition was paid for by the Atlantic colonies of Great Britain, which shows how rapidly they had grown. They were already much larger and stronger than New France, and they decided that they could conquer Quebec, even without help from the British navy.

### "BY THE MOUTHS OF MY CANNON!"

The fleet from Boston arrived beneath the walls of Quebec about the middle of October, 1689. Only a few weeks remained until the St. Lawrence River would be frozen over, but Phips believed that he could capture the fortress within a day or two at most. He had conquered the Acadian French that spring by simply demanding that they surrender, and now he decided to send a message to Frontenac calling on him to give up the city without fighting.

The French soldiers met the messenger as he came ashore. They did not harm him even though he was an enemy, because he came under a white flag of truce. But they did cover his eyes with a blindfold before they began to lead him up the hill to Chateau St. Louis, where the fiery old governor was waiting. On the way, they did everything they could to make the New England messenger think that Quebec was filled with soldiers. He was forced to climb over one barricade after another, while all around the people who were watching rattled guns on the cobblestones and shouted military orders, until the poor messenger was completely bewildered.

At last the New Englander was led into a huge room of the Chateau where Count Frontenac stood, surrounded by his officers. There the blindfold was taken from his eyes. The messenger blinked with amazement at the sight of so many army leaders, all dressed in rich uniforms of gold and silver lace. He had been told that the French leaders were ready to surrender, but now it seemed that Frontenac and his officers were not worried at all! After a moment, however, he saluted the white-haired governor of New France, and handed him the message from Sir William Phips. Frontenac handed it to an interpreter, who read it aloud in French:

"I, William Phips, Knight, demand surrender of your forts and castles undamaged, together with all your persons; when you do this, you may expect mercy from me... If you refuse to do this immediately, I am ready... by force of arms to revenge all wrongs and injuries you have done, and bring you under the Crown of England, and make you wish, when too late, that you had accepted the favour I am offering you.

"Your answer in one hour, blown on your own trumpet to be answered by mine, is required on pain of what will follow."

When the interpreter had finished translating the letter from Sir William Phips, the messenger drew out his watch and handed

it to the old governor. As did so, he reminded the French leader that a reply was needed within one hour. Frontenac listened quietly until everything had been said. At last he spoke: "I shall not keep you waiting so long," said Frontenac to the messenger from Sir William Phips. "Even if your general offered me conditions of surrender a little less harsh, and if I had a mind to accept them, docs he think that these brave gentlemen here would give their consent?"

The messenger was astonished and startled at Frontenac's words, for he had been sure that Quebec would be surrendered willingly. He asked the governor if he could have an answer in writing to carry to Sir William Phips.

"No!" replied Frontenac hotly. "I will answer your general by the mouths of my cannon! He will learn that a man like me is not to be summoned in this fashion. Let him do his best, and I will do mine."

In the fighting that followed Frontenac's reply to the leader from New England, Sir William Phips found out what an able leader the old count was. All his attacks against the fortress were in vain. Cannon-fire from almost overhead poured down on his ships whenever he let them sail close to the shore beneath Quebec. He tried to land an army, but its attack was broken up before it could reach the heights on which the city stood.

Just one week after he had brought his proud fleet into the great river basin below Quebec, Sir William Phips had to give the order to retreat.

As the sails of the ships from Boston disappeared down the St. Lawrence, Quebec went wild with rejoicing. And the hero of the hour was the gallant old governor of New France, who had refused to give up his fortress without a fight.

## TO THE HEART OF THE CONTINENT

THE rich cargoes of furs which Radisson and Groseilliers brought back from Lake Michigan and Lake Superior encouraged other *coureurs de bois* to venture into the western wilderness. Some of the westward-bound canoes also carried missionaries, eager to spread the Gospel among the newly discovered tribes. Since the *coureurs de bois* were strictly forbidden to trade with the Indians, they did not write reports of their travels, as did the better known explorers of history. But many of the trails into the heart of our continent were blazed by these early voyageurs and missionaries.

At first the kings of France tried to prevent their North American subjects from going into the West. New France was still small and weak; she could not easily spare the young men who went off to become fur traders in the wilds beyond the frontiers. They were all sorely needed at home to farm the fields of the young colony and to protect the settlements along the St. Lawrence.

At last, however, France began to realize that if she did not soon move into the West, the English colonists along the Atlantic coast might take possession of it instead. In 1671, a French expedition reached Sault Ste Marie. There it claimed,

in the name of the king of France, Lakes Huron and Superior, and all the country round about "which had been discovered and might be discovered after". In the following year another expedition was sent overland to claim Hudson Bay, but it found that the English had already built forts and were carrying on a busy fur trade with the Indians.

Of all the Frenchmen of the St. Lawrence Valley who listened to the tales of the Indians and voyageurs from beyond the western frontier, none was more interested than a handsome young seigneur, the Sieur de la Salle. The Indians spoke of a great river that flowed through the heart of the continent (they meant the Mississippi), which had never been explored by white men. Perhaps it might lead to the Pacific Ocean. What a triumph it would be to find a route to the western sea, which so many others had sought in vain!

Like most other French-Canadian seigneurs, La Salle was not a wealthy man. But now he was fired with the desire to explore the unknown West, and nothing could stop him. He sold his seigneury on the Island of Montreal, and with the money he received he hired men and canoes and bought supplies for the journey.

It was only three years since La Salle had come out from France, but in 1669 he set forth on his first great expedition of discovery. Instead of following the better-known route up the Ottawa River, he portaged his canoes past the rapids of the upper St. Lawrence and travelled along the southern shore of Lake Ontario, which Champlain and his "young men" had visited over fifty years earlier. Crossing overland towards the south-west, he discovered the Ohio River, but did not follow it downstream to where it joins the Mississippi. By the time La Salle returned to New France, two years later, he had seen enough to believe that France could build herself still another empire in this part of the New World. But he had already spent most of his money to pay for his first journey. How could he carry out the great plans that he had made?

Fortunately, Count Frontenac was made governor of New France in 1672. As we shall remember, Frontenac was almost as ambitious a man as La Salle. The explorer and the new governor came to like each other from the first time they met, and La Salle began to hope that he would have the support he needed to carry out his plans. Shortly after the "Fighting Governor" built Fort Frontenac, he appointed La Salle as its commander.

Because Fort Frontenac controlled the entrance from the Great Lakes to the St. Lawrence River, it quickly became an important military and trading centre. To it came the Indian canoes laden with furs, even those of the Iroquois themselves, who in the past had traded only with the Dutch and English on the Atlantic coast.

But although the new fort helped the fortunes of La Salle, he felt that this was only a beginning. In 1673, the same year that the fort was built, Father Marquette (*mar-ket*) and Louis Joliet (*jo-lyay*) had set out from Green Bay, on Lake Michigan, and reached the Mississippi River. They followed the river downstream far enough to realize, from the direction in which they were going, that it must empty into the Gulf of Mexico instead of the Pacific Ocean. Marquette and Joliet then turned back, without reaching the mouth of the river.

The honour of that discovery was left for another explorer. In 1677, the Sieur de la Salle sailed for France to secure the consent of the king to further explorations in the lands to the south and west.

LA SALLE ON THE UPPER LAKES

From the point above Fort Michilimackinac, the waters of Lake Michigan sparkled in the sunlight as the wind drove the waves across the lake.

Behind the point, by the quiet harbour, stood the wigwams of the Indian village, the cabins of French traders, and the house and chapel of the Jesuit missionaries.

Suddenly, on the height above the settlement, a shout arose. A huge white sail had been sighted on the horizon.

Before long, the ship rounded the point and bore into the harbour. Priests, traders, and Indians crowded to the shore in

wonder and amazement as the deep boom of cannon from the vessel announced her arrival.

For this was the first ship that had ever been launched on the Upper Lakes. She was a little vessel of only forty-five tons, but the Indians at Fort Michilimackinac marvelled at her size as she glided towards them. Truly, the white man had built a great "canoe"!

The ship dropped anchor near the shore in the midst of a little fleet of canoes that moved out to welcome her. The passengers--soldiers, sailors, and gentlemen adventurers from New France--were paddled ashore. They formed a procession and marched towards the chapel in the Indian village. At their head strode a handsome young man, richly dressed in a scarlet cloak with a gold border that glistened in the sun. It was the famous Sieur de la Salle himself. He had just brought the *Griffon* on her first voyage through Lake Erie and Lake Huron to this distant fort of Michilimackinac, at the entrance to Lake Michigan.

In the parade that followed La Salle to the chapel, the onlookers could spy a soldierly man with only one hand, accompanied by a sturdy priest of the Recollet Order. These were La Salle's trusted lieutenant, Tonty "of the iron hand", and Father Hennepin. Father Hennepin had been the first white man to see Niagara Falls, which he visited a little ahead of La Salle during the previous winter.

"And what is the Sieur de la Salle going to do with this fine ship?" asked one of the voyageurs of a sailor near by.

"Ah, he's full of great schemes, the Sieur de la Salle!" answered the man from the *Griffon*. "With this ship he will carry furs from Lake Michigan back to the falls of Niagara. But that's not all. He plans to explore the great river reached by Joliet and Father Marquette six years ago. It is said he bears the king's warrant to build forts and colonies throughout that region. He thinks to build another ship like the *Griffon* on the Mississippi, of which I speak. Then, with ships on Lake Ontario as well, he can move whole cargoes of furs from the West to New France to enrich himself and his good friend the governor, Count Frontenac. What a dreamer, that one!"

"We shall see what comes of these dreams," muttered the fur trader. "He'll have to reckon with those red demons of Iroquois, and perhaps with their friends the English as well. Doubtless he hopes to reach Mexico and shake hands with the Spaniards!"

The sailor nodded. "Ah, but he's stubborn, though. Those five cannon on the *Griffon* there—last winter they dragged them up the cliff beside the falls of Niagara. And it was touch-and-go with the Indians all the time they were building the ship on the river above the falls. Would he give up? Not he!"

"And I say bad luck to him," growled the trader. "There's the end of our business! That ship will carry a hundred canoe-loads of furs. What will be left for us fellows? May the Evil One fly away with him and his schemes!"

"...TO BUILD FORTS AS CENTRES FOR TRADING..."

## DOWN THE MISSISSIPPI

True to his plan, La Salle sailed on south and west over Lake Michigan to Green Bay, where the *Griffon* was loaded with a rich cargo of furs and ordered to sail back to Niagara. As La Salle remained on the shore watching his ship pass over the horizon, he little guessed that she would never be heard of again. No one knows whether storms, hostile Indians, or the treachery of the pilot brought about the ship's disappearance, but no trace of the proud little *Griffon* was ever found. This was a terrible blow to La Salle's fortunes, but he was still determined to explore the Mississippi, and to found on its banks the new French colony of his dreams.

La Salle's first task was to build forts as centres for trading with the Indians. He spent two years in establishing these posts, always under the greatest difficulties. He had to win the trust of the neighbouring Indian tribes, in the face of the Iroquois, who claimed to control the region.

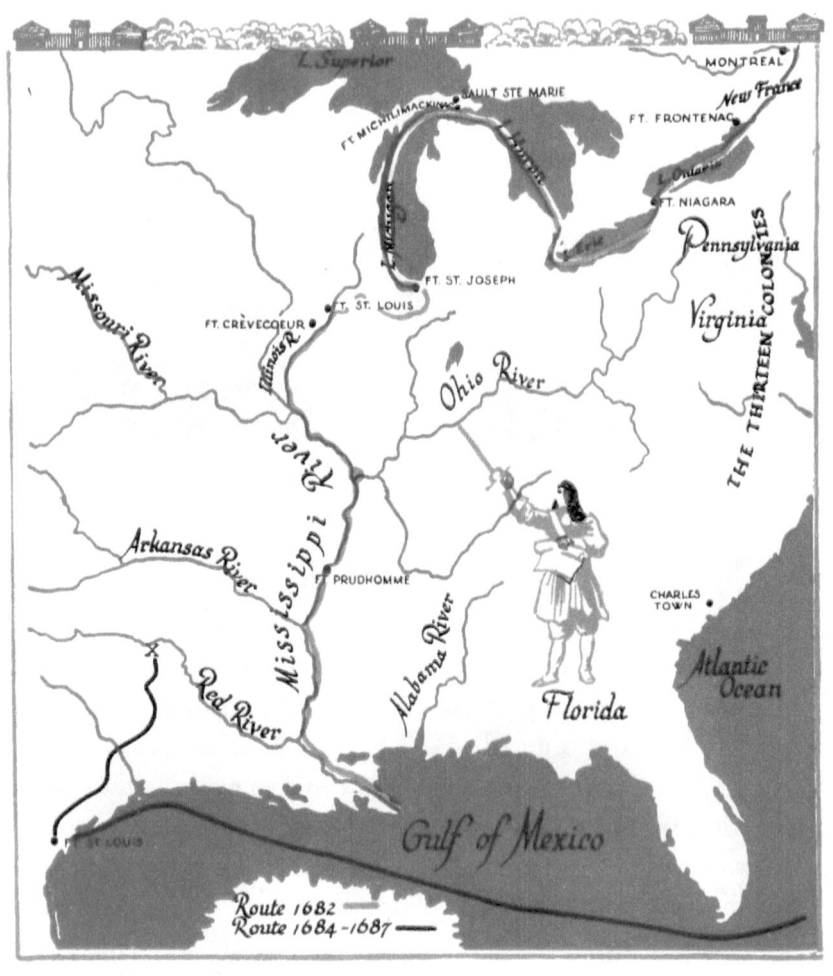

*La Salle's Explorations*

Many of La Salle's men proved treacherous. Tonty was one of the few who remained loyal through every hardship. Frequently supplies ran short. To make matters worse, La Salle's property in New France was seized in payment of his debts.

However, in his third winter in the Mississippi Valley, La Salle began a thrilling canoe journey down the mighty river. With a mixed party of Indians and Frenchmen, he followed its winding course week after week until at last he reached a region of swamps and reedy marshes. Here the river divided into three channels. La Salle broke his party into three groups, each of which followed one of the channels to the Gull of Mexico. On the shore of the Mississippi delta, the three parties came together again, and La Salle proudly proclaimed that all the land about them, and all the lands through which they had passed, henceforth belonged to France. In honour of King Louis, he named the vast country that he had claimed "Louisiana".

The story of La Salle's last expedition is sad. When he returned to France after his long journey down the Mississippi, he secure the backing of the king in a plan to carry settlers by sea to the mouth of the great river he had explored. He was placed in command of four vessels loaded with colonists, and set sail for the Gulf of Mexico filled with high hopes.

Unfortunately, the expedition had a great deal of bad luck. One of the ships was captured by pirates, and another was wrecked. But the worst blow to La Salle's hopes came when he missed the mouths of the Mississippi. One vessel now returned to France, and soon the fourth and last ship was wrecked on the western shores of the Gulf.

For months the little group of survivors followed the brave La Salle overland in search of the Mississippi River. In the spring of 1687, after wandering through Texas for almost a full year, a quarrel arose among the men. During it, one of them turned on their leader and La Salle was treacherously shot.

Thus died one of France's greatest North American explorers, the man who discovered the region where France later built the colony of Louisiana—which covered an area greater than New France itself.

## THE DISCOVERY OF THE GREAT PLAINS

In the hundred years following the founding of Quebec by Champlain in 1608, all the important secrets of the geography of eastern North America were learned. The Mississippi was explored to its mouth by La Salle. The colony of Louisiana was started by the Ibervilles. French voyageurs were travelling regularly to the head of Lake Superior. Even the great inland sea, discovered in Champlain's day by Henry Hudson, was ringed with the forts of the Hudson's Bay Company.

These vast lands covered an area five times that of France and England together. But the race between the two powers in North America had only begun. More than half of the continent still waited to be explored.

If it had not been for the profits to be made from the fur trade, exploration would not have gone on as quickly as it did. Indeed, without the fur trade, there would have been no reason for the English to build posts on Hudson Bay. There would have been little to draw the French voyageurs into the wilds of the Upper Lakes year after year. The very growth of the colonies themselves depended on the fur trade.

Both the French and the English soon learned, however, that the best way to get furs was to build trading posts as close

as possible to the Indian tribes who had furs to trade. As the rivalry between the merchants of the two powers became even keener, they began to send trading parties right into the heart of the continent.

As early as 1690, just over twenty years after the founding of the Hudson's Bay Company, Henry Kelsey set out from the English post of Fort Nelson at the mouth of the Nelson River on a good-will mission among the Indian tribes of the unknown west country. Kelsey travelled up the Hayes River across northern Manitoba, and then followed the Saskatchewan River into the heart of the prairies. Here he visited the Indian encampments, and tried to persuade the natives to bring their furs to the English posts on Hudson Bay instead of to the French on Lake Superior.

Henry Kelsey's journey lasted for two years. When he came back to Hudson Bay, he reported having seen vast herds of buffalo. But although his travels had carried him farther west than any explorer had yet gone, the English did not follow up his work for many years. Indeed, a full forty years passed before a real effort was made to explore the Great West. And then it was a French expedition that undertook the task.

# THE STORY OF THE LA VÉRENDRYES

In the history of Canada there have been many great explorers, but only one great family of explorers.

The father of this family, Pierre de la Vérendrye, was born in Canada. He was the son of the governor of Three Rivers. After serving as a French soldier in Europe, he came back to Canada and went into the fur trade. He married, and had a family of four small boys by the time he was placed in command of a trading post on Lake Nipigon, north of Lake Superior.

The Indians who came to trade with the French at Lake Nipigon told La Vérendrye about a great "Western Sea" lying far beyond the frontier. When La Vérendrye asked the governor of New France to place him at the head of an expedition to search for this Western Sea, the king of France refused to supply the money and men that would be needed. However, the king did grant La Vérendrye the sole right to trade in furs north and west of Lake Superior. This meant that the expedition would have to be made to pay its own way. By agreeing to send cargoes of furs from the West, La Vérendrye was able to secure enough money from merchants in Montreal to hire men and buy supplies to set out.

By this time, three of La Vérendrye's sons, Jean, Pierre, and Francis, were old enough to go with the expedition, and they were as eager to get started as their father. With them, too, went La Vérendrye's nephew, a young army officer who had already visited the Mississippi.

By the fall of 1731, La Vérendrye's expedition reached Kaministiquia at the head of the lakes, near where Fort William stands to-day. This was the most western trading post of the French at that time. Now La Vérendrye's nephew pushed on to Rainy Lake, where he built Fort St. Pierre—named in honour of his uncle. When he returned to Kaministiquia in the spring

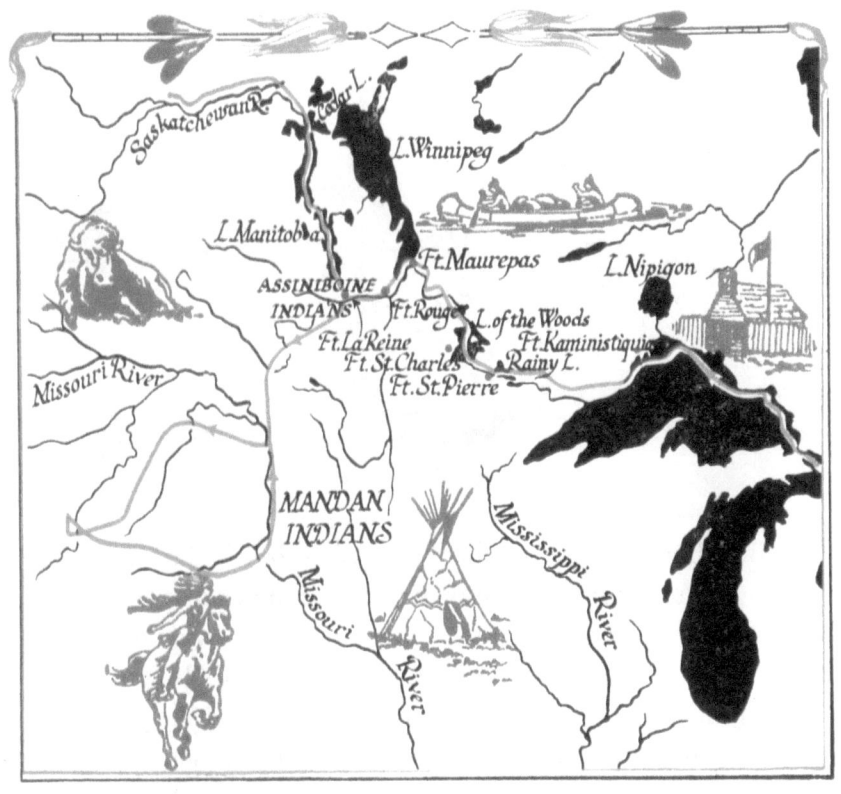

*The Explorations of the La Vérendryes*

with rich cargoes of furs, there was great rejoicing. The whole party now set out towards the West and reached Lake of the Woods, where they built Fort St. Charles.

Next winter, La Vérendrye's eldest son, Jean, pressed still farther into the West. When he reached the point where the Winnipeg River empties into Lake Winnipeg, he built Fort Maurepas. Now the family of explorers had a chain of forts between Lake Superior and Lake Winnipeg, right through the heart of a rich new fur country.

THE LA VÉRENDRYES MEET INDIANS ON HORSEBACK

But things began to go badly. La Vérendrye had to return to Montreal to secure more money from the merchants, although he was already heavily in debt. His brave nephew died at Fort Adaurepas. Then his son Jean was killed by Sioux Indians. But the family went right ahead with their work, and the youngest son, Louis-Joseph, now came west to join his father.

Two more forts were built in what is to-day southern Manitoba: Fort Rouge, at the site of present-day Winnipeg; and Fort La Reine, on the Assiniboine River where we now find the city of Portage La Prairie.

The La Vérendrye family was now in a country quite unlike any that had been explored by Frenchmen before. Instead of rivers winding through thick forests, vast plains stretched before them as far as the eye could see. Turning south, they travelled into the country of the Mandan Indians, but still failed to find the Western Sea. Here, for the first time, the party saw Indians with horses. As we shall remember, there were no horses in North America when the first white men arrived. These animals had descended from those brought to Mexico by the Spaniards.

Three years later two of La Vérendrye's sons, Francois and Louis-Joseph, went again to the Mandan country. They were led from one tribe to another, going south and west, until one day they saw in the distance the "Shining Mountains", as they called them. However, it is not certain whether these were the Rocky Mountains or a foothill range. The La Vérendryes hoped to find the Western Sea beyond the mountains, but the Indians refused to take them any farther. They had to turn back, bitterly disappointed. However, as we know, they were still a vast distance from the sea-coast.

The family continued their explorations. Francois built forts on Lake Manitoba, Cedar Lake (near the mouth of the Saskatchewan River) and at The Pas. He followed the Saskatchewan as far as the forks of the north and south branches where the city of Prince Albert is to-day. He intended soon to go up the river towards the Rockies, but never had the opportunity. Misfortune again struck the family.

La Vérendrye's enemies accused him of doing more fur trading than exploring. This was not fair to the explorer. The expense of building and supplying the forts was so great that La Vérendrye, instead of making profits for himself, was going more and more deeply into debt all the time. While in Montreal in 1749, planning an expedition farther up the Saskatchewan River, the great explorer became seriously ill. A short while later, worn out by the hardships he had undergone, he died.

Although La Vérendrye's sons were anxious to carry on the work they had been doing with their father, the new governor of New France refused to help them. He even handed over control of the western fur trade to his own friends, who had neither the skill nor the enthusiasm of the great La Vérendrye family. But La Vérendrye and his sons had travelled where no white man had ever gone before. And they had added the western plains to the map of North America.

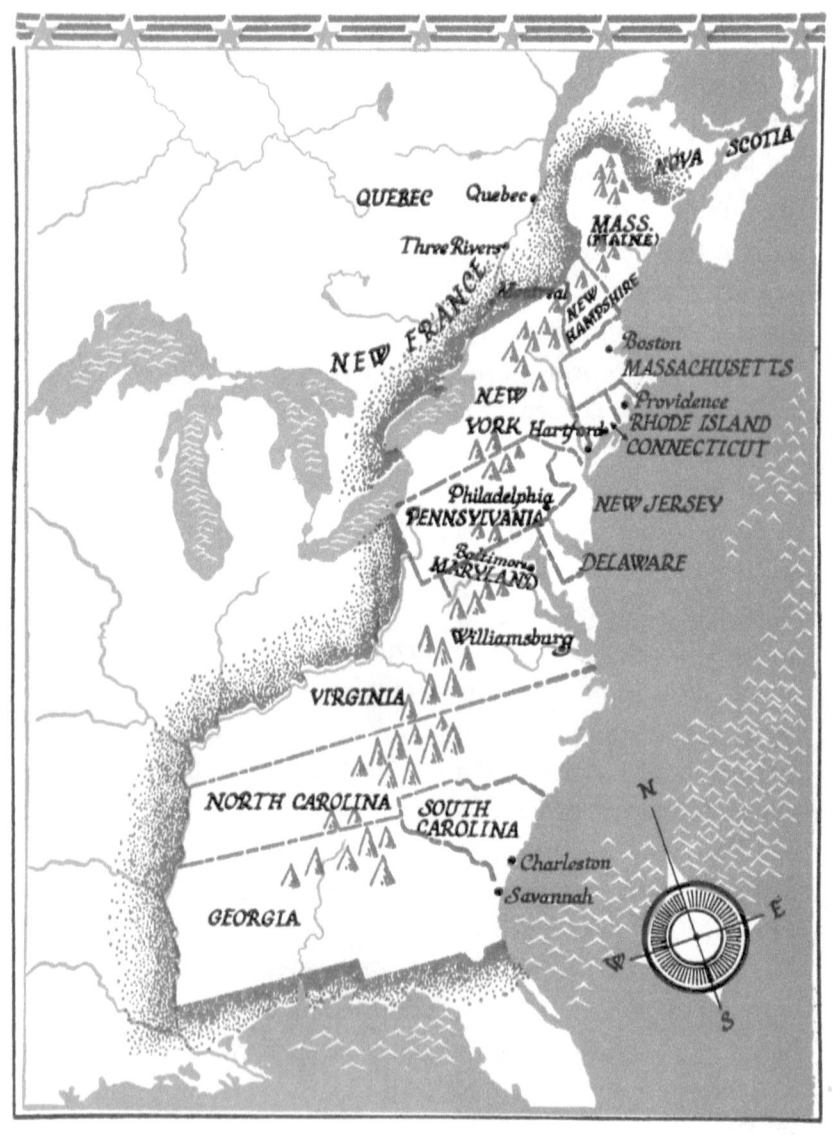

*The Thirteen Colonies*

# THE BRITISH IN NORTH AMERICA

WHEN Champlain brought his first shipload of settlers to Quebec in 1608, it became clear that France planned to colonize the valley of the St. Lawrence. By this time, Spanish colonists had spread northward as far as Florida. The long seaboard between Florida and Acadia still awaited settlement, however. When England joined the race for colonies in North America, she naturally chose this strip of coast for her settlements.

## THE THIRTEEN COLONIES

As early as 1585, Sir Walter Raleigh tried to start an English colony in what is now the State of Virginia. It was not a success. When Sir Francis Drake visited it the next year, the settlers all went home with him to England. Raleigh tried again to get Englishmen to make their homes in the New World, but once more he had bad luck. This time the colonists he sent out disappeared. Perhaps they were all killed by Indians—no one has ever found out.

However, in 1607, the year before Champlain founded Quebec, three new shiploads of English colonists arrived in Virginia. They were sent out by a company of London merchants who had been given control of this part of the coast by the English king. Ever since John Cabot explored the eastern shores of North America, England had claimed to own a part of this continent. The London merchants hoped that the colony would make money for them. They hoped that it would send

VIRGINIAN

PURITAN

them furs, corn, lumber, and perhaps gold and silver as well. During the first few years their new colony barely managed to keep going, but later it became famous for its tobacco crops.

Shortly after Virginia was first settled, Henry Hudson explored the harbour where New York City now stands, and sailed some distance up the Hudson River. He was working for Holland at this time, and it was not long before a Dutch settlement was started at the mouth of the Hudson River. The Dutch named it "New Amsterdam", after the capital of their homeland.

Now there were three countries racing each other for colonies in the northern part of the New World—the French, the English, and the Dutch. We should remember that they all began their work of settlement at about the same time.

A few years later, while Champlain was busy looking after the affairs of New France, another band of English settlers founded Plymouth, near Boston, Massachusetts. These settlers are perhaps the most famous of all who came to the Atlantic Colonies. They had first gone to Holland to escape from the harsh treatment they received at home. Because they wished to be free to worship God in their own way, they had now sailed all the way to America to make new homes. They are usually spoken of as the Pilgrim Fathers, because they had to make such a long pilgrimage to find this freedom.

One by one, other English colonies were started along the Atlantic seaboard as new groups of settlers set out across the Atlantic. Sometimes these colonies were put under the control of one Englishman, who had agreed to send out settlers. Thus William Penn was given a large tract of land on which he settled his followers, the Quakers. Like the Pilgrim Fathers, the Quakers came to North America so that they might worship God in their own way. Penn's tract of land came to be known as Pennsylvania, and to-day it is another of the United States of America.

Unlike New France, the English settlements on the Atlantic seaboard did not form one long colony with a single capital city. Instead, each settlement had a separate beginning and a history all its own. For a long time these English colonies had little to do with one another, and it was not until they all had the same complaint to make to England that they really learned to work together. But that did not happen for almost one hundred and seventy-five years.

In 1664—just six years before the Hudson's Bay Company was founded—a fleet of English warships sailed into the harbour of New Amsterdam and called on the Dutch governor to surrender. The governor would have put up a fight, but his people would not obey his orders to fire. As a result, the English flag

DUTCH                                           QUAKER

was raised over the little Dutch settlement, and its name was changed from New Amsterdam to New York. Little did its people dream that one day their quiet town would be the largest city in the New World.

Here are the names of all the English colonies which were founded along the Atlantic seaboard: Virginia, Massachusetts, Maryland, Connecticut, Rhode Island, New Hampshire, North Carolina, South Carolina, New York, New Jersey, Delaware, Pennsylvania, Georgia. They are usually spoken of as the Thirteen Colonies. It is important for us to remember that all the time France was building her colony in the St. Lawrence River Valley, England was starting these settlements along the Atlantic seaboard.

Then, in 1749, New France learned with alarm that a new English settlement was being built on the Atlantic coast—on territory that had once been held by the French king.

## THE FOUNDING OF HALIFAX, 1749

"Ay, lad, 'tis a grand haven the Colonel will be having up the channel there for His Majesty's fleet." Guy's father nodded towards the broad, quiet bay which reached so far inland behind the new settlement. Father and son were standing atop the bald, rocky height which rose two hundred feet above the tree-tops behind Colonel Cornwallis' town-site on the harbour of Chebucto. Guy had climbed up here often during the three months he had been in the country. His family had landed in July with the first large group of English settlers to come to Nova Scotia. His father had been a lawyer at home, but no one would have guessed it to watch him working with the other colonists that summer. "Too busy to be going picnicking with ye, lad," he had told Guy. "And don't ye be thinking of going beyond the sentries, or the redskins will be after your scalp."

*Acadia (about 1753)*

But at last Guy had persuaded his father to come on a Sunday morning hike. They had set out early, so that they might be back before Mr. Tutty began morning worship. From the height on which they now stood, they could see the missionary's half-finished wooden chapel at the end of the Parade.

"Mr. Tutty says the basin there is six miles long, Father," explained Guy. "With Chebucto harbour as well, would that be room enough to hold the whole British fleet, do you think?"

Guy's father laughed. "Lad," he said, "Bedford Basin there alone, why—it'd handle every vessel afloat on the seven seas!"

"How does Halifax compare with Louisbourg, Father?" asked Guy.

"Confound Louisbourg anyway, lad!" his father answered, "Why, when I touched there on my way from Plymouth to Boston two years ago, I thought it was just the place to bring you and your mother when we left England for good. I'll not be forgetting our good old union flag flying from its citadel when we dropped anchor. Raised there, mark you, by His Majesty's own New England colonists when they thrashed the French in Cape Breton four years ago. What a waste of good colonial blood that was!"

"Why do you say it was a waste, Father?" remarked Guy. "The New Englanders did capture the fortress, didn't they?"

"And is it British now—Louisbourg?" demanded his father.

"Of course it's not! Only last year we signed a treaty with the French king, handing him back Louisbourg just as if we had captured it by mistake. And in return for what, eh? For a city in India, right on the other side of the world. As if New Englanders would have had to worry about India as long as Louisbourg was under the British flag!"

"Will we have to worry about Louisbourg, here in Halifax, Father?"

Guy's father thought for a moment. "We won't, lad," he replied, "so long as the government sends out settlers and soldiers as fast as it says it will."

"Mother thinks you've all done wonders already, Father," Guy added.

"It's been hard work, all right, lad," answered the boy's father. "But so far, the Old Country's been behind us. We're the first large batch of settlers the British government has ever sent to the New World—not that the trading companies haven't done well in the colonies south of us. Ay, but it's been a hard summer for the folk here."

Guy's father was only too right. The weather had been very hot, and much of the food had spoiled. Supplies could be brought from the nearest of the Thirteen Colonies, of course. But the merchants of Boston and New York charged heavily for everything they sold. Then, too, the French had tried to set the Indians against the newcomers. It was not safe to travel far beyond the sentry-posts for fear of attack by Micmac savages.

Worst of all, plague had broken out in the new settlement shortly after the colonists landed. Before autumn, several hundreds of the settlers were dead.

"Look ye, lad, ye can see the whole town-site from here as if 'twere a map," said Guy's father, pointing down at Halifax.

Guy watched as his father named one building after another in the clearing below. Some of the houses were hidden by the trees on the hillside, but the sight was one to be proud of, for only three months earlier the western bank of Chebucto harbour had been unbroken forest. There was not a person, not even the missionary, Mr. Tutty, nor Colonel Cornwallis himself, who had done less than his full share in building the little colony down by the water's edge. Everybody turned carpenter—whether he was by trade blacksmith, shoemaker, mechanic, or farmer.

"Note, lad, the street lines are all staked out already. It's hard to see that when you're down below, although I prepared the deeds myself. You can count the blocks from here, at least those inside the palisade. Three, four, five—yes, that's right.

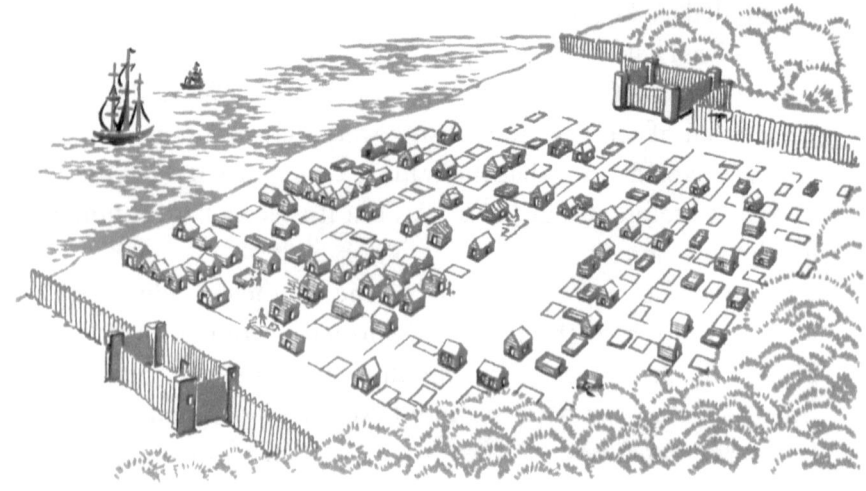

Five blocks along the waterfront by seven deep. Makes more sense than the crooked streets I've seen in Boston. A few more years, and a few more shiploads of settlers, and we'll have to build outside the palisade altogether. Anyway, we're all going to be under roofs this winter. We can be glad of that in this country."

"How many are there here now, Father?" asked Guy.

"Nearly twenty-five hundred, counting the garrison that's come from Louisbourg," answered his father. "'Tis a good enough start, as I say, but we'll be needing much help from home for a while yet. Come, lad, we'd best be getting back down or we'll miss worship."

During the next few years, the colony did receive a great deal of "help from home". Hundreds of settlers arrived in the new year, 1750, and several thousands came during the following three or four years.

Some of the newcomers settled on the eastern side of the harbour, where they started the town of Dartmouth. A number of German immigrants founded still another colony at Lunenburg, using the town of Halifax as a model when drawing their plans. You can find these places on the map of Nova Scotia to-day.

For many years, Annapolis Royal had been used by the British as the capital of Nova Scotia. But now the centre of government was moved to Halifax, which in two short years swelled to a population of more than six thousand men, women, and children. To-day, Halifax is still the capital of Nova Scotia, one of Canada's beautiful Maritime provinces. The rocky height which Guy and his father visited on that autumn morning of 1749 was soon strongly fortified, for it guards the entrance to one of the best natural harbours in the world. Here, safe from the fury of Atlantic storms and enemy submarines, huge convoys of freighters gathered during two world wars to make ready for their trips to Europe. During winter, when the frozen St. Lawrence makes it impossible for vessels to reach either Quebec or Montreal, ocean liners sail into and out of Halifax harbour as usual. And if you look at the globe, you will see that Halifax lies much nearer to Europe than does any other large seaport on the mainland of North America.

When the British chose the harbour of Chebucto in 1749 for their new colony, they indeed chose wisely!

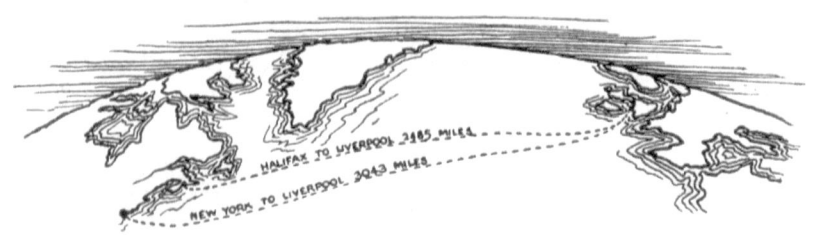

## THREE LETTERS FROM ACADIA

Although France had been forced to surrender Acadia to Britain as early as 1713, few English settlers came to the province until the building of Halifax, half-way through the century. No one knew for certain how much of the country could rightly be called "Acadia", but the British claimed that it included most of present-day New Brunswick and all of Nova Scotia except Cape Breton. The French were determined to hold the south shore of the St. Lawrence from Cape Breton to Canada, and about the middle of the century they built a strong post, Fort Beauséjour, on the narrow isthmus between the Bay of Fundy and the Gulf of St. Lawrence. The British did not allow the "trespassers" to remain long on Acadian soil. Early in the summer of 1755 a powerful force—made up largely of New Englanders—launched an attack against Fort Beauséjour, and two weeks later it was in their hands. But the British governor of Nova Scotia was still worried about the French. Here are three letters which tell what happened next.

*1st Battalion Headquarters,*
*Near Fort Cumberland,*
*Nova Scotia,*
*August 15, 1755.*

My dear Parents:

I hope this letter finds you both as well as when I departed from Boston last May. Five months without mail from your wandering lieutenant must have troubled you sorely. But you will know that I would have written before this if my letters

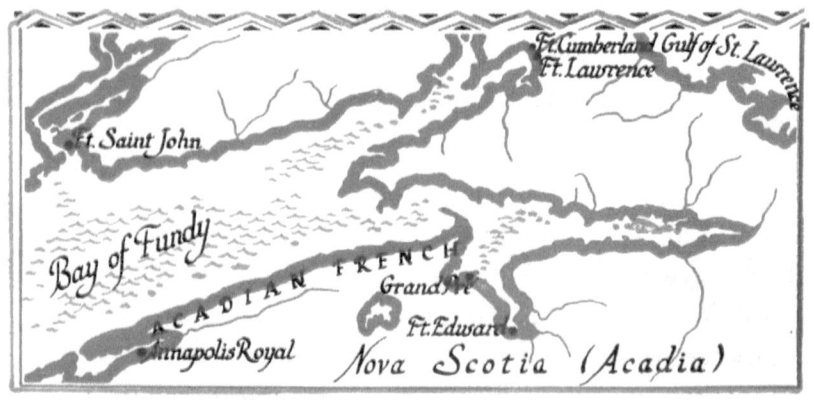

*Settlements on the Bay of Fundy (about 1755)*

could have found their way to Boston. Now I am told that a frigate leaves direct for home in the morning, and private letters will be carried for the officers. So I must put down everything I have to tell you, even if I burn Colonel Winslow's candles until daylight.

The ships you saw us board in Boston harbour last May carried us close to this fort, which the French called Fort Beauséjour. When we captured it in June, we renamed it Fort Cumberland. Fort Beauséjour was built only three miles from our own Fort Lawrence, whose lights I can even now see twinkling in the distance.

Of course, this country has really belonged to Britain ever since the French king surrendered "Acadia" over forty years ago. So the French had no right to build Fort Beauséjour here. However, the French officers we have captured say that this was not part of Acadia, and that therefore it was never surrendered to Britain. Who is right? Although we are at peace with France, you would have found that hard to believe if you had seen us bombarding Fort Beauséjour in June. As you must have read in the New England papers, our men from Massachusetts were magnificent, and we captured the fort after two weeks of fighting.

Although a moment ago I said this land has belonged to Britain for over forty years, I must say that we feel like strangers when we talk to the people who live in these parts. That is because this coast was settled only by the French, there being hardly a man among the farmers I have met who can speak one word of the King's English. These farmers are the "Acadians", of whom we have often heard at home. Many of them came here from around Annapolis Royal, thinking that they were escaping from British rule.

As you well know, the Acadians here and in the Annapolis Valley have long been a great worry to the British governor at Halifax. Most of them refuse still to promise to fight for King George if they are needed.

When we captured Fort Beauséjour in June, we found over three hundred Acadian farmers within its walls. They say that they were forced to fight against us. But this proves that the Acadians will be dangerous subjects if France and England go to war again. Perhaps the chief trouble is that the French at Louisbourg and Quebec will not leave the Acadians alone. Everything possible is done by the French to make this race of farmers believe that they are subjects of King Louis of France, and not of our own King George.

I must stop writing much sooner than I had planned. Colonel Winslow has just arrived from Fort Cumberland, and I am ordered to have my men ready to sail with him in the morning. It is hard to guess where we shall be going, but alas, we are told it will not be Boston. I shall write again as soon as I can. It will be interesting to see what my next address will be!

Your loving son,
Jonathan.

*Written at Lieut-Col. Winslow's Headquarters,*
*Grand Pre, Nova Scotia,*
*August 29, 1755.*

My dear Parents:

Here we are, encamped in the heart of the country of the Acadians! A courier leaves at dawn, hoping to reach Halifax overland in two days. With so many vessels touching there on the way from the Old Country to New England, I am sure you must have this letter within a fortnight.

Fewer than three hundred men came with Colonel Winslow from Fort Cumberland. Strange to say, even our three captains have not yet been told the purpose of this expedition. We already have British garrisons in this part of Nova Scotia—there is one at Fort Edward, not far distant. Some action against the Acadian farmers must be planned, but only Colonel Winslow knows what is afoot.

I must tell you more about these Acadian French. There are said to be about ten thousand of them in all. They are a hardworking people, that I must say. Their farms are as fine as any I have seen in New England. The fall crops are even now being gathered in, and it has been a rich harvest. They raise also cattle, sheep, hogs, and horses. Their apple orchards would be the envy of any of the colonies.

With all this wealth of Nature, the Acadians live simple lives. They have little money, and still less need for it. They make their clothing from the flax and wool raised on their farms. Even their shoes and moccasins are cut from the hides of the wild animals they hunt in the district. Their homes, outside as well as in, are as simple as their lives, two or more large families often living together under one roof.

The Acadians seem to be friendly with the Indians, who have always favoured the French in Nova Scotia. If war breaks out between France and England, we would have a hard fight on our hands in this province, with so many against us! Our men have pitched their tents between the parish church and the graveyard. For myself, I am posted to headquarters as usual, which Colonel Winslow has set up in the home of the priest. The Acadians seem to think we shall spend the winter here in Grand Pre, and they may be right for we know nothing of the business that brings us here. But we shall wait and see...

Your loving son,<br>
JONATHAN.

Lieut-Col. Winslow's Headquarters,<br>
Grand Pre, Nova Scotia,<br>
December 25, 1755.

My dear Parents:

It is Christmas Day, and we New Englanders are alone in Grand Pre.

The Acadians are gone from Nova Scotia, and a sorry part we have played in their going! But we have obeyed Colonel Winslow's orders, and for all that, he has obeyed his. Some of my fellow officers believe that what has been done is wise, but I am sick at heart over it all. Nor am I alone in my feelings, for the colonel himself has said that he has found the work of the past four months more grievous than any he has ever been called on to perform.

Early in September, all the men among the Acadians of Grand Pre, even the boys over ten years old, were herded into the parish church to hear Colonel Winslow read the orders from the governor of this province. New England must have heard by now the harsh sentence that was passed on them. The colonel's words still ring in my ears:

"The duty I am now upon, though necessary, is very disagreeable to me... But it is not my business to question the orders I have received, but to obey them... Your lands and buildings and cattle and live-stock of all kinds are forfeited with all your other possessions, excepting money and household goods... and you yourselves are to be removed from this province."

When Colonel Winslow's orders from the governor were translated into French, the Acadians in the church were stunned by the news. At first they did not seem to believe that they were to lose their homes and to be themselves shipped away to strange lands.

Since that bitter moment in the church, all our time has been taken up carrying out the governor's harsh orders. We had to wait for weeks before the transports arrived to carry away our unhappy prisoners. Now they are all gone, and are being landed at various points on the coast all the way from New England to the mouth of the Mississippi, so they say.

I must add that Colonel Winslow was as just to the poor Acadians as he could be, considering the orders he had from the governor. As far as possible, the people from each village in the neighbourhood were sent together on the same vessels. And one of our own soldiers was given thirty lashes for stealing from one of the prisoners.

In all, we have torn more than two thousand Acadians from their homes about Grand Pre, and shipped them away on the transports. Several thousands more have been captured and sent away from the villages north and south of here.

"AND YOU ARE TO BE REMOVED FROM THIS PROVINCE"

Some of the Acadians managed to escape into the woods, where there is little use hunting for them. But they will have nothing left to return to here after we leave (which can hardly be too soon!). For we are now ordered to burn the barns and homes in the empty villages.

Perhaps it is true that if the French at Louisbourg and Fort Beauséjour had invaded Nova Scotia before we attacked them, the Acadians would have fought against us. If that had happened, we might have lost all our settlements in this province. So there are two sides to the story, are there not?

But even though I know why we have dealt harshly with these Acadians, I shall never feel happy over what we have done this year. Forgive me, but I have no heart to continue writing.

Your son,<br>JONATHAN.

## THE SEVEN YEARS' WAR

WHENEVER England and France were at war with each other in Europe, the English and French colonies were also at war. But as we have just seen, there sometimes was fighting between the colonies even while their motherlands were supposed to be at peace. It seems hard to believe that war had not been declared when Fort Beauséjour was attacked by the English in 1755. That was the year, too, that the Acadian French were removed from their homes in Nova Scotia, and shipped to the other English colonies.

While these unfriendly happenings were taking place in Nova Scotia, there were clashes which were even more war-like between the French and English on their inland frontiers. The rich fur country of the Ohio Valley had been opened by explorers from New France, but now English traders from the Thirteen Colonies were beginning to push across the Alleghanies into this part of North America. Trouble between the rival races here was sure to follow, and before long a bitter struggle broke out in the backwoods.

### THE STORY OF A BRITISH DEFEAT

To strengthen their hold on the Ohio country, the French had built a line of forts, stretching from Lake Erie south to Fort Duquesne, where the city of Pittsburgh is to-day. And at the very moment when the English forces were bombarding Fort Beauséjour in Nova Scotia, another British army was cutting its way through the woods to attack the French at Fort Duquesne!

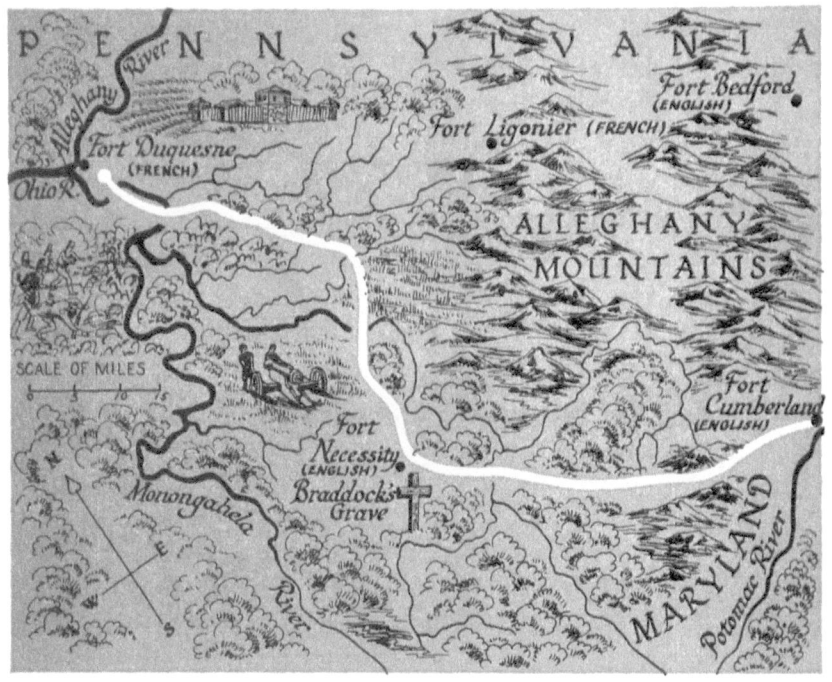

*General Braddock's March*

The commander of this British force was General Braddock. One of his chief officers was a young Virginian, Colonel George Washington. Less than a quarter of a century later, Washington became the first president of the United States of America. Already, Washington had led raids against the French in the backwoods, and his descriptions of the march against Fort Duquesne help us to understand the mistakes which General Braddock's army made.

The way to Fort Duquesne led through heavy forest, and three hundred axe-men went ahead to cut a road for the army. Long trains of pack horses, cannon, and wagons toiled behind. Fearful lest the French send more troops to Fort Duquesne before the attackers could reach it, Washington advised General Braddock to leave most of his equipment behind and push on with the best troops as quickly as possible. Braddock agreed, and chose a strong advance force to go with him ahead of his army. Washington, who went with Braddock, still expected trouble. "My hopes were brought very low," he wrote, "when I found that instead of pushing on without minding a little rough road, the British soldiers were halting to level every molehill, and to build bridges over every brook, by which means we were four days in getting twelve miles." General Braddock's forces were made up of both British regulars and men from the colonies, and they did not get along well together.

Suddenly disaster struck. The French in Fort Duquesne had sent out soldiers and Indians to meet the attackers. Although both sides were fairly evenly matched, Braddock's men were quickly surrounded by enemies who knew far more about forest warfare than they did. Unable to see the French and Indian troops who were firing on them from all sides, the British redcoats made their cannon ready, and blasted away uselessly at the trees which hid their foe.

General Braddock fought bravely, but when his men began to break and flee he was unable to rally them. "We would fight," they answered, "if we could see anybody to fight with!" Even Colonel George Washington had two horses shot from under him, and, although he escaped unhurt, his clothes were ripped by bullets.

Braddock himself was shot down during the fighting. As he lay near death, his men found him and carried him from the field. In a few short hours, over two-thirds of the British troops had been either killed or wounded. Those who were able to escape carried the terrible story of defeat back to the army which was following. Then it was learned that General Braddock had died of his wounds. Wagons, gunpowder, and food supplies

"BRADDOCK ..... WAS SHOT DOWN"

were destroyed, and soon all that remained of the army was in lull retreat eastward.

The first round of the struggle inland had been won by the French.

But bitter as were the clashes between the French and English in America in 1755, they took place only along the frontiers between New France and the British colonies. As long as the two powerful motherlands were not at war, neither tried to overrun the other's empire in North America by planning a real invasion.

However, this picture changed completely in the following year, 1756. For suddenly most of the important countries in Europe were swept into war, and France and England found themselves on opposite sides. In North America, the border fighting now flamed into a struggle for possession of the continent itself.

Which nation would be the victor? Many bitter battles were fought, and much time passed, before the answer could be given. When at last, in 1763, peace was signed, Canada passed from French hands to English. The struggle that brought about that important change is known as the Seven Years' War.

## WOLFE AND MONTCALM

A glance at the map will show that France claimed an area of North America many times the size of the British colonies which stretched along the Atlantic seaboard. But at the opening of the Seven Years' War, there were already almost twenty times as many English colonists as there were French. One might think, therefore, that New France would fall an easy prey to an invading army from the south. But it would be a mistake to judge the strengths of the French and English just by counting the colonists on each side.

In the first place, Great Britain's Thirteen Colonies were thirteen separate settlements and had not yet learned that they could act together. Indeed, for the most part each was in closer touch with England than with the neighbouring colonies, and each had a government of its own. France's empire in North America was quite different, for all the people of New France were ruled by the government at Quebec, which was chosen by the French king.

Moreover, there were only a few routes by which invading forces could strike at Quebec, the heart of New France. At the very mouth of the St. Lawrence River, on Cape Breton Island, the French held the powerful fortress of Louisbourg. There were two other possible openings in the natural armour of forest land which shielded New France against attack from the south. These were the route down the Great Lakes and St. Lawrence River, and the waterway that led north from Lake Champlain down the Richelieu River. Either of these could be held by a small French force under a good general. New France was fortunate when just such a good general was sent to the country in 1756, the year that the Seven Years' War broke out. This new leader was the Marquis de Montcalm.

One of General Montcalm's first moves was to attack and capture the fort of Oswego, a British stronghold at the southeast corner of Lake Ontario. For a while, at least, Quebec would be safe against attack from that direction. Then Montcalm led his soldiers against another British army moving north towards Quebec by way of Lake Champlain and the Richelieu River. At Ticonderoga the two forces came together, and here Montcalm dealt the invaders another smashing defeat.

There was still the third way to reach Quebec—up the St. Lawrence River itself. But the French fortress of Louisbourg in Cape Breton Island, which the British had captured a dozen years earlier, was again in French hands. Until it could be recaptured, it was not safe for a British fleet to risk an attack upstream. In 1758, the British succeeded in landing a strong army on Cape Breton Island. In the siege which followed, Louisbourg was forced to surrender. The way to Quebec lay open!

The news of Louisbourg's fall made many hearts in Canada beat faster. Could the great fortress of Quebec hold off an English attack? The people of New France thought that it could. They did not have to wait long for an answer, for the next year,

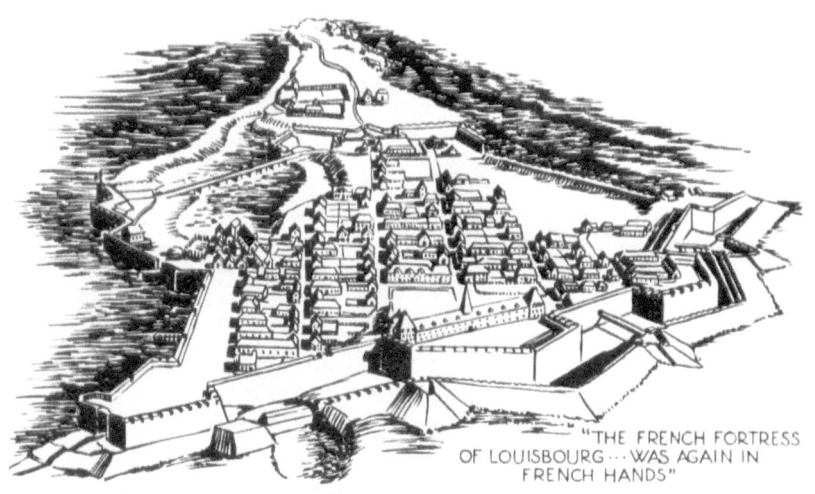

"THE FRENCH FORTRESS OF LOUISBOURG···WAS AGAIN IN FRENCH HANDS"

1759, a powerful British fleet set sail against New France. Soon twenty-two warships, carrying an army of nine thousand troops, were making their way up the St. Lawrence from Halifax.

The commander-in-chief of this powerful fleet was Sir Charles Saunders. The skill he showed in bringing his large force safely up the river amazed the French leaders at Quebec.

The British army was under the command of a clever young English officer, General James Wolfe, who had helped to lead the attack against Louisbourg the year before. Although Wolfe was still a young man of thirty-three, no better leader could have been chosen for such a difficult task. Ever since the fall of Louisbourg, he had wanted to carry the war into the very centre of New France by attacking Quebec. When the king of England was told that this new general must be mad, His Majesty had replied: "Mad, is he? Then I hope he will bite some others of my generals!"

Sir Charles Saunders had brought the British army before Quebec without a fight. It was now up to General Wolfe to capture the great French stronghold.

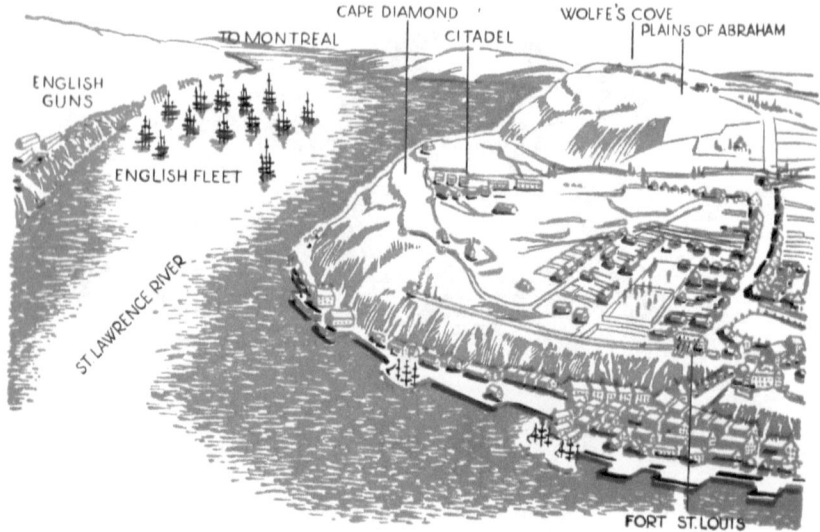

The fortress of Quebec was built on a huge rock which towers more than three hundred feet above the St. Lawrence River. Champlain himself had chosen it in 1608 as the easiest place to defend in the whole valley. Just seventy years earlier, Frontenac had forced Sir William Phips to retreat from beneath the walls of Quebec. Would General Montcalm, too, be able to mock his attackers?

Wolfe landed some of the cannon from his ships, and placed them on the south shore of the river opposite Quebec. From here he was able to lob shells across the St. Lawrence into the streets of the French capital. Montcalm's guns, across the river, replied just as loudly. It did not help the English to be able to "trade shots" with the French, as long as the French flag flew above the fortress.

Of course, all this time Quebec was cut off from France, because the British fleet was on the St. Lawrence River below the town. You might wonder, then, why Wolfe did not choose to wait until Quebec ran out of food and had to surrender.

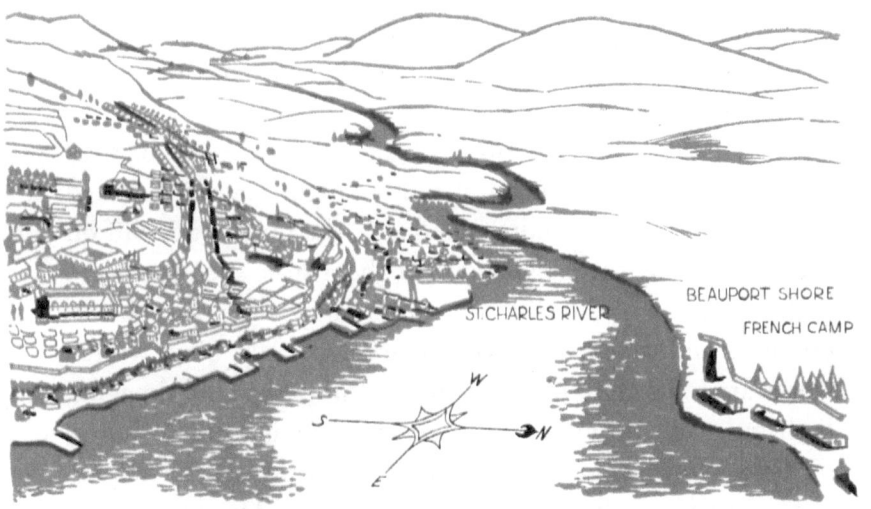

There was a very good reason. By December, at the latest, the river would be covered with ice, and if it stayed, the British fleet would be frozen in for the winter. So you can see that Wolfe had to beat Montcalm right away, or leave New France. And all Montcalm had to do was to keep the English from entering Quebec before winter. Therefore, Montcalm was very anxious not to have to meet the English armies in an open battle, where his poorly trained troops might easily be beaten.

Wolfe did not dare land his men in front of Quebec, beneath the guns of the fortress. One day that summer he tried to march his troops up the north shore of the river to attack the town by land. But the defenders put up so strong a fight that the attack had to be stopped. Montcalm was a clever and gallant general and he made good use of the forces he commanded.

Then Wolfe decided on a daring plan. On the north shore of river a little distance above Quebec, he had seen a small bay where a pathway ran up the side of the cliff. This little bay is now known as "Wolfe's Cove." At the top there were some level farmlands. (One of these farms had been owned by a man named Abraham Martin, and so they were called the Plains of Abraham.) "If only my army could reach the Plains of Abraham," thought Wolfe, "Montcalm would have to come out of the fortress and fight!"

One night Wolfe sent most of his army in ships up the river past Quebec. During the middle of the night, the ships drifted downstream and the soldiers landed at the foot of the cliff on the shore of the little bay. Some of them stole silently up the path to the top of the cliff. They found only a few Frenchmen on guard and were able to overcome them easily. Now Wolfe's whole army began to pour ashore and climb the cliff, dragging their guns and supplies with them. It was a hard task, but by morning Wolfe stood at the head of his army on the heights above, just a little distance from the town itself. Montcalm could no longer avoid a fight to the finish, since Wolfe's men were now ready to storm the town from the rear. Without hesitating, he bravely led his troops against the British.

As the two armies came together, the French troops began to fire into the British lines. Wolfe's men had been told not to shoot back until the command was given. Suddenly the order "Fire!" rang out along the British lines, and the French ranks were torn apart as the British soldiers all pulled their triggers at once. Soon the remaining French troops broke and fled towards the city. In two hours, the Battle of the Plains of Abraham was over.

In the fight, however, two gallant leaders had given their lives. General Wolfe died on the field of battle in the very hour of his victory, shot through the chest by a ball from a French musket. Montcalm, too, had been badly wounded. He was carried into the town, where he died the following day. The English flag was now raised over the captured fortress. New France had fallen at last!

## AFTER THE BRITISH VICTORY

BEFORE winter closed in, the fleet which had brought Wolfe's army to Quebec weighed anchor and set sail for England. But the British flag now waved above the ramparts of the great fortress, and its walls were manned by a British garrison. The district about the city of Quebec was under the command of an English general, James Murray, although the French still held Montreal.

The first winter in Quebec brought misery to the new British garrison. There was not enough fire-wood in the city, food ran short, and the dreaded scurvy broke out among the troops. Stories were heard of a French army on its way from Montreal to attack the newly won capital. Indeed, French bushrangers and unfriendly Indians roamed the countryside all winter long, only too ready to fall upon unwary stragglers from wood-cutting parties sent out by General Murray.

### THE SECOND BATTLE OF THE PLAINS

Then, in the spring of 1760, the French did strike back in force. Under the leadership of General Levis, one of Montcalm's best officers, a large but tired army arrived on the heights outside Quebec's walls, after a difficult journey down the St. Lawrence from Montreal. As Montcalm had done the year before, General

Murray marched forward to meet the attackers before they could storm the city itself. The fight which followed is sometimes spoken of as the "Second Battle of the Plains".

Although few of the troops led by General Levis were trained soldiers, they outnumbered the British almost two to one. Two hours after the fighting began, Murray's forces were in full retreat towards the city. If General Levis had been able to press home his attack, it is likely that the British would have had to surrender the fortress to its former owners!

The little British army which General Murray now commanded inside Quebec was pitifully weak. When would the French troops try to storm the walls? Would the British fleet arrive in time to save the city? During the winter, the frozen St. Lawrence had cut off both sides from the world, but as the spring wore on the hopes of the defenders began to rise again. Meanwhile, the French army outside the gates lost precious time. For General Levis, too, believed that help might come to him up the St. Lawrence. Both sides waited anxiously, wondering whose vessels would arrive first.

Early in May a sail appeared around the bend in the river downstream. Was it British or French? The answer to this question might decide whether Quebec would stand or fall.

Suddenly the British banner broke from the flagstaff of the approaching ship. The city was saved! "The gladness of our troops," wrote one of the officers in Quebec at the time, "cannot be told. Both officers and soldiers mounted the wall in the face of the enemy, and cheered for almost an hour. The gunners were so joyous that they did nothing but load and fire for a considerable time."

The newly arrived ship brought word that a whole British squadron was on its way up the St. Lawrence, and would reach Quebec within the week. The gallant General Levis, who had come so close to winning back what Montcalm had lost, was

now forced to give up his plan to capture the city. A few days later he gave orders to retire. Before General Murray could again launch an attack against the French army outside the gates, it was learned that the besiegers had disappeared in the direction of Montreal.

The French fleet had been driven from the seas, and there was no longer any hope for the French forces which still held Montreal. Soon the St. Lawrence was swarming with British naval vessels, and three separate armies were moving against the few French troops Levis had been able to bring together for his last stand. Even the French-Canadian habitants began to desert the forces at Montreal when Governor Murray announced that they would not be disturbed if they returned to their homes immediately, but that if they continued to fight their homes would be burned by the British troops. Murray carried out his threat, for he tells us that at one place he was "under the cruel necessity of burning the greatest part of these unhappy people's houses. I pray God," he adds, "that this example will be enough. For my nature revolts when this becomes a necessary part of my duty."

Montreal, cut off from any possible help from France, could not hold out for long. Before the summer was over, its garrison surrendered to the attacking armies, and the British flag flew over the St. Lawrence Valley from Montreal to Nova Scotia.

As we have already seen, fighting between the British and French broke out in North America before the mother countries in Europe locked in the struggle of the Seven Years' War. So it was that the end of the fighting in Canada did not mean the end of the war in Europe.

But at last, in 1763, the Seven Years' War was brought to an end by the signing of the Peace of Paris. By this treaty, France agreed to hand over Canada to the British, although she was allowed to keep the little islands of St. Pierre and Miquelon off the south coast of Newfoundland as bases for her fishing fleets. You will find them marked as French possessions to-day.

Britain had gained more by her victory in North America than a vast space of land—already known to be larger than all her other possessions in the New World. The Peace of Paris had also brought her sixty thousand new subjects, whose language, religion, and history were different from those of her other North American colonists. Few would then have believed that these first Canadian subjects of Great Britain would help to build her greatest overseas Dominion, or that her own people in the Thirteen Colonies would soon make war against her and found a new country of their own.

From the first, Britain assured the French-speaking Canadians "the liberty of the Catholic religion". Arrangements were made to move to France any who did not wish to live under British rule, but almost all chose to remain in Canada. To-day the descendants of these earliest Canadian colonists number almost three and a half millions—about one-third of the population of the Dominion of Canada.

### THE WAR CHIEF OF THE OTTAWAS

About four years after Wolfe captured Quebec, a strange meeting took place on the banks of a river not far from Fort Detroit. Almost five hundred Indian warriors had gathered for the great council of the Confederacy of the Three Fires, which was the name given to three of the tribes who lived between Lake Michigan and Lake Huron. In addition to the tribes in the Confederacy of the Three Fires, several other tribes had also been called to the meeting. At last Pontiac, chief of the Ottawas, arose and walked into the midst of the council. On his head waved his war-feathers, and his face and body were painted ready for battle. All the Indians now turned to listen to Pontiac, the cleverest of the chieftains, and the most treacherous in war.

"Why", Pontiac demanded, "does the English king send his redcoats into our country to take over the forts where we have always traded with our good friends the French? Why does he not give us presents, as did the French in years gone by? The French came into our country to trade with us; the English now come to cut down our forests, plant crops, and drive the Indians away forever. To-day New France is held by the English, and it is our turn to be destroyed. We must strike now at these

English forts in our midst! We must drive out and make war on these dogs clothed in red who will do us nothing but harm!"

Then Pontiac told his listeners of his plans to capture the English forts and to kill the English troops. At this time there were not more than a few hundred British soldiers west of Montreal. Against them, Pontiac hoped to throw almost fifty thousand Indian warriors. It is not surprising, therefore, that his plan almost succeeded. It is known in Canadian history as the Conspiracy of Pontiac.

Fort Detroit, which was near by, was the first of the English forts to be attacked by the Indians. Although it never did fall into their hands, the story of how the Indians tried to take it is very interesting because it shows the trickery which Pontiac used in making war.

First, a band of warriors under Pontiac came to the gate of the fort and asked permission to dance the peace dance for the officers inside. The English officer in command of the fort allowed the Indians to come in, and after the dance was over, gave them presents. He did not know that all the time the savages had been inside the fort they had been carefully studying its defences, and counting the number of soldiers and cannon!

However, a young Indian girl visited the fort one night, where she told a story that startled the English officer. "Pontiac", she warned, "will come back with many chiefs to hold a council. Under his blanket each chief will have a gun, sawed short so that it cannot be seen. When Pontiac gives the signal, they will all throw down their blankets and attack you and the other soldiers here in the fort."

A few days later Pontiac did come back to Fort Detroit, just as the Indian girl had warned. With him were about fifty chiefs. But the English were now ready for the Indians. Imagine the surprise of Pontiac when, on entering the fort, he found all the soldiers standing at attention, fully armed, waiting only for

A PLOT THAT FAILED

Pontiac to give the signal to his followers! Pontiac hesitated a while, and then turned and led the Indians away.

The Indians were furious that their trick had been discovered, and soon returned with all their warriors to attack the fort. But although they kept it surrounded all summer long, they were unable to make it surrender.

However, things were not going so well at the other English forts about the upper Great Lakes. One by one, they were attacked by the Indians and destroyed. The soldiers in them were either killed or taken prisoner. Many of them were tortured. By the end of June, there was not an English soldier left west of Lake Erie, except in Fort Detroit. Fortunately, however, this outpost was able to hold off the Indians all through the summer of 1763, and Pontiac at last gave up his attack on it. In the meantime, the English had been able to send more troops into the Indian country, and finally peace was made.

A little while later Pontiac met the English in a peace council at Oswego, on the southern shore of Lake Ontario. Here the

Indian chief and his followers listened carefully to the English general who spoke to them:

"Children," he said, "from me you will always hear what is good and true. You begin now to see the fruits of peace, from the number of traders and plenty of goods at all the garrisoned posts. Keep fast hold of the chain of friendship, that your children, following your example, may live happy and prosperous lives."

Then Pontiac replied. "Father," he said, "we thank the Great Spirit for giving us so fine a day to meet upon such important matters. I speak in the name of all the Indians to the westward, of whom I am the master. It is the will of the Great Spirit that we should meet here to-day, and before him I now take you by the hand. I speak from my heart, for I see that the Great Spirit will have us friends.

"Father," Pontiac went on, "when our great father of France was in this country, I held him fast by the hand. Now that he is gone, I take you, my English father, by the hand, in the name of all the Indian nations. And I promise to keep this peace treaty as long as I shall live." With these words, the war chief handed the English general a belt of wampum. Then he added "Father, when you speak to me, it is the same as if you spoke to all the Indians of the west. Father, this belt of wampum is to strengthen our chain of friendship, and to show you that if any nation shall lift the hatchet against our English brethren, we shall be the first to feel it and to strike back."

Although Pontiac was not punished for his conspiracy against the British, he was no longer the great chief he pretended to be, for now no man trusted him. A short while later he met the same fate that he had dealt so many white men. One evening, as he was walking through the woods, another Indian stole after him and struck him down with a tomahawk. So died the war chief of the Ottawas, probably the cleverest and at the same time the most treacherous Indian leader in Canadian history.

# THE AMERICAN REVOLUTION

THE thirteen colonies planted by Great Britain on the Atlantic coast of North America grew very rapidly. By 1763, when France surrendered Canada to Britain, the number of people in the English colonies was over one and a half millions. Many countries of Europe had fewer people. It is not surprising that the colonies began to think they should control all their own affairs. Until now they had depended on Britain to protect them from the French in Canada, but that danger was past.

It was true that each colony made most of its own laws, but there were still some laws made in England which all of the American colonies were supposed to obey. For the most part, these were not unfair laws; many of them were just and reasonable.

Some of these laws said that the colonists had to pay taxes for defence. Soldiers were still needed to protect the western frontiers against the Indians, and the British government decided that the colonies should pay part of the cost. During the wars with the French, some of the English colonies had shared scarcely any of the expense. The British parliament now made a law setting a tax which everyone would pay.

This seems fair enough, but the colonists were angered because the tax laws were made not by their own law-makers, but by the British parliament in far-off London. "Though born in America," they said, "we are of the same blood as you, and we love liberty. It was our forefathers, too, who won the right many years ago to be taxed only by the law-makers whom they themselves elected."

"THE MERCHANTS OF BOSTON WERE ANGRY..."

For many years there had been laws which controlled the trade of the colonies, but these had not been obeyed very well.

The colonies were not supposed to trade with foreign countries; yet during the war with the French, some of them had even traded with the enemy. When the British now said the laws *must* be obeyed, the merchants of Boston and New York were angry, for they could make much more money if they traded wherever they pleased. The British decided also to make the colonies obey the laws against smuggling—that is, bringing goods from overseas into the country without paying a tax to the government. The profits of smuggling had brought much wealth to the Atlantic ports. They foresaw hard times if this unlawful trade were stopped.

Slowly the idea of breaking away from England to form a new independent nation took hold throughout the Thirteen

Colonies. At first only a few hot-heads actually wished to separate entirely from Britain. But as the British government failed to understand and satisfy the demands of the colonies, more and more people came to believe this was necessary.

In 1774, when feeling in the Thirteen Colonies was running high, the British parliament passed a law which told how the new colony was to be governed and what its western borders were to be. This law was known as the Quebec Act. It said that the boundary was to extend west to the Mississippi River and south to the Ohio. For several years, settlers had been trickling across the Appalachian Mountains into the Ohio Valley. Now the Atlantic colonies learned that they were still not to be given possession of the Ohio Valley, even after they had helped defeat the French!

For many years the Thirteen Colonies had been very jealous of one another, and it was seldom that the mother country, Great Britain, could get them to act together. But now their grievances against Great Britain brought them together at last.

In the autumn of 1774, the Thirteen Colonies held a meeting at Philadelphia. A letter was written by the colonies at this meeting to the people of Canada. It invited them to join in the struggle against the British government, and to send some of their leaders to a meeting which was to be held the following spring.

It was only fifteen years since the French Canadians had laid down their arms after their long and bitter struggle against the British. Would they now join the Revolution and rise against their conquerors?

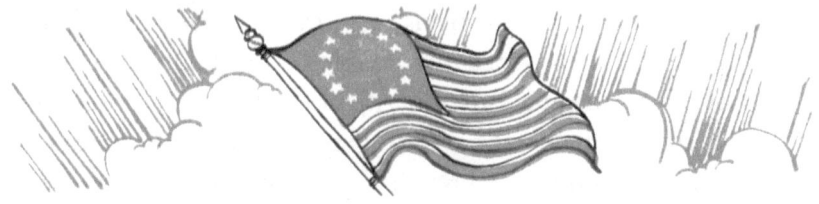

## THE INVASION OF CANADA

The American revolutionists printed their letter and sent it out far and wide in Canada. In it they criticized very strongly the Quebec Act, the law which set forth the boundaries of the "fourteenth colony", and told how the colony was to be governed. The Americans said that the law was full of "injuries and insults" to the people of Canada. What did the people of Canada think of it?

In drawing up the Quebec Act, the British government believed that their new subjects in Canada would be happiest if life went on for them much as it had under French rule. So the French Canadians were promised that they might keep their religion, their customs, and many of their old laws.

The French seigneurs and the Church leaders were pleased by the new Act, since they were allowed to hold much the same positions and rights as they had before the defeat of France. As a result they became strong supporters of British rule, and advised the habitants to be loyal to Britain also.

But the Quebec Act disappointed the habitants. Since the British victory, they had not had to pay the regular dues to the Church and the seigneurs. They did not like having to begin paying them again. On the other hand, the habitants had no reason to believe the things the American colonists told them, or to trust in the promises of those who had been their bitter enemies for many years. It is not surprising, therefore, that most French Canadians were willing to let Great Britain and her rebellious colonists fight it out by themselves. Not many French Canadians took up arms on either side.

In the few years since the British capture of Quebec, only about one thousand English-speaking people had settled in Canada. Many of these had come from the Atlantic colonies, and they felt that the cause of the rebels was just. They were angry, too, because the new law favoured the French Canadians. In the end, they

were a great deal less loyal to Britain than were the habitants.

When the Thirteen Colonies met again in the spring of 1775, no one came from Canada. The Colonies now decided to send armies north to capture the "fourteenth colony". If they succeeded, the British would not be able to use Canada later as a base from which to attack them. They knew that there were very few British soldiers in the country, and they believed that the habitants would be friendly.

Two armies were sent north in the fall of that year. The larger force was commanded by General Richard Montgomery, who had once been an officer in the British army. Montgomery moved against Montreal by way of Lake Champlain. The other army, led by Colonel Benedict Arnold, made a difficult march to Quebec through the wilderness of what is now northern Maine.

Montgomery's advance on Montreal was so rapid that the British governor of Canada, Sir Guy Carleton, had a narrow escape from being captured. Just before Montgomery's troops entered the town, he embarked with several small ships for Quebec. At first the ships made good progress, but then the wind turned against them. While the vessels waited for the wind to change, the Americans caught up with them and demanded their surrender. However, Carleton disguised himself as an habitant, and on a dark night he and a few companions slipped downstream past the American camp-fires. At one place the passage was so narrow that they paddled the boat with their hands to avoid being heard.

By this time Quebec too was in serious danger, for General Arnold's army had arrived from Maine. Its defenders were few, including only about two hundred regular soldiers, and a handful of sailors from ships in the harbour. The fortress ignored Arnold's demands that it surrender, but the defenders were greatly relieved when Sir Guy Carleton arrived safely from Montreal and took command.

Quebec was now the only important place in the whole of Canada still held by British forces. If it fell, Canada would be lost to Britain. Carleton persuaded every man he could to rally to the defence, for Montgomery had now come on from

Montreal to join Arnold for the finishing blow that would win the "key to Canada". It was already late in the month of November, and Montgomery promised to "eat his Christmas dinner in Quebec".

The opposing forces were fairly evenly matched. Of the American troops, many had signed up to fight only till the end of the year, and Montgomery could not count on them after that. Of Carleton's men, only a small part were trained soldiers, and the loyalty of a good many of the others was doubtful. In a message to Carleton, Montgomery described the defenders as "a wretched garrison, consisting of sailors unacquainted with the use of arms, of citizens incapable of the soldier's duty, and a few miserable emigrants"!

Carleton would not even reply to Montgomery's demands for surrender, for he looked on Montgomery as a rebel and a traitor to his king.

December wore on. Christmas Day passed. Still the Americans waited. Still the British refused to yield.

On New Year's Eve it began to snow, and under cover of the storm Montgomery launched his assault. He himself led an attack from the west, while Arnold led one from the east. Montgomery's men hardly reached the defences when they were driven back, and Montgomery himself was killed; his body was found in the snow next day by the British soldiers. Arnold's men were more successful, and won their way into the Lower Town. But Arnold was wounded, and his forces were suddenly attacked from both sides and made to retreat.

The Americans continued to besiege Quebec until spring. During the winter they ran short of supplies, and the habitants became unfriendly and unwilling to give any assistance.

In the spring, when the ice went out, a British fleet appeared on the river, and the besiegers fled—"leaving their dinner cooking", it is said. One eye-witness wrote: "They left cannon, muskets, ammunition, and even clothes; we found the roads strewn with these, while bread and pork all lay in heaps on the highway... Look which way soever one could, men were flying and carts driving away with all possible speed."

Carleton, who hoped that the rebels might still be won back to their loyalty to Britain, treated them kindly. He ordered that the wounded Americans should be searched for and brought to hospital. When the prisoners were better, he let them all go back to their homes in the Thirteen Colonies.

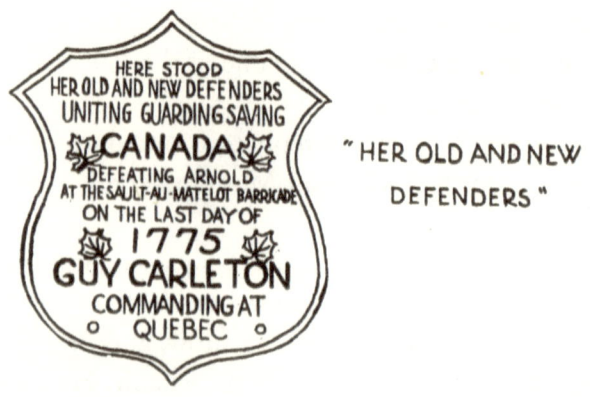

" HER OLD AND NEW DEFENDERS "

## THE FATHER OF HIS COUNTRY

Who is the greatest man in Canadian history? That is a hard question to answer. Even when you have studied much more Canadian history than is told in this book, you will not find it easy to make up your mind.

But if you should ask any boy or girl who goes to school in the United States, "Who is the greatest man in American history?", the answer would come like a flash—"George Washington!"

For there might never have been a United States of America, if it had not been for George Washington. It was he who led the Thirteen Colonies in their fight for independence. During the Seven Years' War, he had fought beside British soldiers against France; now Britain was his enemy, and as we shall see, France became his friend.

The Revolutionary War went on for several years, and often it looked as if the colonists could not possibly win. British troops took New York, and held this important city throughout the war. A British army captured Philadelphia. Here the Thirteen Colonies had met in 1776 to sign the "Declaration of Independence", which said that they would no longer be colonies of Great Britain, and that their people were no longer subjects of the king of England. While the British army spent the winter comfortably in Philadelphia, the Revolutionary forces starved and froze in their camp only twenty miles away. Later on, the British troops overran the whole of Georgia and South Carolina. But General Washington would not give up, even when the future seemed darkest.

Two years after Montgomery's attempt to capture Quebec, a British army of 8,000 men set out from Canada by way of Lake Champlain. It planned to meet another British army advancing up the Hudson River from New York, and thus cut off New England from the southern colonies. But by some strange error, the British general in New York did not receive the order to start. At Saratoga, a much larger force of Americans surrounded the army which had come from Canada, and it had to surrender.

This great victory turned the tide for the rebelling colonists. France had been watching the war in North America, and now decided that since the Thirteen Colonies could do so well by themselves, it would be worth while to help them against her old enemy. She declared war on England. The French navy kept the British fleet busy at sea. Guns, ammunition, and clothing were sent from France to the American armies, and finally French troops were landed to help.

At last, in 1781, General Washington cornered a British army of 8000 men at Yorktown in Virginia, and forced it to lay down its arms. This was the end of the war. Two years later, a peace treaty was signed by Great Britain with the United States.

At the close of the war, George Washington said farewell to his army and returned to his home in Virginia. But soon his country called him again, for in 1789 he was chosen to be the first president of the United States.

The Thirteen Colonies had won their independence from England. But although a new flag had been raised in North America, the people who lived under it were largely of British descent. Many of the laws and liberties which the people of the United States still treasure are the laws and liberties of England.

## "HIS MAJESTY'S LOYAL SUBJECTS"

IN the British forces which opposed George Washington, there were many soldiers who came not from England, but from the Thirteen Colonies. These men felt that, in spite of the mistakes the mother country had made, it was not right for the colonies to take up arms against her. They joined the British armies in order, as they thought, to save the colonies from ruin.

In addition, there were many thousands living in the Thirteen Colonies who did not take up arms, but who hoped with all their hearts that the rebellion would be put down.

As the war went on, the colonists who were fighting so hard for their independence grew very bitter towards those of their neighbours who remained loyal to the British king. Angry mobs carried off the belongings of the loyalists, burned down their homes, ill-treated them, and sometimes even put them to death.

When people were known to favour the British side, they were often fined heavily and put into prison. Their lands were taken away, and they lost their jobs.

When the war was over, many of the colonists who had fought against the Revolution were afraid to go back to their homes. Others, who had been able to stay in their homes during the war, were now forced to leave. Many, indeed, did not wish to remain in a country which was separate from Britain. Where were all these people to go? A large number of the loyalists returned to England. Others went to the British West Indies. About fifty thousand came to Nova Scotia and Canada, where they were known as the "United Empire Loyalists".

At this time Nova Scotia included what is now the province of New Brunswick. In the whole region there lived only about 17,000 people, and most of these had come from the Thirteen Colonies to settle in Nova Scotia before the Revolution. When the Loyalists of New England had to seek new homes under the British flag, they turned to Nova Scotia.

## THE LOYALISTS IN THE MARITIMES

Nova Scotia began to receive Loyalists shortly after the beginning of the Revolution, and after it was over a huge tide of Loyalists poured in—between 30,000 and 40,000 in all.

The first fleet to arrive in 1783 carried seven thousand Loyalists, half of whom went to the St. John River where they built a settlement known as Parrtown. Parrtown has since become the city of Saint John—one of Canada's great ice-free ports on the Atlantic coast.

At Port Roseway (later called Shelburne), on the south-west shore of Nova Scotia, a town was begun which at one time had 10,000 people living in it. The story is told that when the first

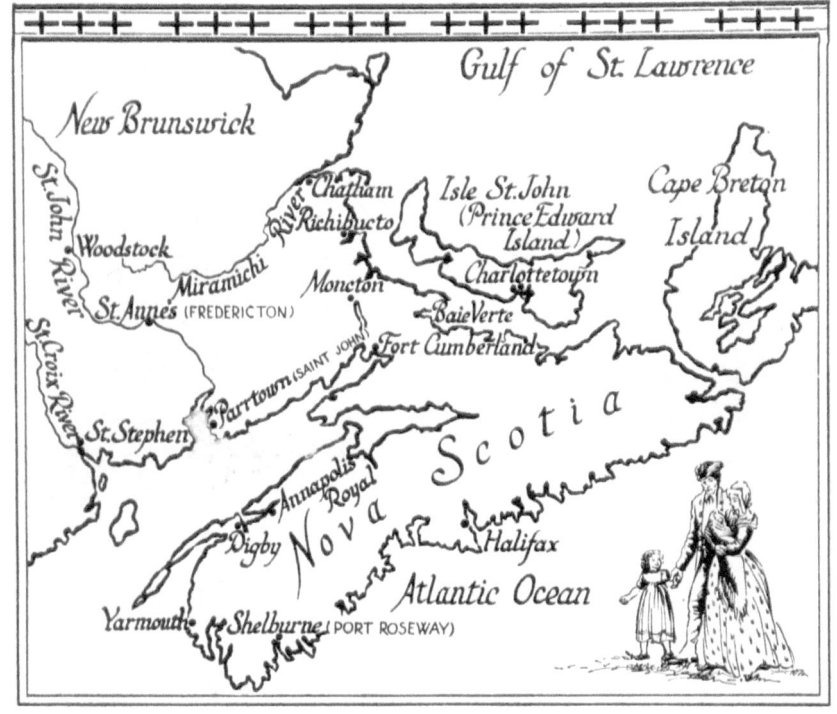

*Loyalist Settlements in the Marines (About 1784)*

Loyalist Settlements in the Maritimes {about 1784) Loyalists arrived they asked one of the few settlers in the lonesome place, "How came you to stay here?" The man answered: "Poverty brought me here and poverty kept me here!" The settlers might well have heeded the warning. Although their town did well for a few years, it did not continue to grow and in the end most of the people had to move away.

Life was hard at first in the wilds where the Loyalists had to build their homes and plant their crops. One woman tells in her diary of coming to shore at Saint John: "It is, I think, the roughest land I ever saw. We are all ordered to land to-morrow, and not a shelter to go under."

Fortunately, the Indians were not hostile. A party which landed sixty miles up the St. John River told of meeting savages the day after they arrived:

"Next morning we discovered a fleet of ten Indian canoes slowly moving towards us, which caused considerable alarm with the women. Before they came within gunshot, one who could speak English came to let us know, 'We all one brother!' They were of the Micmac tribe and became quite friendly, and furnished us plentifully with moose-meat."

The British government did its best to help the newcomers. They were given free land, and supplies of food, clothing, and lumber were provided to keep the new settlements going until they could look after themselves. Nevertheless, it was impossible for the British government to take care of so many settlers all at once, and bitter winters and poor crops during the early days were terrible trials indeed.

As a result of the coming of such large numbers of new settlers, Nova Scotia was divided into two colonies in 1784. The new province was named New Brunswick, and the newly named town of Fredericton on the St. John River was chosen as its capital.

The Loyalists suffered great hardships, but their labour and sacrifices prepared the way for those who followed. Their descendants have spread to every part of Canada, and many Canadian boys and girls are proud to-day to say that they are of "Loyalist stock".

### THE LOYALISTS IN CANADA

Shortly after the peace treaty was signed in 1783, some seven thousand United Empire Loyalists arrived in Canada, which then included both Quebec and Ontario. Most of the newcomers settled along the shores of the St. Lawrence River above the rapids upstream from Montreal, and on the northern shore of Lake Ontario. A Loyalist settlement sprang up near Niagara and a smaller one at Detroit. Unlike the Nova Scotia Loyalists, who went by sea, most of those who came to Canada crossed overland from the Thirteen Colonies. Here, too, the British government did what it could to help the new settlers get started. But in 1787 the crops failed, and the next year went down in history as "the hungry year".

Many stories have been told of the sufferings of the Loyalists at this time. "Not many miles from Picton," says one story, "a beef bone passed from house to house and was boiled again and again in order to extract some nourishment." A letter said about the Niagara district: "the children leaped for joy at one robin being caught, out of which a whole pot of broth was made"!

The coming of the Loyalists changed the whole picture in Canada. Up to this time almost all the white settlers had been French, but now there were two different groups in the country—one French-speaking, and one English-speaking. The French and the English colonists were accustomed to quite different ways of living. Laws had already been made for Canada which, it was hoped, would make the French people contented and happy subjects of the British king. These laws did not suit the new English-speaking settlers in the least.

When the Loyalists came to Canada, very few of them stopped in present-day Quebec, where most of the good farming land was already held by French-speaking Canadians. This made it possible for the parliament in Great Britain to try to please the English and the French at the same time, by dividing Canada into two separate provinces. The western province, which had mostly English-speaking people, was called Upper Canada; and the eastern province, which had mostly French-speaking people, was called Lower Canada. It was hoped that this arrangement would make it possible to give each province the laws best suited to the people living in it. A governor was appointed for the whole country, and a lieutenant-governor for each province.

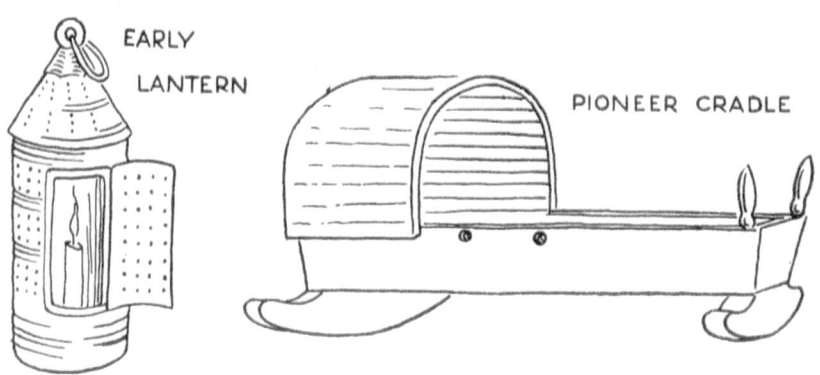

SOAP MAKING

CLEANING GRAIN

## "THE DIARY OF MRS. SIMCOE"

The first lieutenant-governor of Upper Canada was Colonel John Graves Simcoe. He was a British officer who had commanded loyalist troops in the American Revolutionary War. Governor Simcoe was an able and hard-working man; he foresaw that Upper Canada would one day become a great province, and he did his best to start it on the way.

Governor Simcoe's wife came to Canada with her husband. She was skilful at drawing and water-colour painting, and made many sketches of scenes in Upper Canada. Her pictures and a diary which she kept while here tell us a great deal about Upper Canada in those early days.

Most of the southern part of Ontario, which is now so thickly settled, was then covered with dense forests. Only here and there along the St. Lawrence River and Lake Ontario were the forests broken by settlers' clearings and rough cabins. There were almost no roads, and when Colonel and Mrs. Simcoe journeyed from Montreal to Newark (now Niagara) in 1792, they travelled chiefly by water. At night they sometimes went ashore to sleep in a settler's home, or, more often, they pitched their tents on the bank of the St. Lawrence.

Kingston was the largest settlement in the province. Mrs. Simcoe described it as "a small town of about fifty wooden houses and merchants' storehouses". At Kingston, the governor and his wife embarked on a small ship and sailed to Niagara—a voyage which took three days.

At Niagara, a small wooden building which had first been built as a naval storehouse had been set aside for the governor's use. Mrs. Simcoe found the building "undergoing a thorough repair for our occupation, but still so unfinished that the Governor has ordered three tents to be pitched for us on the hill above the house."

Four days later Mrs. Simcoe had her first view of Niagara Falls. She was as thrilled as any visitor to-day by what she described as "the grandest sight imaginable".

Governor Simcoe called together the first parliament of Upper Canada at Newark in September, 1792. Only sixteen members had been elected, and some of these could not come because it was harvest time and they were busy in the fields. But Simcoe opened the little parliament with as much ceremony as he could, and the members voted on several important laws at this first meeting.

One of Governor Simcoe's chief problems was the defence of Upper Canada, for he feared there might soon be war between England and the United States. This fear was shared by his wife, who said, "I am always glad to have large parties at dinner, for when I sit alone I do nothing but think of the threatened war in this country."

The governor took what steps he could to prepare the province to defend itself. He formed the settlers into groups which drilled as soldiers whenever they could, and he equipped a small fleet to sail on the waters of Lake Ontario.

When Simcoe came to Upper Canada the British regiments guarding the province were camped at Kingston and Niagara. Since Niagara was on the American border, Governor Simcoe decided to begin a military barracks and naval base across Lake

THE SIMCOES AT YORK, 1793

Ontario at Toronto. The governor named the settlement York, in honour of the King's son, the Duke of York. Simcoe did not plan, however, to make York the capital of Upper Canada. He favoured a place in the western part of the province, where the city of London is now, because he thought an inland town would be safer from attack. After he left Upper Canada, however, York became the capital.

Governor Simcoe built roads to open up the province and aid in its defence. His soldiers began a highway, Yonge Street, which ran from Toronto to Lake Simcoe (named by the governor after his father). Dundas Street, leading from Niagara to the western part of Ontario, was also begun by Simcoe. Both these highways are in use to-day, but they do not look much like the rough, barely cleared roads of Simcoe's time.

Upper Canada's chief need, however, was more people. When Simcoe came, there were only about 10,000 in the whole province. It was Governor Simcoe's aim to secure more settlers, so that the land would be cultivated and food grown for many people. He often said that the day would come "when every acre of land from the Ottawa to the Detroit River would so respond to the call of the farmer that the sickle would never be idle and the people never be in want."

To attract more people, Simcoe advertised in the United States that settlers could obtain free grants of land in Upper Canada. There were a good many loyalists still living across the border who were glad to take this opportunity to make their homes again under the British flag. Of course, there were others who came more for the free land than because they cared what flag waved over them.

Mrs. Simcoe's diary tells us that "a great many settlers come daily from the United States, some even from the Carolinas, about 2,000 miles. Five or six hundred miles is no more considered by an American than moving to the next parish is by an Englishman."

Governor Simcoe made many long journeys through Upper Canada. Sometimes he had to travel where there were no paths for horses or waterways for boats or canoes. In February, 1793, Mrs. Simcoe wrote to a friend in England: "Colonel Simcoe is gone to Detroit, on foot the greatest part of the way, a journey of about 400 miles, but as I am convinced the exercise and air will do his health and spirits great good I rejoice in his absence, though it will be a month or six weeks."

Sometimes Mrs. Simcoe travelled with the governor. She tells in her diary of visiting many settlers' homes. She had a sharp eye for good or bad housekeeping, but was a very "good sport" about hardships. She tells of the dinner a settler gave her at Stoney Creek, near the present city of Hamilton. Not everything on the menu would appeal to us!

"They prepared me some refreshment at this house, some excellent cakes, baked on the coals; eggs; a boiled black squirrel;

tea, and coffee made of peas, which was good. The sugar was made from black walnut trees, which looks darker than that from the maple, but I think it is sweeter."

On more than one occasion Mrs. Simcoe met Joseph Brant, a famous Mohawk chief who had settled in Upper Canada. The British Government had granted him and his tribesmen land along the Grand River because of their loyalty during the Revolution. The city of Brantford is named after Brant, and the Mohawks still live by the Grand River.

In the summer of 1796, the Simcoes returned to England. But the people of Ontario will always remember Governor Simcoe because he did so much to help their province when it was just beginning. They will remember Mrs. Simcoe because of her interesting diary and sketches of Upper Canada which show us what it was like during its first five years.

## FURS OF EMPIRE

WHEN we think of the numbers of freighters that ply the waters of Lake Ontario and Lake Erie to-day, it is hard to believe that these lakes were not part of the first water route to the West.

Even during the early days of British Canada, fur traders paddled their canoes up the Ottawa River from Montreal, and crossed over by way of Lake Nipissing and the French River to Georgian Bay. They travelled up the St. Mary's River to Lake Superior, avoiding the rapids at Sault Ste Marie by a small lock which they had built themselves. Every spring these traders set out from Montreal in huge canoes laden with goods to trade. In the autumn they returned by the same route, their canoes riding deep in the water, heavy with rich furs from the Far West.

Although the Ottawa route was direct, it was difficult. At many places the canoe men had to carry goods and canoes for long distances over rough trails, to avoid falls and rapids. La Vérendrye, the famous French explorer and trader, had found that it cost him so much to bring goods from Montreal that he was continually short of money.

The Hudson's Bay Company was able to carry goods by ship direct to its trading-posts, which were built at the mouths of rivers flowing into the Bay. Since the Indians brought their furs down the rivers to these posts, the Company did not have the trouble and expense of going after them.

After La Vérendrye had built trading-posts west of Lake Superior, however, the Company found that many of the Indians were taking their furs to the French, instead of making the journey to Hudson Bay. The Indians liked English goods better than French goods, but not so much better that it seemed worth while going so far.

Like a modern business firm which finds competition becoming keen, the Great Company now sent one of its men on

HENDAY AND THE BLACKFOOT CHIEF

a "good-will tour". In 1750, Anthony Henday travelled as far as the foothills of the Rockies, where he spent the winter with the Blackfoot Indians. He was probably the first white man to see the Rocky Mountains, since it is doubtful if the La Vérendryes really travelled far enough west. But Henday seems to have been a better explorer than salesman, for he was able to persuade only a few of the natives to bring their furs all the way to Hudson Bay. Most of the Indians still preferred to deal with the French, who went right into the country where the native tribes roamed. Henday himself reported that one old chief "made little answer; only said that it was a long way off and that his people knew not the use of the canoe."

When the British captured Quebec in 1759, the Hudson's

Bay traders thought that they would now receive all the furs. But they were rudely surprised. Lone traders, who came to Montreal from New England and the British Isles, lost no time in getting into the western fur trade. These new traders proved to be just as bold and adventurous as the French, and they brought better and cheaper goods.

Alexander Henry was one of the first of these new traders to go into the West. He made his first trip in 1761. Two years later he narrowly escaped with his life at Michilimackinac when the fort was attacked by Pontiac's warriors.

The number of traders grew rapidly. They built warehouses at Montreal, and hired French-Canadian voyageurs to take the canoes on the long voyages to the West. Soon they were finding their way across the plains as far as the La Vérendryes had gone, and even farther. Some of them reached Lake Athabaska.

But the Hudson's Bay Company was not asleep. In 1769, one of its men, Samuel Hearne, made a long and difficult journey from the mouth of the Churchill River to the Coppermine River. He followed the Coppermine to where it empties into the Arctic Ocean. On the return journey, Hearne travelled farther west and discovered Great Slave Lake. In 1774, he built Fort Cumberland on the Saskatchewan River route leading to Lake Winnipeg. This was the first inland post of the Hudson's Bay Company. It showed the Montreal traders that the Company was not going to let them win away the fur trade without a struggle.

After the American Revolution, the traders from Montreal were no longer able to go into the fur country south of the Great Lakes. But they became busier than ever in the Canadian West. At first they were rivals, but soon they found that it was better to work together and share the profits. Then, in 1784, a group of the most successful Montreal traders joined together to form the North West Company. Henceforth, it was the chief rival of the Hudson's Bay Company.

## TO THE NORTH-WEST

"Well, Duncan," said my father, "here's the lad!"

The tall man rose quickly from the heavy book of accounts he had been studying, and came across the dusty warehouse to greet us. He and my father shook hands warmly, for they were old friends, and then he turned to me. His blue eyes were pleasant but keen in his dark, weatherbeaten face. Father introduced me:

"This is Angus. Angus—Mr. Duncan McKenzie, partner in the North West Company!"

"Sit you down, William, and you, too, Angus," said Mr. McKenzie. "So you are the lad who's made up his mind not to be a lawyer? I do not blame you—how your father's kept to his dusty law-books all these years I canna understand!"

"Now, now, we can't all be adventurers like you, Duncan," answered my father. "A quiet life suits me well enough. But Angus—he will not bide at home here in Montreal, but longs to be off to the Far West. As I told you, he's a good, industrious lad, and if you have a place for him in the Company, I doubt not he'll serve you well."

"I am sure of that," said Mr. McKenzie heartily. "But Angus, would you be willing to sign up for seven years' service, wherever we might send you? But hold, I'll first tell you both a bit about service in the Company.

"We have four ranks of Company servants. First, as you know, there are the canoemen—the French-Canadian voyageurs who handle the freight canoes."

"PORTAGE"

Well did I know the voyageurs, who swaggered about Montreal in the winter season in their bright caps and sashes. Just once, however, had I seen them speeding by in one of their great canoes. I had been on a visit to my uncle's farm on the St. Lawrence just above Lachine, where the fur-trade canoes start off on their long voyages. Suddenly, around a bend in the river, appeared a long North West canoe, pennants flying, voyageurs singing, paddles flashing in the sun. I was only ten years old then, but how I longed to be in that great canoe! Eight years had passed and my wish was as keen as ever.

But Mr. McKenzie was speaking. "I don't need to tell you how splendid these men are. I have made hundreds of voyages to Fort William, and beyond, and I never cease to admire and value their skill. They can paddle as long as light lasts, and rise with the sun to paddle all day again. They carry the canoes and 90-lb. bales of goods on their backs over long, rough portages. Some of our canoes are nearly forty feet long, you know, and hold four or five tons of goods.

"These hardy fellows risk their lives time and again. On almost every portage we see crosses which mark a place where brave men have died—at one rapids I counted more than thirty!"

I was glad that my mother, who was none too happy about my becoming a fur trader, could not hear this. My father said nothing; perhaps he thought that if Duncan McKenzie had made hundreds of voyages safely, I might do the same.

"In spite of the hardships and dangers, the voyageurs are always gay and cheerful. Barring the skirl o' the pipes, William, there's no grander music than the singing of the voyageurs. Ay, they're fine tunes: *C'est l'aviron!, En roulant ma boule!,* and the rest."

Duncan McKenzie paused and filled his pipe. I thought he had forgotten about me. But he went on:

"Besides the voyageurs, we hire French-Canadian guides who are of great help to us in pushing our trade. They can speak the languages of the different Indian tribes, and they know all the best canoe routes. We pay them well, but they earn every penny.

"Next come the clerks, and that is where we might use you, Angus. We need young men with education to keep tally of the goods and furs during the journeys to and from Fort William. At Fort William, strict accounting must be made of goods and stores. Then, after a clerk has finished his seven years, he usually becomes a partner, as I did, and may be stationed here at Montreal and travel with the brigades to Fort William. Or he might be placed in charge of a district in the West.

"During your service as a clerk, we pay only a small wage, but you will always know that as a partner you will one day

share in the profits of the Company. Every clerk knows this, and it's no wonder all the lads work like beavers."

"I suppose that is what you mean by 'the spirit of the North West Company'," said my father.

"Indeed it is!" answered the Nor' Wester. "Every man knows he's working for himself, not just for wealthy owners overseas. Mind, I respect the men of the Hudson's Bay Company for their faithful service, but it's not to be expected they would show the boldness and daring of our wintering partners."

"The wintering partners stay in the West, don't they, Mr. McKenzie?" I asked.

"Well, Angus, as you're aware, our western trading-posts are so far away that we have had to build Fort William as a halfway meeting point. Here our brigades from east and west meet and exchange goods for furs. The wintering partners remain in the West all the year round, making the journey once a year to Fort William. At Fort William they pass on the furs they have gathered in the winter's trading with the Indians, and then return to their posts with the loads of trade goods we have brought them. Indeed, some of our wintering partners are now so far afield that the summer is not long enough for them to make the trip to Fort William and return, so we easterners go on to meet them at Rainy Lake."

I thought that I should very much like to be a wintering partner, and some day travel to the Rocky Mountains and beyond, like Sir Alexander Mackenzie, the famous North West explorer of whom I had read.

"Fort William must be a very busy place," said Father.

"That it is. Why, at the height of the season, I have known three thousand men to be there at one time. It's a town in the wilderness—and a fort as well. Inside the fortifications are a large house with a great dining-hall, a council house, storehouses, blacksmith's shop, workshops, a house for the doctor, sleeping quarters for partners, clerks, and guides—and a jail, which the voyageurs call 'the butter tub'."

"I daresay the 'butter tub' is well filled," said Father with a rather severe look, "if what I have heard of behaviour at Fort William is true."

Mr. McKenzie grinned. "I'll admit there are gay times; but what would you expect? The men come in from long, dangerous journeys, and lonesome winters on the plains; it is no wonder they want to have a good time together before they set off again."

"I'll wager the partners make merry with the rest, eh, Duncan?"

"To be sure we do. Our dining-hall is 60 feet long by 30 feet wide, and as many as 200 have sat down there to dinner at one

THE "ARITHMETIC" OF THE FUR TRADE

time. But do not think we ever neglect business for pleasure. The summer is short, and everyone has to work hard. Especially the clerks"—he smiled at me—"if the furs are to be valued, counted, and pressed into bales for the trip to Montreal, and the blankets, tobacco, kettles, ammunition, and other trade goods are to be sorted and made into packs for the western canoes, which are smaller than ours. Both pork-eaters and lard-eaters must get back before the frosts close the waterways."

"Pork-eaters? Lard-eaters?" said I, in surprise.

"The pork-eaters are called so by the westerners, because on their voyages the food of the Montreal men is chiefly dried peas cooked with salt pork. The Montrealers call the western men

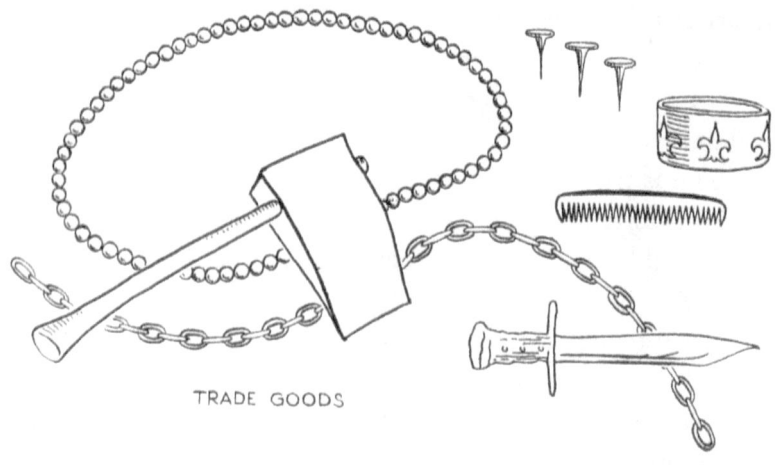

TRADE GOODS

MAKING PEMMICAN

lard-eaters, because they eat pemmican. Pemmican is made by the Indians, of dried buffalo meat, pounded, and then mixed with lard. I didn't care much for it at first, but one gets used to it—especially when there's nothing else to eat."

"I don't know how Angus would take to that," said Father, laughing. "His mother thinks he is mighty hard on the victuals, and his poor father has had to grind hard at the law for eighteen years to nourish the six feet of him."

"Well, you've given him health and strength, and with the sharp wits he must have from his father, he should go far in the fur trade. What do you say, Angus, are you coming with us?"

And that is how I came to join the North West Company.

"BALING THE FURS"

## TO THE WEST COAST

IN the year 1579, Queen Elizabeth's famous captain, Sir Francis Drake, was sailing up the western coast of North America. It was two years since Sir Francis had set out from England in his little ship, the *Golden Hind*. Cruising far southward, he rounded the tip of South America. Then he sailed up the western shores of the continent until he reached the Spanish colonies of Peru and Mexico. There he found what he was looking for—Spanish treasure-ships, whose captains little expected to meet an English sea-dog on the Pacific Ocean.

Soon the hold of the *Golden Hind* was stuffed with plunder from the Spanish ships. But her captain was uneasy. He had still to win his way home to England, and the Spaniards would certainly be watching for him when he turned back towards Cape Horn.

Why not continue north? Most sailors were then quite sure there was an ocean passage through North America. Drake wondered if he could find its western entrance farther up this

unknown coast. But as he sailed north, he met such "extremity of cold", "vale, thick fog", and contrary winds, that he finally turned back.

Sir Francis now landed on the shore of northern California, and claimed that "province" for the Queen of England. Then he set sail westward across the Pacific. He forged bravely on, across the Indian Ocean, around the Cape of Good Hope, and up the western coast of Africa. At last he reached England and Queen Elizabeth again. This was the first English voyage around the world.

Two centuries passed before any other English sailor followed Drake to the north-west coast of North America. In the meantime, tremendous events had taken place in the eastern part of the continent. The French built their empire in eastern America, and lost it. The American colonists had begun their fight for independence.

During all this time, little had been learned about Canada's Pacific coast. Explorers sent by the Russians proved that Asia and North America were separated by the narrow strait named after its discoverer, Vitus Behring. Having reached Alaska, the Russians began to visit farther down the coast, trading for furs with the Indians. And there were visitors from the south as well. The Spaniards had started settlements in California, and were beginning to explore the north-west coast of the continent.

At last, in the very year that the Thirteen Colonies declared their independence of Great Britain, another great English sailor set out on a voyage of discovery which took him to the northwest coast of North America. This famous explorer was

Captain Cook. The parliament of Great Britain had offered to pay twenty thousand pounds to anyone who found a north-west passage which ships could use. Every attempt to find a route from the eastern side had failed, but it still seemed possible that a search from the west would be successful.

Cook sailed up the coast of British Columbia in 1778, exploring the bays and inlets. He stopped at Nootka Sound, a

harbour on the west coast of Vancouver Island, and stayed there about four weeks. His sailors busied themselves trading with the natives for the handsome sea-otter skins they wore.

After leaving Nootka, Cook continued north around the coast of Alaska until he had just passed Behring Strait. He was now at the north-west tip of the American continent. Here his ships were stopped by a wall of ice, which rose above the sea "ten to twelve feet high"; the ice extended "from west by south to east by north, as far as the eye could reach". Cook rightly concluded that any passage from the Pacific to the Atlantic was so far north that it would be blocked by ice and useless to ships.

On the return journey, the English ships stopped at Canton, China. Here the overjoyed sailors found that the sea-otter skins purchased from the Indians at Nootka brought a very high price from the Chinese. So valuable were they, that "the rage with which our seamen were possessed to return and buy another cargo of skins, to make their fortunes at one time, was not far short of mutiny." The news spread, and a rich fur trade began which lasted for about forty years. Sailors visited every Indian village they could find, looking for furs. As a result, the northwest coast was thoroughly explored. Once more the fur trade had led the way!

The Spaniards claimed the whole of the western coast—even though they had not colonized it—and it was not long before trouble arose. A Spanish expedition was sent to build a fort at Nootka, on the western side of Vancouver Island, and a Spanish governor was placed in charge. One of his first acts was to seize several English trading ships which were at Nootka. For a time it looked as if there might be war between England and Spain, but in the end a treaty was signed which gave both countries equal rights to trade along the coast.

The next important British visitor was Captain George Vancouver. He was sent out by the British government in 1791, with orders to make maps and charts of the coastline. This exploration took two years, for Vancouver did his work thoroughly. He explored Puget Sound, where the city of Seattle stands to-day, and the fine harbour off the Strait of Georgia on which the city of Vancouver has been built. He sailed north through Queen Charlotte Strait, and proved that the island which has been named after him was not, as Cook had supposed, a part of the mainland.

One of Vancouver's stops along the northern coast was at Cascade Inlet. If he had touched at this spot only six weeks later, there might have been a famous meeting between him and another great British explorer. Who was this other explorer, and where had he come from?

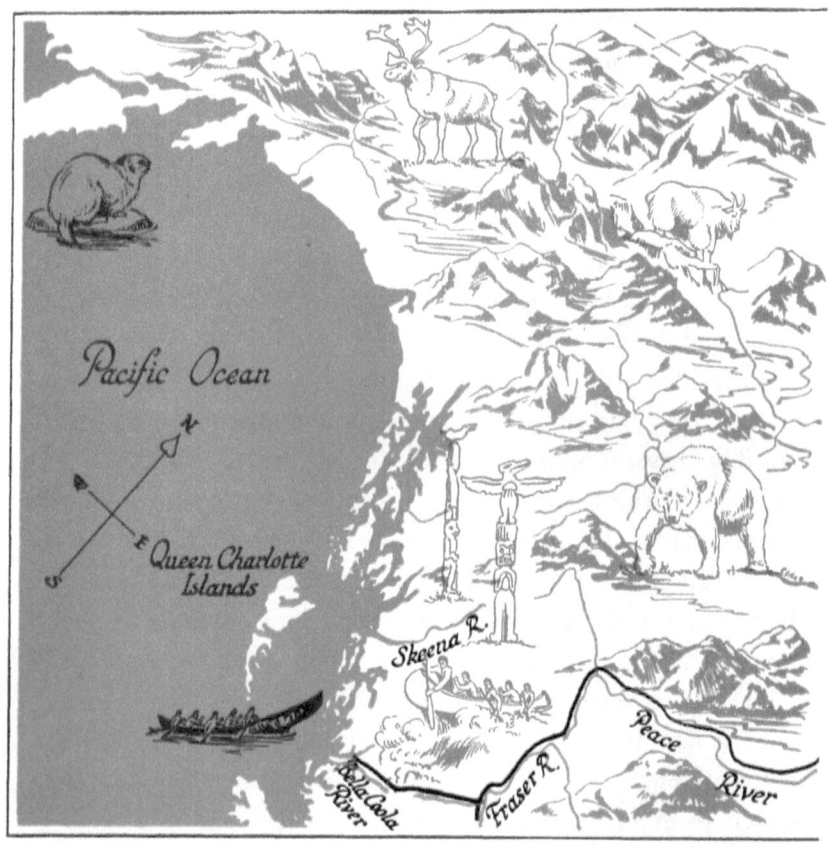

## OVERLAND TO THE PACIFIC

On September 8, 1794, Mrs. Simcoe, wife of the first lieutenant-governor of Upper Canada, made an interesting note in her diary:

"Mr. Mackenzie, who has made his way to the Pacific Ocean, is just returned from thence, and brought the Governor a sea-otter skin as a proof of his having reached the coast."

We can imagine how interested Governor and Mrs. Simcoe must have been to hear the tales the explorer told of his journey

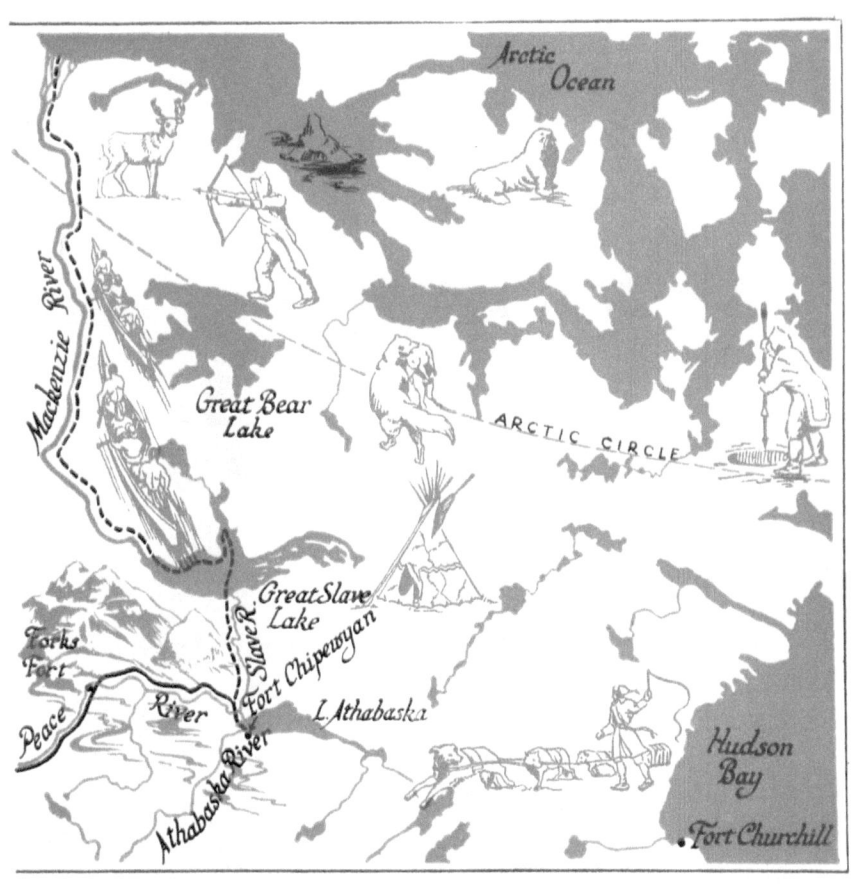

to the coast, and of the strange ways of the natives who lived there. For Alexander Mackenzie was the very first white man to reach the Pacific Ocean by crossing overland from either Canada or the United States.

Mackenzie was a young fur trader of the North West Company. Five years earlier, he had made up his mind to try to find a way across the continent to the Pacific. He was in charge of the Company's post at Fort Chipewyan on Lake Athabaska, and from the Indians who came to the fort with furs he heard tales of a great unknown river. He hoped this river might lead

"I..... PERCEIVED THAT THEY WERE WHALES....." MACKENZIE

to the Pacific coast, which white men had visited up to this time only by sea.

With five white men and several Indians as companions, Mackenzie set out in the spring of 1789 from Fort Chipewyan. The explorers crossed Lake Athabaska, followed the Slave River to Great Slave Lake, and entered the strange river of which the Indians had spoken. It was a lonely journey. They met a few natives who warned them "it would require several winters to get to the sea, and that old age would come upon us before the period of our return," as Mackenzie wrote in his diary. When the travellers reached the "land of the midnight sun", the days were so long they paddled many miles each day. But by this time Mackenzie realized that they were not going in the direction of the Pacific and so this river could not possibly lead to the western ocean. He called it "River Disappointment", but it was later named the Mackenzie, in his honour.

On a July evening the weary paddlers beached their canoes at a point where the river was divided into channels by low islands and sand-bars. After they had rested a time, they saw that the water was rising, and some of them got up and moved their baggage higher on the bank. They thought the wind had caused the rise. But the next day they sighted Bowhead whales. Now they realized that it was an ocean tide that had made the water rise the night before. They must be near the sea!

Mackenzie had now explored one of the great rivers of America. After a winding journey of fifteen hundred miles—which took only six weeks—he had reached the Arctic Ocean. But he was by no means satisfied with his great achievement. He still wanted to find a route to the Pacific.

As a fur trader, Mackenzie was interested in the valuable sea-otter skins Captain Cook had told about. Moreover, Alexander Mackenzie was a true adventurer and a born leader of men, and he was determined to find a way to the Pacific Ocean itself. He laid his plans carefully, and even made a trip to England to buy better instruments for exploring, and to learn to use them.

By 1793 he was ready at last, and started out with ten other persons in a single large canoe. They went up the Peace River, which flows from the Rocky Mountains into the Slave River.

The explorers found the going very difficult. Sometimes they had to drag their canoe upstream through foaming rapids, pulling it by a line while they themselves clung to the edges of cliffs. Mackenzie said later, "one false step of those who were attached to the line, or the breaking of the line itself, would at once have sent the canoe, and everything it contained, to instant destruction." Sometimes the adventurers had to carry the canoe and their supplies over difficult portages. At one point on the Peace River they took three whole days to get the canoe over the side of a mountain.

After six weeks of danger and toil, Mackenzie and his men came to a "Great River", which we now know as the Fraser. It was wild and full of rapids. After they had travelled down it for

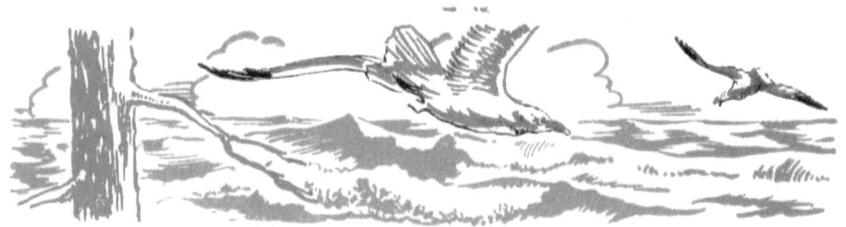

some distance, they met a group of Indians who warned them the river was so long and violent they would never reach the sea.

What were the explorers to do now? Their supplies were running low, and it was impossible to get clear directions from the natives. One Indian demanded, "What can be the reason that you are so anxious for a knowledge of this country; do not you white men know everything in the world?" Mackenzie replied that the white men certainly were acquainted with every part of the world, "that I knew where the sea is, and where I myself then was, but that I did not exactly understand what obstacles might interrupt me in getting to it!"

Acting on the best advice he could get, Mackenzie turned back up the Fraser, and then crossed to a small river flowing west. Soon he began to hear stories from the natives about other white men visiting the coast. He decided he could not now be very far from the ocean. One Indian told him that they were approaching a river "which was neither large nor long, but whose banks were inhabited; and that in the bay which the sea forms at the mouth of it, a great wooden canoe, with white people, arrived about the time when the leaves begin to grow". The Indian was speaking of the Bella Coola River, but to reach it the explorers had to leave their canoe behind and make a difficult journey overland. For nearly two weeks they struggled through the forests before arriving on the bank of this river. Here they obtained dug-out canoes from the Indians. At last the way downstream lay open. After a few days of paddling, they sighted the Pacific Ocean!

Because the Indians were unfriendly and supplies were short, Mackenzie soon had to turn back from the coast. Before he left, however, he wrote on a great rock, in a mixture of "vermilion in melted grease", this message:

"Alexander Mackenzie, from Canada, by land, the twenty-second of July, one thousand seven hundred and ninety-three."

### ACROSS THE ROCKIES

Alexander Mackenzie had found one route across the Rocky Mountains to the Pacific Ocean. The fur traders hoped, however, to find a better one farther south. They knew that the streams flowing westward from the "height of land" must empty into the Pacific, and they now began to explore them.

During the summer before Mackenzie made his journey to the Pacific, the mouth of one great mountain river, the Columbia, had been discovered from the sea. The traders now tried to

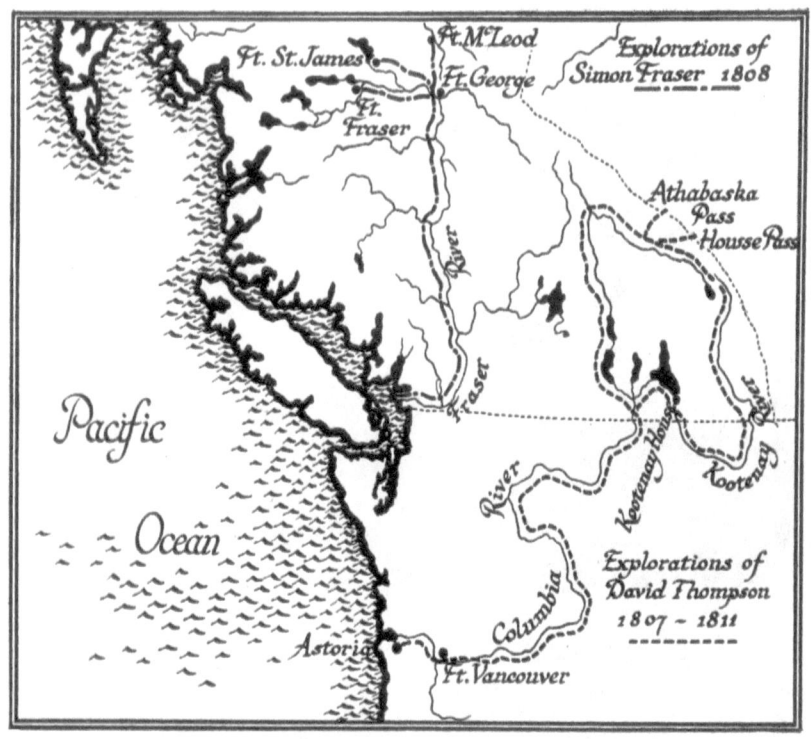

*Fraser and Thompson Explore the West Coast*

find its source, for it seemed likely that this river would offer an easy route from the heart of the Rockies to the Pacific Coast.

Twelve years after Mackenzie's journey, the North West Company began to build trading-posts across the Rockies. A young partner in the Company, Simon Fraser, was sent to follow Mackenzie's route up the Peace River. Fraser reached the "Great River" which Mackenzie had found, and began a fur trade with the Indians, building several trading forts on the headwaters of the river. Then, in 1808, he set out to explore the "Great River", hoping that it was the Columbia.

It was a terrible task. Time and again, only the amazing skill of the voyageurs saved the lives of the explorers on the wild waters of the river. However, Fraser and his party kept on until they reached its mouth, only to find that they were far north of the point where the Columbia was known to flow into the Pacific. Fraser had explored an entirely different river! Fittingly enough, it has been named after him.

During his journey, Simon Fraser had been surprised to learn from the natives that another party of white men was descending a river which ran parallel to the one he was on. This party was headed by another Nor' Wester, David Thompson. The river Thompson was exploring was that which Fraser had sought--the Columbia!

David Thompson was a noted geographer and surveyor, who had already spent ten years mapping the country between the Great Lakes and the Rocky Mountains. He explored the Columbia to its source, and then followed it to its outlet on the Pacific, which he reached in 1811. He built trading-posts in the Columbia River region on both sides of what is now the boundary between Canada and the United States.

With the building of posts west of the Rockies, the North West Company was now trading in furs from the Great Lakes to the Pacific Ocean. It was transporting goods and furs by river, lake, and portage, through the vast area between Montreal and the Western Sea.

We can look at the map of Canada and follow the long route of the fur traders. Down the Athabaska and Churchill Rivers, down Lake Winnipeg, the Winnipeg River, and the Rainy River, to Fort William. From Fort William, the canoes of the "pork-eaters" took the furs to Montreal by the Ottawa River route of which we have already read. Here at last was a "North-West Passage"—even if it was very different from the one which men had sought in vain for over two hundred years.

## THE WAR OF 1812-1814

SO strong is the feeling of friendship between Canada and the United States to-day that there are no longer any forts for defence along the three thousand miles of frontier between the two countries. Canadian and American troops have fought side by side to help win two world wars. In time of peace as well, our two nations have shown a spirit of good neighbourliness towards each other that sets an example to the whole world.

It is hard to believe that these two great countries were not always such good neighbours. But we shall remember that when the Canadian people refused to join in the War of Independence in 1775, Canada was invaded and almost captured by American armies led by Arnold and Montgomery. When General Arnold came over to the British side later during the war, he became, in the eyes of Americans, one of the greatest traitors in the history of the United States.

The United Empire Loyalists who came to Canada after the close of the American Revolution certainly did not feel kindly towards the government of the new United States. Many years passed before these differences of opinion could be forgotten, and unfortunately Americans and Canadians found themselves at war once again before they learned to understand and trust each other. There were many people who fought against each other in this new war who could remember the bitter days of the American Revolution, for this was the year 1812, and the United States was still less than thirty years old.

At this time England was fighting a great war in Europe against the French, who were led by the Emperor Napoleon. The British navy had swept the French fleet from the seas in the famous Battle of Trafalgar, and now it was trying to stop goods from reaching France and her allies on the continent of Europe. The United States was not at war with Napoleon, and felt free to trade with both sides. You can imagine how angered the Americans became, therefore, when the British fleet began to stop their ships on the way to European ports. The British searched these vessels for runaway English sailors, and it was

said that some of the men they arrested were really American citizens. Sometimes they even forced the American ships to land at English ports. Britain certainly was not seeking to anger the United States, but she was fighting for her life against an enemy who had already conquered most of the countries of Europe. She needed all her sailors to man the fighting ships which defended her shores. When she did not pay attention to American protests, the United States finally declared war. There were other reasons, too, why the United States was willing to fight Britain a second time. Some Americans believed that their young country would be safer if all North America north of the Gulf of Mexico could be brought under the "stars and stripes". Then there could no longer be any doubt as to which nation would own the western part of North America, where settlement was just beginning. And because Canada was British, it was bound to become a battleground.

England could spare very few soldiers to help defend Canada against invasion, and in almost every land battle of the war, the British and Canadian forces were much smaller than the American. But the British regulars in Canada were experienced soldiers, and the Canadian volunteers—though not so well trained—were determined to fight hard to protect their country. Many Americans did not favour the war at all, and refused to have anything to do with it. Often the American soldiers were given very little training and sometimes they flatly refused to obey their officers. During the first part of the war the American armies did not have capable generals. But the people of the United States did believe that victory in Upper and Lower Canada could be won easily. "We can take the Canadas without soldiers," said their Secretary of War. "We have only to send officers into the provinces, and the people will rally round our standard."

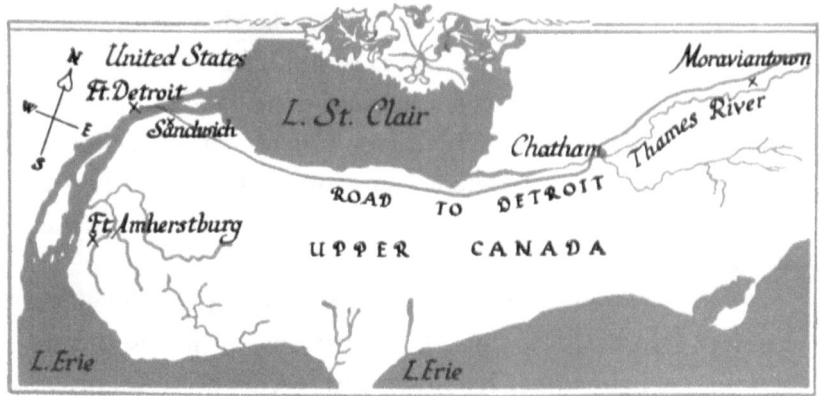

*The Detroit Frontier, 1812*

### THE STORY OF A SHAWNEE CHIEF

In the wilds to the south and west of Lake Erie dwelt a tribe of Indians known as the Shawnees. As new settlers from the young United States of America began to clear this part of the country, the Shawnees and their neighbouring tribes grew fearful lest they should be driven from their homes.

The Shawnees had a great chief named Tecumseh. Tecumseh knew that his people might have to fight, but he also knew that they could not fight the United States alone. However, Tecumseh had heard that there was going to be trouble between the Americans and the British to the north, and this gave him an idea. He travelled to Upper Canada to see the British leaders. He told them that he and many thousands of Indian warriors were ready to fight on the side of Canada against the United States.

When war broke out between Great Britain and the United States, Tecumseh and his warriors made their camp on an island in the Detroit River. The British were very much worried about the American forces in Fort Detroit, which lay near by. They knew that if the Americans crossed the Detroit River and entered the western part of Upper Canada, they would have to rush more troops from Niagara to hold the invaders back. This they did not want to do, because there were not enough British troops even to guard Niagara. Canada was in very great danger in 1812, because there were more than sixteen times as many colonists in the United States as there were on our side of the border.

As soon as fighting broke out at Detroit, Tecumseh led his warriors into battle against the Americans, as he had promised. In one fight alone, Tecumseh and seventy of his followers were able to trap a force of two hundred American soldiers on horseback. Tecumseh planned this attack so well that over half the Americans were killed, while only one of his warriors lost his life.

A few nights after this fight, Tecumseh was awakened by the booming of cannon. "Have the Americans crossed the river?" he asked himself. He soon learned, however, that the cannon had been fired to welcome the British commander-in-chief—General Isaac Brock. It was two o'clock in the morning, but Tecumseh hurried with his chiefs to meet the famous British general.

General Brock was very glad to meet Tecumseh. The two leaders shook hands, and the British general thanked the Indians for their help. "I desire my soldiers", Brock told Tecumseh, "to take lessons from you and your warriors, that I may learn how to make war in these great forests."

This pleased Tecumseh greatly. Pointing at General Brock, he turned to his chiefs, and exclaimed, "Hoh! This is a man!"

Late into the night, Brock and Tecumseh sat together working out a plan for the attack on Detroit. When the Indian leader went back to his camp, it was almost daylight. But the plan was a good one, because almost as soon as the attack began, the American general surrendered. Three days after their meeting, General Brock and Tecumseh were in Fort Detroit.

Brock now returned to Lake Ontario, where the Americans were getting ready to attack across the Niagara River. But Tecumseh's work was not finished, and he stayed on. The next year the Americans sent fresh troops to recapture Detroit, and the new British leader there was forced to retreat. Tecumseh did not like the idea of retreating, but he ordered his warriors to fall back with the British, fighting as they went. At last, Tecumseh persuaded the British general to stop retreating and meet the Americans who were following them. As soon as the British leader agreed to do so, Tecumseh called his Indians together for a council meeting.

"Brother warriors," he cried, "we are now about to enter a battle from which I shall never come out. My body will remain in the field of battle."

Tecumseh was right. The British soldiers were tired and hungry before the fight began, and the Americans soon broke through their lines. Only a handful escaped altogether. In the height of the battle, Tecumseh caught sight of the American leader. Shouting his war-cry and waving his tomahawk above his head, he rushed through his warriors to strike him down. But the American leader saw him coming; aiming his pistol at the Indian chief, he shot Tecumseh through the heart.

That night, after the fighting was over, some of the Indian warriors who had fought with the British returned to the battle-field. Almost at the edge of the American camp they found the body of their fallen leader, and carried it away.

There is no monument to-day over the grave of this great Indian chief. For only the Indians knew where they had buried their dead leader, and they kept their secret well.

### "AT QUEENSTON HEIGHTS"

General Brock had prepared Upper Canada against invasion as well as he could, since war had been feared for several years. Volunteer soldiers had been trained carefully, and along with the British regulars, were stationed at posts along the border.

Even though Canadians were encouraged by Brock's capture of Detroit during the early days of the war, they knew that the danger of invasion was still great. The greatest danger now lay along the Niagara River, between Lake Erie and Lake Ontario, where the Americans had gathered about seven thousand troops.

When General Brock left Tecumseh at Detroit, he hurried to the Niagara River frontier. Here he found fewer than fifteen hundred men to guard the Canadian shore against an attack by the Americans from across the river. If the Americans gained a foothold on the Canadian bank, they might overrun the Niagara Peninsula and reach the Dundas Road—the main highway joining York, the capital, with the western part of the province. Upper Canada would then be cut in two.

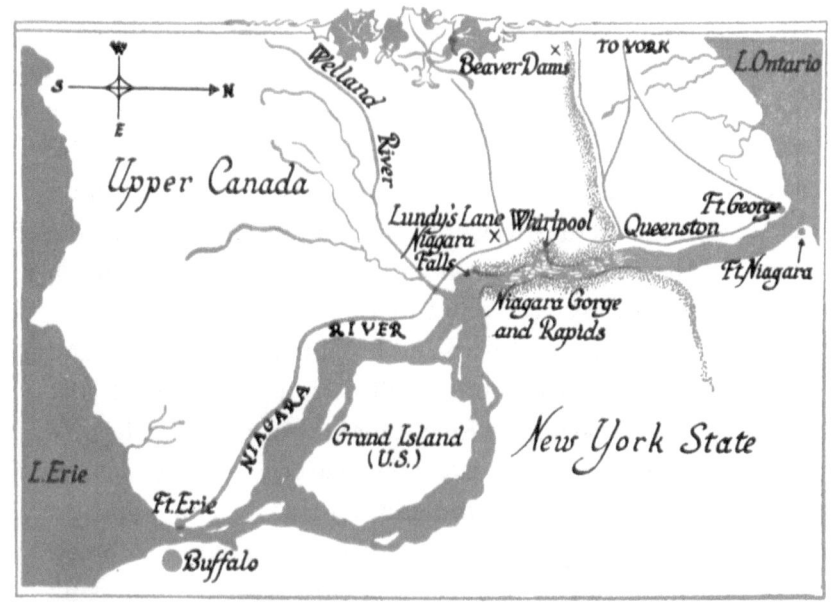

*The Niagara Frontier. 1812*

General Brock was at Fort George, at the mouth of the Niagara, on the night of October 12. Shortly after midnight, the Americans began to cross the river at Queenston. At first it was not clear whether this was to be their main attack, or was to be only a feint to draw the main British force away from Fort George. Leaving his second-in-command, General Sheaffe, a brave and able officer, with orders to follow with the troops from Fort George if the American main attack turned out to be at Queenston, Brock rode along the river to see for himself what was happening. On the way he met a messenger with news that a great many of the enemy had crossed the river, and more and more were coming over. On learning this Brock sent the messenger to Fort George with orders to General Sheaffe to hurry the soldiers along as quickly as possible.

The village of Queenston lies at the foot of Queenston Heights, a steep cliff some 350 feet high, rising from the edge of the Niagara River. A British gun had been placed on the top of the Heights, but the Americans climbed a steep and narrow path that brought them up behind the British gunners, who then had to beat a hasty retreat. Brock rallied his men for a charge, and, with drawn sword, led them up the steep hill. The ranks of the Americans broke and success seemed sure, when Brock himself was struck down by a shot, and almost instantly killed. Dismayed, the British and Canadian lines faltered and then retreated to the foot of the hill, carrying their dead leader with them, and leaving the Americans in control of the Heights.

The Americans did not enjoy their success for long. General Sheaffe, who now took command, rallied his men, and by a brilliant and daring movement struck inland with his forces. Led by Indian guides, he made a surprise attack on the flank of the Americans, who then had to fight with their backs to the river. Although they still greatly outnumbered the British and Canadians, about fifteen hundred of them having already crossed the river, they were soon overpowered. Two thousand of the enemy waiting on the American side, who were ordered to reinforce their comrades, refused to cross the river when they saw what was happening. The Americans on the Heights now tried desperately to escape. Some managed to row back across the river; others tried to swim, but many were drowned. Some even threw themselves over the cliff. Most of them, however, surrendered to the British and Canadians.

It was a costly victory, for the British had lost a great leader and a great soldier in General Brock. A lofty monument in his honour now stands on the Heights on which he fell. It reminds us how courage, patriotism, and brilliant military skill once more saved Canada from a larger and more powerful invading army.

## AN EVEN STRUGGLE

So long were the land and sea frontiers of the United States that the story of the War of 1812-1814 is a story of many separate clashes, which happened at widely scattered points. In some of these battles the Americans were victorious; in others they were defeated. Indeed, sometimes both sides claimed to have won a battle, but in the end neither side could rightly claim that it had won the war.

The outcome of the struggle disappointed those Americans who believed that the British would be driven from North America, for when peace was made the borders were left unchanged. And the British, too, were disappointed. They owned the strongest fleet in the world, yet they lost most of their sea battles with the enemy! This was because the Americans cleverly avoided fighting more than one British vessel at a time, and although the United States had few warships, those they did have were larger and stronger than most of the ships of the Royal Navy. However, the British fleet controlled the shipping lanes of the Atlantic, and by the end of the war American overseas trade was crippled.

Once, when the British frigate *Shannon* met the enemy's frigate *Chesapeake* off Boston in 1813, the sea duel did go against the United States. After barely fifteen minutes of fierce fighting, the American vessel surrendered and was taken into Halifax by her captors. But victory such as this was unusual for the British in this war.

American and British ships also fought against each other on the Great Lakes. Because of the falls at Niagara and the rapids on the St. Lawrence, each side had to keep separate fleets on Lake Erie and Lake Ontario. Early in the war, the American navies won control of both lakes, which made the defence of Upper Canada doubly difficult. There was always the danger that the enemy ships might land an army at the rear of the forces defending the land frontiers. This actually happened in the spring of the second year of fighting.

Early in 1813, the United States fleet on Lake Ontario appeared suddenly off York and began to pour troops ashore. The little capital of Upper Canada was quite unable to defend itself, since most of the troops were on the Niagara frontier on the other side of the lake. The American troops that overran the city did not stay long, but during the fighting and confusion, the parliament buildings were burned to the ground, and several of the public buildings were robbed.

On Lake Erie the Americans defeated the British fleet, shortly after Detroit had been captured by Brock and Tecumseh. The English general whom Brock had left in command was unable to bring up supplies by ship across Lake Erie. Land transportation was much too slow and difficult. As we have already read, the British were thus forced to give up Detroit and retreat overland. It was during this retreat that the famous Shawnee chieftain made his last stand.

The threat of invasion of Canada by land did not end with the American defeat at Queenston Heights in 1812. Both the Niagara frontier and the country south of Montreal saw bitter fighting during the remaining two years of war. Fortunately the

American attacks across both these borders were broken up by the British and Canadian defenders, although they were usually heavily outnumbered by the enemy.

In the fall of 1813, an American army of some five thousand men moved north from Lake Champlain towards the St. Lawrence. On the Chateauguay River, just south of Montreal, it was met by a smaller British army, which included a number

of French-Canadian troops under de Salaberry. De Salaberry cleverly stationed buglers in the woods about the Americans, and when the signal to sound the bugle calls was given, the noise was so great and came from so many directions that the invaders believed that they had met an army of at least ten thousand! After a short fight, in which the French-Canadian troops shared fully in the victory with their British and Canadian comrades, the Americans ordered a retreat and fell back towards Plattsburg.

On the Niagara frontier, the struggle see-sawed back and forth through 1813 and 1814. At first the Americans succeeded in overrunning most of the Niagara Peninsula, but the British counter-attacked and landed on the American side of the river, where they acted even more recklessly than the United States troops that had occupied York. The towns of Lewiston and Buffalo were set on fire, and any provisions which could not be used were destroyed.

The bitterest land battle of the war was fought at Lundy's Lane, near Niagara Falls, in the summer of 1814, when over eight hundred men on each side were wounded, and many killed. Both sides claimed it as a victory, although the Americans ordered their troops to withdraw after the fighting.

During the fall of the same year, the British launched a counter-attack against the United States. An army of ten thousand regular troops, most of them fresh from Europe where they had at last defeated Napoleon's armies, was led south from Montreal towards Lake Champlain. But disaster was waiting for them there. Both the British and the Americans had ships on Lake Champlain, although the British fleet was the stronger. When the powerful land army reached the American fort at Plattsburg, it was ordered to hold back until the British fleet attacked the American ships in the harbour near by. Valuable time was lost, for the fort would have surely fallen if the British troops had stormed it immediately. Instead, the commander of the British fleet was ordered to engage the American warships, and in the fighting which followed the English vessels were completely beaten. Meanwhile, the British army was not allowed to attack, and when the lake battle was over it began to retreat northward to Canada.

But the war was rapidly nearing its end. The British fleet on the Atlantic had almost stopped American ocean trade, and more and more British troops and supplies were being poured into Canada. On Christmas Eve, 1814, peace was signed at last—a peace that was to grow more and more real as time went by.

## THE RED RIVER COLONY

MANY of the French voyageurs, clerks, and traders employed by the fur companies spent their whole lives at the western posts. Often they married Indian women and raised families in the West. Their children were known as Metis (*may-tees*).

The Metis were true sons of the plains—mighty buffalo hunters, skilful traders, and fine canoemen. They earned their living either as employees of the fur companies, or by supplying pemmican to the fur traders. The valley of the Red River, south of Lake Winnipeg, was the district in which much of this pemmican was made.

The number of trading posts increased rapidly. While the North West Company was building forts farther and farther west, the Hudson's Bay Company was also adding new posts. At some places there were forts of both companies, often within gun-shot of each other. Near the trading-posts were the homes of the Metis families. Over the plains the Indian tribes still roamed, following the buffalo herds on which they chiefly depended for food.

Then, in 1811, rumours of a great change began to be heard in the West. Settlers—settlers from overseas—were on their way to the Red River Valley. And these strangers were not coming to join the fur trade. They intended to begin farming in the heart of the "fur traders' preserve"!

## THE STORY OF LORD SELKIRK

When Sir Alexander Mackenzie's account of his explorations was published in England in 1801, many people were thrilled by his story of courage and adventure. One of those who read it was a great Scottish nobleman, Lork Selkirk. Not only did it interest him, but it gave him an idea.

In Scotland at this time, many of the farmers were being driven from their homes. The land-owners from whom they rented their small farms had decided to use the lands for shee-praising. So when Lord Selkirk read about the rich prairies lying west of the Great Lakes, he began to think that these poor Scottish farmers might find new homes if they could be taken to British North America.

Lord Selkirk had never expected to be wealthy, because he was the youngest of seven brothers. It was therefore unlikely that he would ever inherit the title and estates of his father. But his brothers all died, and at the age of twenty-eight he found himself one of the richest men in all Scotland. Perhaps it was because he had always thought that he would have to earn his own living that he now felt he should use his wealth to help others. Mackenzie's descriptions of North America had given him an idea how to do this, and he was ready to spend his own money to see that it was carried through.

From the Hudson's Bay Company, of which he was part-owner, he now obtained a large grant of land in the North-West. This grant covered an area more than three times the size of Scotland itself. But when we recall the size of the original grant to the Hudson's Bay Company from which this was made, it does not seem so enormous.

History has shown that Lord Selkirk was not mistaken about the possibilities of the West, but he did fail to foresee the hardships that his settlers would have to face. The North-West The

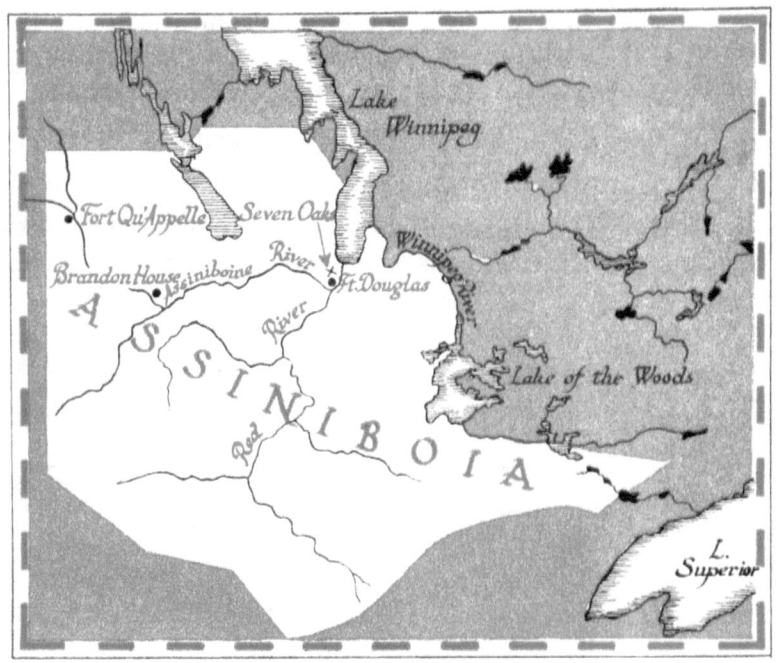

*The Red River Colony*

Red River Colony Company had no desire to see a colony started in the heart of the country from which it drew rich cargoes of furs. It knew that settlers would drive away the buffalo, on which the traders and the Indians depended for food. So even before Lord Selkirk's first group of Scottish settlers set sail for the New World, employees of the North West Company went among them to try to discourage them from the voyage. The Hudson's Bay Company traders were no more anxious to see the country settled than were the traders of the North West Company, but they could not say very much because of Lord Selkirk's share in the Company.

The first group of settlers landed at York factory on Hudson Bay in 1811. They spent the winter there, and went on to the Red River in the spring in flat-bottomed boats which they built themselves. They went by way of the Hayes River, Oxford Lake, and the Nelson River, to Lake Winnipeg, and down the Lake to the Red River. About forty miles up the Red River, they landed. They had scarcely brought their boats to shore when a crowd of Metis, dressed as Indians, came racing up on their horses.

FORT DOUGLAS, RED RIVER

They had been sent by the Nor' Westers to frighten away the colonists. However, the settlers refused to be frightened by the yells and threatening actions of the Metis. Soon they built a fort, which they called Fort Douglas after Lord Selkirk's family.

Unfortunately, the journey from York Factory took so long that it was the end of August before the settlers arrived at the Red River. This meant that they had to face the winter with only the supplies they had brought with them and with what food could be obtained by hunting the buffalo. Indeed, when the buffalo moved south during the winter, the colonists had to follow them. In the spring, they were able to return to their settlement. But because they had only hoes with which to work the soil, their planting was not a great success. Additional settlers arrived from the homeland, but they, too, found the going hard.

In an effort to keep food on hand for the colony, the governor ordered in 1814 that no provisions should be taken out of the settlement for one year. This angered the North West Company's traders, who depended on pemmican from the Red River, to carry on their travels. They attacked Fort Douglas, and destroyed it along with the buildings of the settlement. By threats and promises, they persuaded some of the settlers to travel east to Upper Canada; others were driven north to the shores of Lake Winnipeg.

When Lord Selkirk heard of the sufferings of his colonists, he set sail for America himself. He had arrived at New York when the news of the attack on Fort Douglas reached him. A new governor, Robert Semple, was now sent to the Red River along with another party of settlers. Fort Douglas was rebuilt and the settlements restored. The North West Company's traders were desperate, however, and Lord Selkirk still had good reason to worry about the future of his colony.

Once again trouble broke out between the colonists and the North West Company's traders. Governor Semple, with a number of the settlers, met a band of traders at a place called Seven Oaks. A fight broke out, and Semple along with twenty of his men were shot down. The traders then went on to the settlement, took over Fort Douglas, and once more scattered the colonists. The news of this further tragedy reached Lord Selkirk at Sault Ste Marie, from where he was ready to travel west with about one hundred Swiss soldiers who were anxious to settle in the Red River Colony.

By this time Selkirk was furious at the North West Company. He led his Swiss soldiers on to Fort William, where there was a great post of the Nor' Westers, and made prisoners of several of the partners of the Company whom he found there. He sent them back to Canada to stand trial for the death of Semple and his men. Then he went on to the Red River, where he recaptured Fort Douglas, and set about the rebuilding of the colony. He now laid plans for schools, churches, and highways, and made a treaty with the Indians, who admired him very much.

But further trouble was arising for Selkirk in Eastern Canada. The North West Company claimed that he had acted unlawfully in seizing Fort William. A law-suit was brought against him, and he was ordered to pay damages. Selkirk, on the other hand, could not obtain punishment for the traders who had murdered Semple and his followers. Unable to secure justice, he returned to Britain disappointed and broken in health. Three years later he died.

For a long time, "Kildonan"—as Selkirk had named the Red River Colony—faced difficult times. Only the hardiest and most determined of the settlers remained to see better days, to-day, however, Kildonan is a part of the great city of Winnipeg. Lord Selkirk's faith in the future of the Red River and the West has been more than justified.

## THE END OF FUR TRADE RIVALRY

The coming of settlers to the Red River Valley was not the only problem of the fur traders. The rivalry between the Nor' Westers and the Hudson's Bay Company was proving very costly to both. Furs were growing scarcer and the traders had to travel longer and longer distances to obtain them. Both companies were losing money. At last, in 1821, they decided to join hands and become one. The name of the Hudson's Bay Company was kept, and the North West Company was no more.

The first governor of the united Company was George Simpson. He had come to Canada from Scotland, and risen rapidly in the service of the Hudson's Bay Company. Now, at thirty-four years of age, he was chosen to rule a vast fur-trading empire. The choice was an excellent one. Simpson expanded the business of the Company, and reduced expenses. He protected the Indians by forbidding the sale of liquor to them. For nearly forty years he governed the region from the Great Lakes to the Pacific, and governed it well. It is no wonder that he was called "the little Emperor"! These were, however, the closing days of the empire of the fur traders. From the East, great changes were coming; the western plains soon would cease to be a "fur traders' preserve".

## SETTLERS FROM OVERSEAS

NOT long ago a newcomer to this continent was travelling across the country, wondering where he and his wife should make their new home. Although he still did not speak English very well, wherever he stopped he found the people very friendly and glad to answer all his questions. They were also willing to tell him about themselves, whether they were born here and how their families first came to the New World.

"I didn't feel bad about my broken language any more or my stranger ways," wrote the immigrant later. "I saw everybody is a foreigner. Only difference, some came early and some came late."

*Some came early and some came late!* When we think of our vast Dominion, and especially of its large cities linked by great railroads and modern highways, we are likely to forget that it is not very long since there were no white men at all in Canada. Even to-day, there are few families that have entirely forgotten where their forefathers came from.

From where, then, did our almost twelve million Canadian citizens come? When did they come? How did they come?

Of every ten people in Canada to-day, about five would find that their ancestors came from the British Isles. About three could trace their families back to France—and these three would be

French-speaking. The remaining two would he descended from settlers who came out from other countries of Europe, perhaps Germany, Poland, Russia, or Italy. It is easy to remember these few figures.

Of course, this does not mean that you would be likely to find ten such Canadians living next door to one another just anywhere in Canada. And it does not mean that many people might not have Polish grandparents as well as English grandparents, for Canadians often have the blood of several nations in their veins. Then, too, we shall remember that the oldest Canadians of all are the Indians and Eskimos who were here when the white man came.

We have already read in this book of several early "waves" of immigration to Canada. The intendant Jean Talon speeded the coming of immigrants to New France after the colony had been growing only slowly for many years. After Canada became British, English-speaking traders and merchants began to arrive from New England. Following the American Revolution, large numbers of United Empire Loyalists began to pour into the country from the United States, with the result that the new provinces of New Brunswick and Upper Canada were created.

After the War of 1812-1814, a new flood of settlers from overseas began. Most of them came from the British Isles—England, Scotland, or Ireland. Of course, many of the people who left the Old Country between 1815 and 1850 went to Australia and New Zealand, which were just beginning to be settled. But most of them—over eight hundred thousand in all—came to Canada, which lay much closer to home, and where often the only price for land was hard work.

The hardships in the backwoods were many, it is true. But they were often no worse than the hardships which had driven the newcomers from their homes in the Old Country to begin life again in the New World. And for some, indeed, the greatest hardships of all were met on board the overcrowded sailing vessels which plied the North Atlantic during the "Great Migration", as the years between 1815 and 1850 have sometimes been called.

What must one of these sea voyages have been like?

Few of the immigrants could afford to travel "cabin class", and we have been left many vivid accounts of daily life between decks in the "steerage", where men, women, and children were shut together for one or two months at a time during the Atlantic crossing. Perhaps we should be able to picture life aboard one of these immigrant vessels better if we read the story of one of the newcomers. Here are a few paragraphs from a diary, such as might have been kept by the fifteen-year-old daughter of an English immigrant family in the year 1832.

**STEERAGE DIARY, 1832**

*March 26.* We have been moving slowly down the Thames all day and must be nearing the Channel, for I can feel the ship roll as I write. The crowding between decks seems worse because there are neither windows nor port-holes through which to see outside. There are over a hundred and fifty passengers with us in the steerage, and some of them seem a pretty rough sort.... There are rows of berths along both sides of the ship, and down the centre is a long plank table with rough benches, where we shall gather for our meals. It is the only place I have found for

writing, though the two lamps they allow us by day do not give much light.

If Father's business had not failed, we might have been able to buy cabin passages. The steerage is no fit place for Mother, or for myself either, for that matter. Still, I must not complain, for I am sure that we shall make up all that we have lost, once we reach the colonies.

I wonder if I shall ever get used to our fellow-passengers, a dozen of whom are seated on the bench opposite me as I write. Some of them are tradesmen, I can see—carpenters, cobblers, and the like, for they all brought their tools aboard with them. Others must have the same plan as Father, that is, to take land in Upper Canada where they say one may have a hundred acres for the asking. I wonder if Father will like farming! The Thompsons, who went out two years ago, wrote that the hardest part is at first, since as much land as possible must be cleared before the first sowing.

Already there is grumbling over our food for this voyage. They are supposed to give each of us a pound of meat or bread daily, although the children will certainly get less. But the day's rations, given out after roll-call, just before we hoisted anchor this morning, were not more than half that amount. And the bread was already sour. We brought a few provisions with us, of course, but they cannot last long. What will it be like a month from now? For they tell us it may be ten weeks before we reach Montreal.

There is an open fire-place built on each side of the fore-deck, where the cook will serve out our daily rations. Both have been covered all day by the pots and pans of the passengers, and they say the fires will be put out at seven o'clock. So far we have been unable to get near them ourselves, but perhaps we shall have a turn at cooked food to-morrow.

*March 28.* Only three days out from England, and already the steerage is becoming unbearable! The slice of salt beef handed each of us yesterday was so rotten that it could not be eaten, at least not by our family. We have been allowed hardly a quart of drinking water per person each day, and the mate laughed at me when I asked about water for washing.... The sea is very rough, and many of the passengers spend the whole time in their berths. Mother, too, is ill and remains abed, but she does not complain. The fire-places on the fore-deck continue overcrowded, as indeed they must remain until the end of this unpleasant voyage.

Father learned just this morning that his solicitor, Mr. Johnson, is a cabin passenger on our ship, and we have been promised permission to visit him soon. The captain told Father that the cabin passengers could not be asked to visit the steerage. Truly, we are treated as though we were convicts being deported to Australia rather than colonists bound for Upper Canada...

"THE STEERAGE IS NO FIT PLACE..."

*March 30.* We were allowed above this morning, Father and I, to meet Mr. Johnson. 1 felt ashamed of my shabby appearance, for it has been impossible to wash. Mr. Johnson was very kind, but I fear it was more pity than politeness that led him to invite us into his cabin. He is travelling alone, and in great comfort compared with those of us in the steerage. But his passage cost him thirty pounds, and that is six times the fare Father paid for each of us to travel between decks. So he dines as well as we ever did at home, and has all the pleasant trimmings of a hotel into the bargain—a sofa, rocker, curtains, carpets, etc. I fear I wept when we had to go down again between decks, where the air was so stifling that we could hardly enter....

*March 31.* It is Sunday, and there was a simple service for Protestant passengers and Mass for the Catholics on the foredeck early this morning. But the sea is very rough, the food grows worse, and the rations smaller. Some of the emigrants in the open berths next to us are a noisy lot, and Father warns us that

they are given to thieving and that we must be careful. They play cards most of every night by the light of candles which they stick against the wooden hull of the ship—a most dangerous practice. Their loud talking troubles Mother greatly, for she is still quite-ill. The air between decks remains so heavy that we must manage to bring her outside soon, for Father is as worried about her as I am....

*April 6.* This past week has been a nightmare, for we have been shut between decks and driven before a storm ever since I last wrote in my diary. The allowance of drinking water has been cut even further, for they say that two of the supply casks were smashed during the gale. At that, it is hardly possible to drink what they give us, its odour is so frightful. They have sent down a keg of vinegar, which we mix with the water to smother its taste.... Worse still, one of the emigrants has been taken suddenly ill, and there is talk that the plague has begun among us. No one will go near him, but we must all breathe the same air until the hatches are removed and we are allowed on deck again.

*April 15.* Our misery is too terrible to describe. The cholera is spreading rapidly, and eleven have died in less than a week. Fortunately, Mother is better, the storm is over, and we are allowed on deck again by day. Some of the poor emigrants have not lived more than ten hours after being struck down with the dread disease. Their bodies are thrown overboard immediately, with hardly more than a few words read by the captain by way of a burial service. The sailors are all afraid to come between decks, where we are forced to spend the nights, for fear of being taken with the disease.

*April 25.* It is a full month since we sailed, and no sign of land yet. The cholera has lessened, and indeed it may be ended, for those who are now ill seem to be getting better. But in all, twenty of the emigrants and two of the sailors were buried at sea, the last of them a week ago. The weather is fine at last, and although it is very cold we are allowed to sleep on deck if we choose.

*May 11.* We are well inside the Gulf of St. Lawrence at last, and can see the high, wooded shore of Gaspe on our left, or "to port" as the sailors say. Our rations are no smaller, fortunately, though it is sad to think that this is because so many died last month. Some of the men, including Father, went fishing in one of the boats while we were over the Grand Bank off Newfoundland. The cod they brought back was a welcome addition to our diet after the bad beef that we had been forced to eat.

*May 18.* We have landed, but our water journey is not yet ended. We are on Grosse Isle in the St. Lawrence River, just downstream from the Island of Orleans. All the vessels from home must anchor here, and the colonists are brought ashore to be checked for sickness. There were six ships here when we arrived, and more come up the river with every tide. There are several hospitals on the island, but they are terribly overcrowded with cholera cases from the incoming ships. Many of the vessels come in loaded with emigrants from Ireland, who seem to have had an even worse time at sea than we did. Our own passengers were well enough when we landed yesterday, though some were barely strong enough to walk. But we hear that one was taken down with cholera this morning, which makes one doubt the wisdom of bringing all the newcomers together on this island. We hope to be allowed to leave this afternoon. Father was wise enough to buy our sea passage right through to Montreal, although most of the people will be put ashore at Quebec.

*June 1.* We are encamped at a pleasant spot on the bank of the St. Lawrence, with only one more rapids between us and Prescott. The Durham boat, which has carried us up the river from Lachine, near Montreal, is tied close in to shore a stone's throw from where I am writing. It is a strange craft, about a hundred feet long, and could carry a heavy cargo on its deck if there were not so many passengers. The French-Canadian crew raised a large square sail over it to take us through Lake St. Louis, but they had to work hard with the poles to bring us up the current of the river. More than once we were drawn by horses on the bank, and sometimes by the men themselves, as we passed through the canals around the worst rapids. The crew is taking a well-earned rest at the moment, while some of the passengers busy themselves at quoits as a remedy for the stiffness that results from cramped quarters on an open deck.

"...THE STREETS ARE FILLED WITH NEW COLONISTS..."

*June 7.* Kingston at last! And what a beautiful place it is, even though it is unlike any town I have ever seen in England. The streets are filled with new colonists like ourselves. Some arrived to-day from Montreal by a new route that has just been opened. Instead of following the St. Lawrence as we did, with its swift current and overcrowded locks, they went up the Ottawa River to Bytown, from where they came on to Kingston by the new Rideau Canal. It is a much longer journey, but they say it is safer. However, we found the last two days of our journey from Prescott pleasant enough, for we were taken in tow by one of the new steamships that have just been built on Lake Ontario.

Unfortunately, the cholera has followed us here, and over one hundred cases are reported in Kingston alone. The newspapers are full of news telling of the spread of the disease, and indeed all Upper Canada is in a state of alarm over it.... Father says we shall leave Kingston for his grant on the river as soon as possible. For myself, I look forward to the adventure that is in store for us, though I know that hard work lies ahead.

## UPPER CANADA, 1832

As the lands along the lakes and rivers of Upper Canada were taken up by families like the one described in the diary above, settlements began to spring up inland as well. Indeed, by the eighteen-thirties the countryside of present-day Ontario was beginning to take shape. Of course, the roads were poor in comparison with our modern highways, and there were no railways yet.

It was in 1832, too, that an English missionary came to Thornhill, a village on Yonge Street just north of present-day Toronto. When he returned to his home in England a few months later, he wrote a book about his stay in Upper Canada. Here are some of the things he had to say about the country as it was then:

"Horses are not, at first, of much use to settlers except for riding, as they cannot be safely used among the stumps of trees, being quicker in their movements than oxen, and not so steady. After the stumps have entirely decayed, which takes place in from six to ten years except where pines have stood, horses can be used with the same advantages as in other countries.

"The price of a good horse is from fifty to eighty dollars; of a yoke of oxen, from fifty to sixty; of a cow, from eight to sixteen; and of a full-grown fat hog, four dollars. In winter, good beef, venison, etc., can be purchased at four cents per pound. In summer no venison can be obtained, and other kinds of meat

are from six to eight cents per pound. Fish is very cheap and good: sixteen white-fish, each weighing two pounds, for a dollar.

"The whole surface of Upper Canada is laid out in lots of equal divisions. The country is cut throughout by roads at a mile and a quarter distance from each other, either completed or marked out. One set of roads runs east and west, the other north and south. They therefore form blocks of land, perfectly square, each containing a thousand acres, and each side of which is a mile and a quarter long. The block is next divided into five farms, of two hundred acres each, being a quarter of a mile broad, and a mile and a quarter long, and each facing on two roads, while two lots out of every five have a road on three sides.

"The value of land in Canada is increasing regularly and rapidly. For instance, Yonge Street was first settled thirty-seven years ago. At this time, land on it was given to any person who asked for it. A few years after, a lot was worth from fifty to a hundred dollars. A lot now is worth from four to eight thousand dollars on many parts of Yonge Street. Land has generally been found to double its value every three or four years. A person possessing money and wisdom is sure to improve his wealth by

EARLIEST TYPE    LATER LOGS SQUARED AT ENDS    SQUARED LOGS

moving to Upper Canada. He loses many of the comforts of a highly polished life, but I consider his gain much greater than his loss.

"Nothing is so clear a proof of the richness of the soil as the number and size of the trees. They are magnificent. In most places, no boughs branch off from the trees till forty or sixty feet from the ground. The surface of the ground between them is beautifully open, and a person may walk for miles up and down, in the very heart of the woods, without other obstruction than mouldering giants of the forest which lie upon the ground. Some of the fallen trees are four feet thick, and where these lie on the ground they form fences which a man can pass neither under nor over.

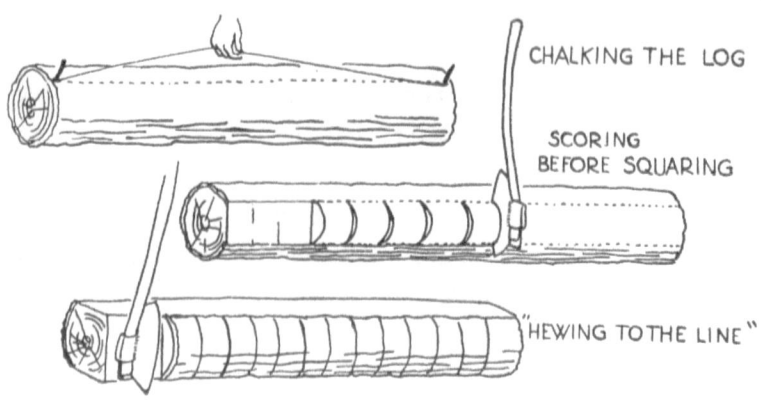

CHALKING THE LOG

SCORING BEFORE SQUARING

"HEWING TO THE LINE"

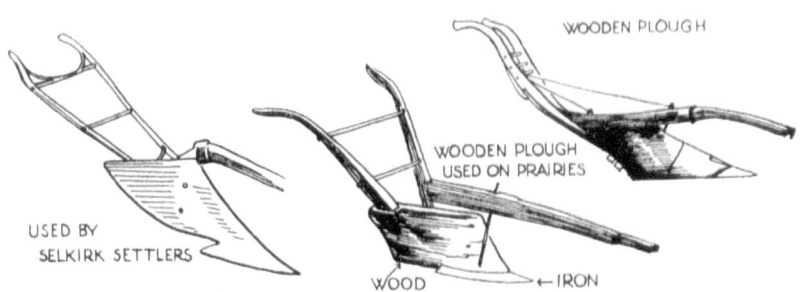

"The richness of Canadian soil is a powerful attraction, not only to Europeans, but to Americans also who prefer it to many parts of the States. No year passes without witnessing the emigration into Canada of great numbers of Yankees, as well as of great numbers of people from the United Kingdom of Great Britain and Ireland, who had resided for years in the States.

"Persons of idle and lazy habits, or of no regular trade or business, ought never to enter Canada. The country having to be cleared before it can yield produce, more labour is required at first from the farmers than in a long-settled country. Indeed, where every respectable person is employed, there is no place for idle people. They will not be encouraged, nor succeed in any way."

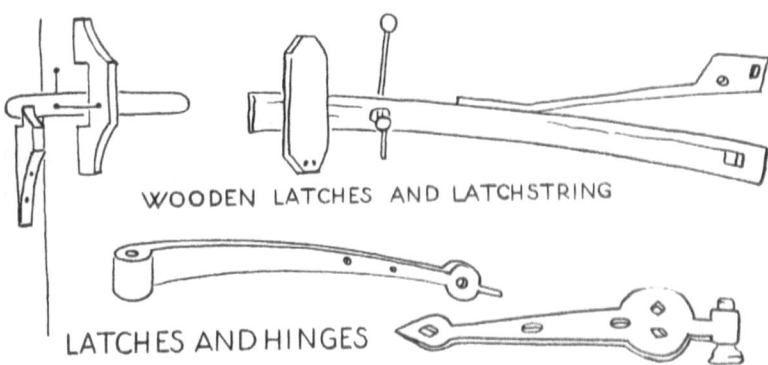

## RULING OUR LAW-MAKERS

UNTIL little more than a hundred years ago, Great Britain's possessions in North America were separate colonies, and each had a government of its own. Even the Thirteen Colonies along the Atlantic seaboard did not join hands until just before the American Revolution, about fifteen years after Wolfe captured Quebec.

The five British colonies of Upper Canada, Lower Canada, New Brunswick, Nova Scotia, and Prince Edward Island, each had an assembly to which the colonists were allowed to elect members. But the law-makers whom the colonists elected to these assemblies only helped to make the laws for their colonies. The members of an assembly might note that a certain law should be passed. But it often happened that the lieutenant-governor of the colony, together with the small group of people he had chosen to advise him, might not be willing that it should become law. And no law could be made without their consent. Thus the real power in each of the British colonies was in the hands of the governor of the colony and the small group of men he had gathered about him as his "councillors". To-day, the approval of the governor general must still be obtained for the laws passed by the parliament of Canada. But the men who advise the governor general are chosen from parliament itself, that is, from the law-makers elected by the people. So we can now say that the people really control their government.

In the days of the colonies, the lieutenant-governor was usually sent out from Great Britain, since he was the king's representative. But his advisors were chosen from the most important people in the colony. It is true that he was usually careful to choose the wisest men he could find, but he was more likely to choose wealthy businessmen and politicians of the towns, than farmers or fishermen. Soon the people began to complain that they were not being governed by the law-makers they elected to their assemblies, but by small groups of wealthy land-owners and businessmen chosen by the lieutenant-governor to advise him what laws should be passed and what laws should not be passed.

In Upper Canada, the fact that the law-makers in the assembly had to pay attention to the wishes of the lieutenant-governor's wealthy advisors soon led to serious trouble. Upper Canada was the youngest of all the colonies, and settlers were still flocking in to become farmers. Since all land first had to be granted by the government, it was possible for the councillors to give the best farming land to people who would be friendly to them. It was also possible that some of them might accept money secretly for granting land, or for giving citizens government jobs.

At least, that is what William Lyon Mackenzie was saying in the year 1826.

# THE LITTLE REBEL

A visitor to the town of York, Upper Canada, on June 8, 1826, would have been much surprised if he had passed by the office of the *Colonial Advocate* that evening. The *Colonial Advocate* was the newspaper published by William Lyon Mackenzie, who happened to be out of town.

The doors and windows of Mackenzie's newspaper office had been smashed in, and a crowd of young men were dumping his printing type into the water of the bay near by! The crash of hammers could be heard inside the building, where their companions were busy breaking up the press on which Mackenzie printed his newspaper. Strangely enough, no one who watched the law-breakers made any effort to stop them.

Who were these young men of York and why were they wrecking the printing office of the *Colonial Advocate*? What

had William Lyon Mackenzie done that made them act so foolishly?

Ever since he came to the colony from Scotland six years earlier, Mackenzie had been complaining about the government he found in Upper Canada—as the southern part of present-day Ontario was then called. Just two years had passed since he began to publish his newspaper, the *Colonial Advocate*. Now his complaints against the government of Upper Canada were being read by a great many people. Mackenzie said that the lawmakers of the colony were controlled by a handful of people who were more interested in becoming rich and powerful themselves than in helping the citizens of Upper Canada. He said that even the law-makers elected by the people were too willing to obey the wishes of the lieutenant-governor and his councillors. The young men who wrecked the printing-office of the *Colonial Advocate* that evening came from the families of the men who, according to William Lyon Mackenzie, made up this "ruling class".

Many of the people of Upper Canada thought Mackenzie was wrong to criticize the government as he did in the *Colonial Advocate*. They felt that it was disloyal to speak or write against the lieutenant-governor and his councillors, because the lieutenant-governor was the representative of the king himself in the colony. But even so, few people thought Mackenzie deserved to have his printing-office raided by a band of rich young ruffians, and now many of the citizens of Upper Canada took his side. Therefore, when Mackenzie learned the names of the law-breakers who had done the mischief, he had them brought into court. Not only did he receive enough money in damages to repair his shop and buy a brand-new printing-press, but he had a fair amount left over as well. Now that he could again set up in business, Mackenzie went to work afresh—attacking the little group of men around the lieutenant-governor even more violently than before.

'— AND BUY A BRAND-NEW PRINTING-PRESS...'

Soon the band of Upper Canadian businessmen who controlled the colony's law-makers were being spoken of as the "Family Compact". The members of the Family Compact did not all come from one family, but they sometimes acted as if they did. On the other hand, many of them were very clever and capable men, and much of what Mackenzie said about them was unfair. But as long as the Family Compact was able to stay in power and persuade the lieutenant-governor to agree only to the laws it favoured, the law-makers whom the people of the colony elected were powerless.

Here are some of the charges William Lyon Mackenzie made against the Family Compact of Upper Canada:

1. Mackenzie said that new grants of land to settlers in Upper Canada were not being made fairly. He claimed that the best farming country was often given to those who paid money secretly to members of the Family Compact or their friends.

2. Mackenzie said no one could obtain a government job unless he was a member or a friend of the Family Compact.

3. Mackenzie pointed out to the readers of the *Colonial Advocate* that the government was making large grants of land to the Church of England and was not helping other Protestant churches. Often these "church lands" were left uncleared for

years, while new settlers had to make their homes on poorer land. A large uncleared church grant would often lie between a settler and his nearest neighbour.

4. Mackenzie complained bitterly about the way the government had failed to improve the roads in the colony. He said that the tax-money was spent unwisely and often wasted in order to help the family Compact and its friends.

In short, William Lyon Mackenzie was trying his best to show that almost everything which the government of Upper Canada was doing was unwise or even dishonest. Of course, he was not the only person in Upper Canada who said that things needed setting right. The next ten years saw the bitterest political struggle in the history of our country. On the one hand were the members and friends of the Family Compact. On the other were the "Reformers"—including William Lyon Mackenzie.

At first it seemed likely that the Family Compact's power might be brought to an end quickly and peacefully. Mackenzie and many other Reformers were elected as members of the assembly of Upper Canada. Unfortunately, however, the Family Compact continued to control the lieutenant-governor, and the Reformers could not persuade him to get rid of his old advisors.

Trouble between the Reformers and the Family Compact grew rapidly worse during the next few years. Some people began to say that the Reformers wanted Upper Canada to break away from Great Britain and become a separate country. Others said they wanted to make the colony a part of the United States of America. Of course, very few Reformers demanded changes such as these. Most of them were as loyal to Britain as the lieutenant-governor himself. For a long time, even William Lyon Mackenzie asked only that the lieutenant-governor's advisors should be elected, instead of being "chosen". If this had been done, it would have meant that for the first time the people of Upper Canada would have controlled all their law-makers.

Unfortunately, there are always some leaders who, if they cannot get their way by peaceful means, want to fight those who disagree with them. William Lyon Mackenzie was such a man, and it is hard to forgive him for what he did next.

"Will the Canadians declare their independence", his newspaper screamed, "and shoulder their muskets?" William Lyon Mackenzie had decided to lead an armed rebellion against the government of Upper Canada!

Early in December, 1837, little groups of settlers armed with pike-staffs and muskets began to gather on Yonge Street a short distance north of Toronto—which was the name given to York when it became a city just three years earlier. The leader of these men, who were nearly all farmers from the country near by, was William Lyon Mackenzie. For weeks past, he had been riding the roads through the backwoods of Upper Canada, telling the settlers that the time had come to take up arms against the government of the colony. Now about seven hundred of them had arrived, ready to march against Toronto as soon as Mackenzie gave the word. Mackenzie had thought that many more would have answered his call to arms, but he decided not to wait for other followers to appear.

The Family Compact leaders in Toronto made hasty plans to meet the rebels. Although most of the government troops had, foolishly, been sent out of the city, it was not long before there were more armed citizens inside Toronto prepared to defend it than there were rebels ready to attack it. Besides, the government forces were much better armed than Mackenzie's followers, and when the fighting began there was little doubt who would win.

When we think of some of the battles between the Americans and the British just twenty-five years earlier, the fighting that took place between the government troops and Mackenzie's rebels on December 7, 1837, seems very unimportant. But the

fact that Canadians were now fighting against Canadians made men even in distant England realize that many things needed to be set right in the colonies.

William Lyon Mackenzie and his rebels were soon put to flight by the troops and armed citizens from Toronto. Although the Family Compact leaders did their best to have Mackenzie arrested, he managed to escape by travelling on foot all the way to the Niagara River, where he crossed over to the United States. Here he found men who were willing to follow him in still another attempt to overthrow the government of Upper Canada. With his new followers, who were mostly Americans, he seized a Canadian island in the Niagara River just above the falls. For a few weeks during the spring of 1838 he made a stand here against British and Canadian troops, but when they began to shell the island from the mainland he was forced to retreat to the American shore. The Mackenzie Rebellion was over.

A few years later, William Lyon Mackenzie was pardoned by a new Canadian government for having led the Rebellion of 1837 in Upper Canada, and he returned to this country. Great changes had taken place while he had been in exile. The old Family Compact group had disappeared. Upper Canada and Lower Canada had been united under a single government. Most of the complaints which he had once made in the *Colonial Advocate* had been forgotten.

But perhaps the most important fact was that all these changes took place peacefully after the defeat of Mackenzie's rebels north of the city of Toronto. During the years that William Lyon Mackenzie had been living in the United States, it had been decided that the lieutenant-governor's advisors should be chosen from among the law-makers elected by the people. The people of Great Britain's colonies in North America had at last succeeded in gaining control over *all* their law-makers. But how that had been brought about is a story we shall come to later.

### THE STRUGGLE IN LOWER CANADA

After Canada became British, the people of Lower Canada were given a much larger share in the making of their laws than they had ever had when Canada belonged to the king of France. The French-speaking people of Canada appreciated the rights which were given them by the British government. But there was a further reason why few French Canadians, after the

"PAPINEAU WAS RAPIDLY GROWING POPULAR"

beginning of the eighteenth century, had any wish to see their colony governed again by its old rulers.

Just thirty years after the English army under Wolfe captured Quebec, a terrible revolution broke out in France. The French king was taken prisoner and executed, and many of the country's religious leaders were killed or forced to undergo great hardships. French-speaking people of Canada were then, as now, good Catholics, and they were horrified by this revolution in the homeland of their ancestors. They now looked on Canada, not France, as their homeland.

But the people of Lower Canada felt their government could still be improved. Lower Canada now had an elected assembly, but it was having even more trouble getting along with the governor and his councillors than the assemblies in the other colonies.

For most of the people of Lower Canada were French-speaking, just as the people of Quebec are to-day. They were, therefore, much annoyed to find that the French-speaking lawmakers whom they elected could not get the English governor to agree to all the laws they wanted to pass. This was because the governor had chosen most of his councillors from among the English-speaking merchants of their colony. These businessmen owned most of the lumber and grain, and they wanted the assembly to tax the people of Lower Canada to pay for the building of canals, which would make it easier to ship their goods. They were anxious, too, to have more English-speaking people brought into Lower Canada from Great Britain. Naturally, these wishes of the governor's English-speaking councillors were not the wishes of the French-speaking law-makers in the assembly of Lower Canada. When the elected assembly refused to help pass the laws the governor's councillors wanted, it became difficult to carry on the business of governing the colony.

While William Lyon Mackenzie was busy criticizing the Family Compact in Upper Canada, Louis-Joseph Papineau was rapidly growing popular as the leader of the French-speaking people of Lower Canada. Papineau, like Mackenzie, gradually grew more and more bitter in his attacks against the governor and his English-speaking councillors. Then, in the fall of 1837, his followers took up arms against the government. Indeed, fighting actually broke out in Lower Canada before William Lyon Mackenzie marched his rebels against Toronto.

As in the other colonies, there were many clear-thinking people in Lower Canada who refused to try to change the method of government by fighting. The leaders of the Catholic church spoke openly against the rebellion, and the fighting did not spread throughout the colony. Papineau himself fled to the United States only a few days before William Lyon Mackenzie escaped the government forces of Upper Canada by crossing the Niagara frontier. Two rebellions had been fought and lost in British North America at almost the same moment! Like Mackenzie, Papineau returned in later years to Canada and found that most of the reforms he sought had been brought about peacefully in his absence.

**NOVA SCOTIA'S GREAT LEADER**

One winter's day in Halifax, a little over a hundred years ago, people were hurrying along the streets in the frosty weather. But nearly all of them stopped to look up at the grim old Court House as they passed by. From the way they nodded and shook their heads, it was plain something of great importance was going on in the building.

"How do you think it will turn out?" said one stout old gentleman to a friend.

"I wouldn't have given a penny for Howe's chances a few days ago," said the other, "but he spoke for six hours yesterday, and there wasn't a dry eye in the courtroom when he finished. I don't know what the jury will decide, but the people are with him, to a man."

"They say he couldn't find a lawyer in Halifax to defend him," said the old gentleman sadly.

"They were afraid to fight the Compact," replied his friend. "But Joe Howe needs no lawyers. He's the best speaker and the best writer in Nova Scotia. He knows his books, and he knows people too. When he was a boy his father taught him to read the

"HE HAS BEEN READING AND STUDYING EVER SINCE"

Bible and to study good literature. Why, he went to work in his father's printing-shop when he was just thirteen years old, and he has been reading and studying ever since. He bought his newspaper, the *Novascotian*, when he was only twenty-four. For seven years now, he's been travelling around the country getting stories for his paper; I'm told he has stopped for a meal or a bed in nearly every farmhouse in the colony. Yes, indeed, *everybody* knows Joe Howe!"

"Some high-and-mighty folk in Halifax are no friends of his," said the stout gentleman, shaking his head at the Court House. "Because he printed that letter saying that the men who control our city are dishonest, they are trying to put him into prison."

Both men watched the Court House anxiously. Suddenly the doors swung wide. An excited crowd streamed out, shouting with joy. On their shoulders rode Joseph Howe. The jury had found him "not guilty", and the people of Halifax were carrying him home in triumph!

A year later, Joseph Howe was elected by the people of Halifax to the assembly of Nova Scotia. He at once became the leader of those who were trying to change the method of government. As in the other British colonies of North America at this time, the people's law-makers in the assembly of Nova Scotia had little real power. The governor made the laws with the help of the few men he chose to advise him. Like William Lyon Mackenzie, Joseph Howe had to struggle against the governor and a Family Compact. Like Mackenzie, Howe was an editor and a printer, and sat in the assembly elected by the people. But in no other way were they like one another.

Joseph Howe's father was a United Empire Loyalist, who had come to Nova Scotia with his young bride during the American Revolution. As his gifted son once said, "He left all his household goods and gods behind him, carrying away nothing but his principles and the pretty girl!" These principles were also the principles of Joseph Howe, who was equally devoted to Britain and the empire. In all his struggle to secure for Nova Scotians the control of their own government, Howe never forgot or failed to remind his hearers that he was only trying to obtain the same rights which British subjects in the motherland possessed. "I wish to live and die a British subject," Howe once said, "but not a Briton only in name."

At this time, leaders in Britain feared that if the people of a colony were allowed to make their own laws, they would soon wish to be entirely independent, like the United States. Joseph Howe said, "The idea of independence from the mother country never crossed my mind." He told the British leaders that the colonists were proud of being British, and would always remain loyal to the mother country. He said that this loyalty would only be strengthened by the governor choosing his councillors, not from a few wealthy men in the colony, but from the law-makers elected by the people.

When rebellions broke out in Upper and Lower Canada, Howe's enemies said that he, too, was stirring up rebellion. But Howe published in the *Novascotian* a letter he had written two years earlier to a friend in Lower Canada. In this letter Howe had said that he sympathized with the Reformers, but that he feared if they kept on as they were going they would end in rebellion. He said the people of Nova Scotia would never take up arms against the British government.

While the rebellions in the Canadas made British leaders realize that the troubles in the colonies were serious and that changes must be made, it was Joseph Howe, and a few others like him, who made the British government see that the colonies were ready to govern themselves. It was Howe's great loyalty, as much as his ability as a speaker and a writer, that led men in the colonies and in England to believe in Joseph Howe and the cause for which he fought.

## THE CRY FOR REFORM

The people of the other Atlantic colonies, New Brunswick, Prince Edward Island, and Newfoundland, followed the example of Nova Scotia in the struggle to gain control of their government. In these provinces the same changes came at last, and came peacefully.

Although the people of New Brunswick at first had no more control over their lieutenant-governor's councillors than had the people of the other British colonies, there was little talk in this "Loyalist province" about rebelling against the government. Indeed, when the Papineau rebellion began in Lower Canada, several regiments of soldiers were sent from New Brunswick to Quebec. But in much the same way that Joseph Howe was demanding changes in Nova Scotia, a young lawyer named Lemuel Wilmot was calling for peaceful reform in New Brunswick.

The Family Compact that surrounded the lieutenant-governor in New Brunswick contained many good and able men, just as did the Compacts in the other provinces. But its members felt sure that if the assembly were allowed to control the lieutenant-governor, it would not be long before the colony would cease to be British.

The two rebellions had been crushed as quickly as they broke out, because most citizens wanted reform without rebellion.

But the "cry for reform" from colonists who were determined to control their governments lasted many years, and gradually it became clear that they were going to win the right they demanded.

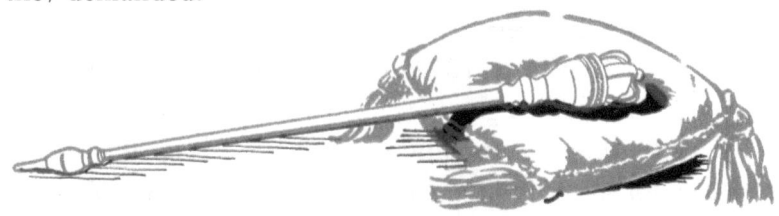

## "GOVERNMENT BY THE PEOPLE"

IN 1939, King George VI and Queen Elizabeth came to Canada, and during their stay visited every province in the Dominion. At Niagara Falls they crossed the river to view the great cataract from the American side. As they crossed the border, they were greeted by large crowds of cheering citizens of the United States.

Just about one hundred years earlier, a new governor general of the British colonies paid a similar visit to the United States shore at Niagara Falls. This official was Lord Durham, and as governor general he represented the British Crown in North America. But times were different a hundred years ago, and the people who crossed the border with Lord Durham were much worried about his safety. It was less than twenty-five years since the close of the War of 1812, and British and Americans still had not learned to be good friends.

Lord Durham's companions received a pleasant surprise, however, for the Americans gave him a warm welcome. As Lady

Durham wrote later, many "took off their hats, an unusual mark of respect among the Americans". After the visit was over, Lord Durham gave a large banquet on the Canadian side of the river, and many American citizens were included among the governor general's guests.

Friendly meetings between leaders of both countries are commonplace to-day, but just before Lord Durham's time some of the people in the United States were again talking about driving the British from North America. Only a few months had passed since some Americans had helped William Lyon Mackenzie hold out against British troops who were trying to capture him on a little island just above the falls on the Niagara River. During that fight, a handful of Canadians rowed across the river, set fire to Mackenzie's ship, and sank her. Since the ship was American property and had been in dock on the American side of the river, many United States newspapers claimed that the peace had been broken by the Canadian "raiders". A short while later, some Americans destroyed a Canadian ship on the St. Lawrence River, and this aroused bitter feeling on the Canadian side of the border. It began to look almost as if there might soon be another war.

But Lord Durham wrote to the President of the United States. He said that it would be foolish for two countries to quarrel because of the reckless acts of a few people. The President agreed, and the threat of further fighting passed.

Perhaps the Americans should not be blamed for sympathizing with Mackenzie and his followers. Like the Americans in the Revolution, Mackenzie had fought against real injustices, even though his rebellion had been put down. Now, however, Lord Durham had been sent to Canada to learn how the British government could correct the injustices which had caused the two rebellions of 1837. His task was to find out how Canadians could live at peace with one another, as well as with their neighbours.

LORD DURHAM AT KINGSTON

**A FAMOUS REPORT**

What steps did Lord Durham take to bring peace to Canada? First, he freed nearly all the rebels who had been put in prison. Some of their leaders, however, he sent away to Bermuda, where they would not be able to cause more trouble in Canada.

Then Lord Durham set to work to find out everything he could about Canada. He did not ask just the rich people, or those who lived in the towns, or those in the government. He also asked the poor people, the settlers in the backwoods, and the men who had been struggling for better government. He travelled through Lower and Upper Canada as far as Niagara, seeing the country for himself.

Unfortunately, however, Lord Durham had enemies as well as friends in the British government. These enemies criticized him so much that before long he resigned as governor general. He spent in all only five months in the colonies, but in those five months he learned enough to write a famous "Report" for the British government after his return to England.

In this Report, Lord Durham told all about Canada as it was at this time and about what he believed could be done to make it stronger and happier. He suggested that Upper and Lower Canada be united and governed by one assembly. He also recommended that some day *all* the British provinces in North America be joined together. But most important of all, Lord Durham said that the assembly elected by the people of Canada should control the government of the country. Before this time, the people had been allowed to elect law-makers, but the governor and his advisors had often refused to agree to the laws passed by the assembly. Each province had really been ruled by its governor and a Family Compact—the little group of men who advised him.

Lord Durham said that if the colonies were given the same right to govern themselves as the people of Great Britain, they would become even more loyal than before. Most people in Lord Durham's time felt that to give colonies so much freedom would encourage them to break away, as the United States had done. We know now that Lord Durham was right. He was the first British statesman to foresee a British Commonwealth of Nations such as we have to-day.

Most of Lord Durham's advice about Canada was sound. He made one bad suggestion, however. He thought that when the two provinces were united, French Canadians might be made to adopt the English language and English customs. Lord Durham failed to understand how deeply French Canadians cherish their own speech and ways. To-day, we realize that Canadians, even though they speak different languages, can get along together if they will try to understand each other's point of view.

Worn out by his five months' toil in Canada, Lord Durham returned to England. He was deeply hurt at the harsh criticisms he had received. Before another year had gone by he fell ill and died.

During the years that followed, many of the changes Lord Durham had recommended were made. In 1841, the two Canadas were united under one government. Upper Canada now became known as Canada West, and Lower Canada was renamed Canada East. Lord Durham had advised that a system of local, or "municipal", government should be set up in the colonies, and in due course this, too, was brought about.

The new government of Canada West and Canada East met first in the city of Kingston, which lies almost exactly half-way between Toronto and Montreal. Within three years, however, the capital of the two colonies was moved to Montreal, where most of the country's business firms were located. Here the government of the two Canadas was carried on for the next six years.

### "CABINET" GOVERNMENT

When Lord Elgin, governor general of Canada, opened the newly elected assembly in 1848, he found in it two important groups, or "parties". These parties held very different opinions. On the one side were the supporters of the old Family Compact, who were called "Tories". On the other side were the "Reformers", who had supported the people's right to control all the branches of government. Since more Reformers than Tories had been elected, Lord Elgin asked the Reform leaders to recommend which men should advise him.

The group of men chosen in this way was known as a "cabinet". The members of the cabinet were called "cabinet ministers". No longer did the governor choose his advisors himself. Instead, they were the choice of the party which had won the greatest number of seats in the election.

It was now clear that the cabinet would carry out the wishes of the people. The question that remained to be answered was: Would the governor always carry out the wishes of the cabinet? Must a governor give his consent to *every* bill passed by a colonial parliament? *Must a governor be willing to sign a bill even though he does not favour it?* Some politicians, especially in Britain,

REFORM LEADERS
HINCKS, LA FONTAINE, BALDWIN, AND LORD ELGIN

doubted if the colonies could safely be allowed the last word in making their own laws. They said that a governor general should not sign a bill, thereby making it law, just because it had been passed by the colonists' law-makers. They said that if the governor general did not agree with such a bill, he should refuse to let it become law, or at least that he should send it to the British government for approval.

"I WAS RECEIVED WITH CHEERS AND HOOTINGS"—LORD ELGIN

### LORD ELGIN'S DECISION

Suddenly trouble arose. Early in the spring of 1849, rioting broke out in Montreal against the government. It was only twelve years since the rebellions in the two Canadas, and now there was trouble again. But this time the reason was different. It was not because the governor had refused to agree to a law which the assembly wanted, but because he had consented to agree to it!

Before 1837, the wishes of the assembly had very often been blocked by the governor and his Family Compact advisors. Now, in 1849, the assembly had passed a bill to which the Family Compact party was very much opposed, and the governor general decided to sign the bill because the majority in the assembly wanted it. But those who opposed the bill were so angry that they broke into rioting. Many of these opponents were the very men who had upheld the governor in 1837!

The name of this famous bill was the Rebellion Losses Bill.

If it were passed and became law, a fairly large amount of money would have been paid out to those people of Canada East whose property had been damaged during the Papineau rebellion twelve years earlier. Many people now feared that rebels as well as loyalists would be paid damages for the losses they had suffered during the rebellion, since it was difficult to say who had fought for the government and who had fought against it. "No reward to the rebels!" became their cry in 1849. When they tried to force their wishes on their government, some of them became rebels themselves.

The important thing for us to remember about the Rebellion Losses Bill is not *what* it was about, but that there were many people who felt that it should not have been passed. Lord Elgin himself did not think it was wise. But the people's representatives had passed it. Would the governor general, then, make it law by signing his name to it?

As Lord Elgin's carriage stopped outside the council chamber of the Canadian government, rumours began to fly about Montreal that he intended to sign the bill which was opposed by so many "loyalists". Of course, most of the people of Montreal and the surrounding country were quite willing to accept the bill as law, and took no part in the argument. If they had done so, what followed might have been even worse than it was.

Lord Elgin knew that he was being called upon to make an important decision. Should he sign the bill, or should he ask the British government to decide whether or not it should become law? His mind was already made up when he entered the council chamber. The responsibility, he had written in a letter to England, "rests, and ought, I think, to rest, on my own shoulders". When the bill was now handed to him, he signed it immediately.

What happened next is best told in Lord Elgin's own words:

"When I left the House of Parliament, I was received with mingled cheers and hootings by a crowd which surrounded the entrance of the building. A small knot of individuals, made up of persons of a respectable class in society, pelted the carriage with missiles they must have brought with them for the purpose." Fortunately, no one was injured, but the worst was yet to come.

As the law-makers continued with their business in the House that evening, the loud roars of an angry mob suddenly split the air and a shower of stones and rocks began to crash through the windows on both sides of the meeting-room. In a few minutes, the crowd was inside the building, and the members of the assembly escaped as best they could. When the rioters reached the chamber of the assembly, their work of destruction began in earnest. Furniture was smashed, tables overturned, lamps, books, and papers were scattered about the room. At the height of the disturbance, a cry of "Fire!" suddenly was heard, and in a few minutes the building was in flames. Although fire-engines arrived, the angry mob refused to let them be used until the fire had spread too far to be put out. By morning, only the ruins were left of the parliament of the united Canadas.

Although the assembly called special meetings elsewhere in the city, mobs continued to meet also and several leaders of the government that had passed the Rebellion Losses Bill narrowly escaped injury at their hands.

A few days later, Lord Elgin returned to the city to attend a meeting of the government. As he passed through the streets, his party was once more surrounded by angry rioters who began to pelt his carriage with stones, bricks, and even rotten eggs. Later, on his way to his residence just outside town, he was again overtaken by the mob, and barely managed to escape.

Twice the brave governor general had risked his life by facing angry mobs. And he had done so only to carry out the wishes of their law-makers. How many of the rioters realized that he was establishing the right of the people to govern themselves? How many of them stopped to think that the governor general was protecting *their* rights, by obeying the wishes of their elected law-makers?

Parliament met no more in Montreal, for the next eight years the law-makers held their meetings in either Toronto or Quebec, until in 1858 Queen Victoria chose Ottawa as the capital of the two Canadas. Not many more years were to go by before Ottawa was to become the seat of government of a country much greater than the united provinces of Canada West and Canada East.

Many people said that the rioters who had attacked the government in Adontreal in 1849 should have been put down with greater force. Some persons even said that the troops should have been ordered to fire into the crowds. But Lord Elgin was determined that no blood should be shed if it could possibly be avoided, just as he was determined to carry out the wishes of the assembly. He had to risk his own safety and face the insults of the mobs. But not a life had been lost.

"Yes, I see it all now," said a friend of Lord Elgin some months after the troubles were over. "You were right—a thousand times right—though I thought otherwise then. I admit that I would have reduced all Montreal to ashes before I would have endured half what you did; and I should have been justified, too."

"Yes," replied Lord Elgin. "Your course would have been justified, but it would not have been the best course. Mine was a better one."

*The Beginning of British Columbia*

# THE STORY OF BRITISH COLUMBIA

WHEN the North West Company and the Hudson's Bay Company were united in 1821, the new company appointed Dr. John McLoughlin to rule the vast territory stretching from the Rockies to the Pacific and as far south as California. Dr. McLoughlin had been in charge of the North West Company's post at Fort William, where a young Scotsman, James Douglas, served under him. It was Douglas who now became chief trader in McLoughlin's new headquarters at Fort Vancouver, on the Columbia River, over two hundred miles south of the present city of Vancouver.

However, the United States, which had bought California from Spain, also claimed much of this far western area. It was agreed by Britain and the United States that until the boundary was decided, both Americans and British should be allowed to trade and settle in this part of the country. Large numbers of American pioneers soon came. Many would have died of starvation or been killed by the Indians if McLoughlin had not fed and protected them. He saw that their coming might end his own rule, but he said, " Wherever wheat grows, men will go, and colonies will grow."

When Dr. McLoughlin saw that much of his "empire", including Fort Vancouver, might soon become American, he sent James Douglas north to build a fort on Vancouver Island. The new post was named Fort Victoria, in honour of the Queen. It was said to have been "built with blankets", because the Indians who built the stockade were paid with one blanket for every forty stakes. The fort was completed in record time!

VICTORIA —

It soon became necessary for Great Britain and the United States to reach an agreement about the ownership of the West Coast. The British were claiming all the land as far south as the Columbia River, and the Americans were demanding all the land as far north as Alaska, which was then still owned by Russia. In 1846, a peaceful settlement was made, when Britain and the United States signed the Oregon Treaty. The boundary was to continue to follow the 49th parallel across the Rockies to the sea. All of Vancouver Island, however, was to remain British.

When the Oregon Treaty fixed the United States boundary north of Fort Vancouver, the headquarters of the Hudson's Bay Company was moved to Fort Victoria. Douglas succeeded McLoughlin as western head of the Company, and it was not long before he became governor of Vancouver Island as well.

For seven years Douglas ruled the peaceful little colony. Then, in 1858, a gold rush to the Fraser River began. Miners and prospectors stormed into the Hudson's Bay post at Victoria, seeking supplies and means of getting into the mountains of the mainland. There was no government on the mainland, since up to this time there had been no need for one. Only Indians and a

-1863

few trappers and fur traders lived there. But Douglas proclaimed British rule and British law, and soon the British government backed him up by making him governor of the mainland as well as the Island. With the aid of an upright and stern judge named Matthew Begbie, Douglas now brought law and order to the mining-camps which were springing up so rapidly. When the rush was over, most of the miners left the country, but those who remained formed the backbone of the population of the province of British Columbia.

In 1863, Douglas was knighted by Queen Victoria. One year later he resigned as governor and retired from politics. He spent the remainder of his life in Victoria, the city which he had founded. Soon the Island and the mainland were united into one colony, which was called British Columbia, and Victoria became its capital.

Governor Douglas was responsible for the building of the famous Cariboo Trail. This was a long and difficult road which wound for five hundred miles through the mountains into the gold-mining country. Thousands of gold-seekers passed over it. Here is a story that tells what the journey must have been like.

## ON THE CARIBOO ROAD

"Stage is waitin'!" shouted the owner of the Eighty-Three Mile Inn, as he poked his head through the doorway.

Hastily I swallowed the last of my ham and eggs. They weren't very good, but the crisp mountain air had made me hungry. Besides, they had cost me three American dollars.

I hurried out to the waiting stage-coach. The six horses champed impatiently; the driver was on the box, and the guard waited to climb up beside him. I jumped in and settled into an outside seat. One after the other, the passengers clumped out into the chilly grey morning and took their places in the stage.

The long whip cracked.

"See you Friday, Charlie," shouted the owner of the Eighty-Three to the stage-driver, as we clattered off. I looked back after a minute and saw the log building and the waving man just disappearing out of sight around the bend.

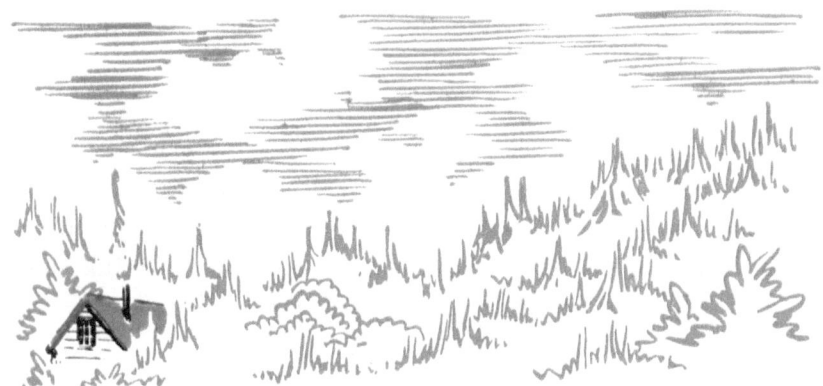

Leaning out and peering ahead, I decided the Cariboo Road looked much as it had the day before. What a ride we had had! I hadn't been so thrilled—or scared—since our ship had bucked a fierce gale rounding Cape Horn. The trip by Hudson's Bay steamer up the Fraser River from Fort Langley to Yale was tame in comparison, though it too had seemed exciting at the time. What a ride! My eyes had ached from staring up at the heights where our road led, and from looking down, down to the river running swiftly at the bottom of the canyon. As the horses swung the heavy stage around the sharp curves, time and again I had expected we would go right over the edge.

Every bone in my body had ached from the shaking as we drove over the hard rock road. But I was eighteen years old, strong and healthy, having lived on the farm until the longing for adventure drew me away. When we reached the roadhouse where we spent the night, I fell asleep at once and never knew till morning how hard the bed was.

On that first day's ride I had learned that our driver, however reckless he seemed, knew every turn of the road by heart. My fellow travellers, to be sure, did not seem worried. Whether the coach was tearing along a narrow shelf of rock hanging over the river, or across a platform supported by a cribwork of logs wedged against the mountainside, or over a shaky wooden bridge, seemed all one to them. The grizzled miner opposite me did not even pause as he reeled off story after story.

What stories they were! Old Sandy had a yarn to match every sandbar in the river. He had seen hundreds of dollars' worth of gold washed out of the sands of the Fraser. But the gold seldom stuck to the fingers of those who found it. Old Sandy had stories of the precious dust being wasted in gambling and drink, and of men waylaid and slain for the gold they carried.

"Aye, lad," Sandy said to me, "Ye're three years too late."

"Well," I said, "I've a good job promised me in the mines at Barkerville."

"A job!" replied Sandy in great scorn. "And what's a job? Working pumps in a mine that's owned by a company! Now, back in '61 and '62—that's when fortunes were found in the Cariboo. Twenty thousand of us there were, hunting for the gold in '63—not many more than five thousand are left now."

"Made their fortunes and retired, I suppose," said I, with a grin.

"Now, laddie, dinna joke about it. Some struck it rich. Others found naething, and died o' the scurvy or starvation, or left poorer than they came. Some, like me, made a fair bit and spent it all. Flour was sixty pounds a barrel. Ten pounds for a pair o' boots! I saw ye look pained this morning when ye paid for your breakfast. I mind when I would have paid twa pounds for an egg like that one ye sniffed at so suspeeciously. It took a fortune to live."

"Well, Sandy," spoke up the man sitting beside me, "I've heard you had a pretty good time while your money lasted. It didn't all go for flour and shoes!" Everybody laughed, Sandy included, and the man went on. "This road has been a boon to the mining country. The cost of freight is only a fraction of what it used to be, and though prices are still high a man can live on what he earns at the mines.

"You all know I'm an old Hudson's Bay man. I remember when there was no road here at all—only Indian paths and portage trails made by us fur traders. It is remarkable that in three years such a road as this should have been built—over four hundred miles long, through the most difficult and dangerous country—"

Suddenly we were all lifted from our places and abruptly seated again, as the coach lurched to a halt.

We looked out.

"Washout!" called the driver, pointing at the road ahead. The rocky "fill" had been washed away; only a narrow track remained of the regular eighteen-foot roadway.

"We're going across," called down the driver. "Anybody want to get out and walk?"

Nobody did. The stage-coach moved slowly forward. But what were the wheels on my side travelling on? I couldn't see anything below—not for a long, long way down. I stopped looking, and even stopped breathing. The wheels on the other side scraped the cliff as the coach crept by. Suddenly, a whip cracked above us, and we were off again.

"A difficult and dangerous country, gentlemen, as I was saying," continued the Hudson's Bay man. "Over two hundred thousand pounds this road cost—four hundred pounds a mile."

"I wouldn't give a shilling for that piece we just passed," said Sandy, and we all laughed.

"British Columbia was fortunate in having for her first governor James Douglas—Sir James he is now, since Queen Victoria made him a knight," said the Hudson's Bay man, when we had quieted down. "He's the man who built this road. Just one of the great things he did for this colony.

"There's talk, now Sir James has retired, of joining British Columbia and Vancouver Island into one colony," he went on. "And, by the way"—turning courteously to me—"I hear rumours of a union of the Canadas and the Maritime colonies. You are lately from Canada West, I believe; have you heard anything of such a union?"

"I recall there was a report in the Toronto *Globe* last fall about something of the kind," I replied. "A conference in Charlottetown, Prince Edward Island, I think. But I hadn't heard much about it before I left. Of course, people have talked about it off and on for years."

WE WERE AT BARKERVILLE...

"Aye, people are always talking," said Sandy. "Next they'll be talking about *us* joining up with Canada—and not even a road or railway between us!"

On we drove for three days, with a pause every twelve or thirteen miles for change of horses. They were days of dust and jolting, of dazzling white mountain-peaks and green mountain rivers. They were days filled with tales of treasure-hunting, both humorous and sad. Then, as we neared the end of another twelve-mile stage, the horses began to move faster instead of slower, the driver yelled and cracked his whip furiously, the dust rose in a thick cloud about us. We jerked to a stop. As the dust settled I saw unpainted, low frame buildings straggling along the main street of a mining town larger than any I had passed through. From the narrow wooden sidewalk three or four weary miners and a lonesome-looking old Indian stopped to stare at us. A prospector trudged by, urging three pack-mules along the road. A long string of oxen pulling two freight-wagons lumbered past down the trail by which we had come.

We were at Barkerville—the end of the Cariboo Road.

## LIFE ACROSS THE COLONIES A CENTURY AGO

TO-DAY a traveller may board a train in Montreal in the evening, and arrive in Fredericton or Saint John the following morning. He may even make the trip in a few hours by airplane. A hundred years ago, before the coming of the railway, such an overland journey meant many days of travel, and often severe hardship. In those days, summer travel on the newly invented steamships was much preferred to winter travel overland by sleigh. Nevertheless, even winter travel was often easier than journeying during the spring months. During spring, what roads there were often turned into rivers of mud and slime, through which the horse-drawn coaches and carriages could hardly move.

A spring journey from Kingston to Saint John in the 1840's, therefore, was likely to be such an adventure that a traveller could write a whole book about it. At least one traveller did just this, and the following story is based on the account he left us.

## SPRING JOURNEY, 1844

In the beginning of April, 1844, I left Kingston, the capital of the Canadas for these past three years, and travelled to Montreal, where the government has now been moved. The journey of one hundred and eighty miles, with my family, was most disagreeable. We travelled in an open post-wagon, for a closed carriage was thought too heavy for the roads, which were now breaking up after the winter's frost.

The driver and I were forced to walk a good part of the distance, to relieve the exhausted horses. On the first day, we made the thirty-six miles to Wright's Tavern, after having toiled the whole way through melting drifts of snow and, where there was no snow, through heavy mud. Here we were put into a garret-room, the window of which had several panes of glass missing. We remained here (I cannot say rested) until another postwagon came at three o'clock in the morning, whereupon we went on again.

We passed through Brockville and reached Prescott, first being tumbled about on the frozen roads and then being dragged through the soft mud, which began as the rising sun warmed the surface of the road. Opposite the rapids, just below Prescott, the wagon became stuck fast in a deep mud hole. Passengers and baggage were taken off to "lighten ship", and using rails from the fences on the side of the road, we painfully hoisted the wheels out of the slough.

We sleighed across the ice of the Ottawa River, even though it was becoming unsafe. One horse, indeed, broke through, but fortunately the water was shallow where this accident happened.

At last, after four days and three nights of most unpleasant travel, we reached Montreal. Later in the summer, the road would have been good enough, though no doubt very rough in places. But at this season of the year, there was no other means of making the journey or we should have sought to use it.

In Montreal, I left my family and continued on my way towards Saint John, in the province of New Brunswick. The next stage of the trip was the most pleasant of all, for a steamship was already running to Quebec, and on this I took passage. It was a pleasant change to be able to rest inside the cabin as we glided down the smooth surface of the river, instead of paying for the right to help the horses pull the wagon, as had been necessary on the road to Montreal. But my comfort was not to last long.

At Quebec, I crossed by ferry to the south shore of the river, where I continued my land journey. A light wagon had been held there, and in it six of us embarked for Riviere du Loup, a hundred miles down the southern bank of the St. Lawrence. I found this part of our journey interesting, for I did not know French-speaking Canada. The shore was everywhere well cultivated, and the many houses along the way made a cheerful

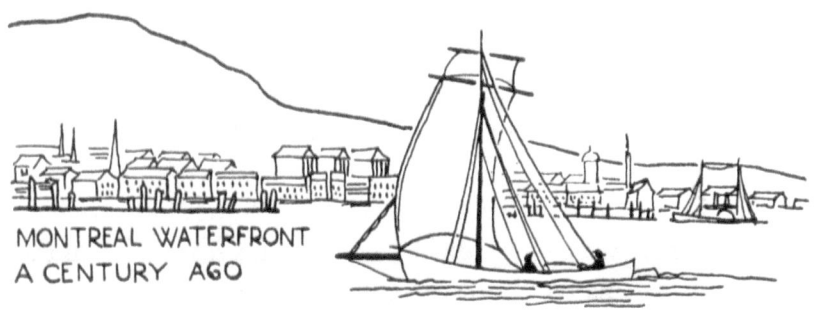

MONTREAL WATERFRONT A CENTURY AGO

scene. As we passed close to the water, we saw nets set out on the wet sands of the shore where the tide was out. These were so placed as to catch fish at high tide, which could be removed from the nets while the water was low.

This was the country of the original French colonists, the *habitants*. The habitants are a contented and likeable race of people. The men are usually clad in thick linen shirts and grey coarse cloth, manufactured by the women. The women in summer wear printed blouses, and blue or red skirts with broad-brimmed straw hats. In winter, we were told, they often wear grey coats like the men.

The French-Canadian houses present a pleasing picture with their white-washed walls and high, curving roofs. Inside, there is very little furniture, but everything is spotlessly clean. In the more comfortable homes, coarse white and striped carpeting is laid on the floors in winter. A heavy iron stove is usually placed in the wall between the two rooms, into which most of the houses are divided. In winter, it serves both for heating and cooking. In the hot summer months, the cooking is done under a shed outside, while the baking takes place in a white clay oven raised on posts in front of the house.

The habitants are all Roman Catholics, and their churches are usually very large, being ornamented outside with two belfry spires. Formerly, a father gave his sons a portion of his land when they married. Now, many of the young French-speaking Canadians move away to take land at a distance from the banks of the St. Lawrence. Many have moved into the Eastern Townships, that fertile part of Lower Canada that lies east and south of Montreal.

At Riviere du Loup we found two small hotels for travellers, though there were few guests in either at this season. From the chief businessman in the place we received the latest information concerning the condition of the route which still lay ahead of us. We also had the latest news from Halifax and Saint John, for we were now travelling the mail route between Montreal and the East.

We now started out on the hardest part of the whole journey—the Temiscouata Portage, which leads from Riviere du Loup into New Brunswick. In order to reach Lake Temiscouata, which was our immediate goal, we broke up into small groups of two or three. Each group was put in a separate caleche, or little cart, along with some of the baggage.

The Temiscouata Portage is difficult at the very best seasons of the year, but the melting of the snow makes the passage in May one of unbelievable hardship. We were deep in the woods when we reached the Riviere Verte, where a toll is taken for the portage. The toll-post is looked after by an old curly-headed sergeant, who has lived there since 1815.

With great labour, we got the first night to St. Francis River, where we slept. Snow still lay in the woods, and water rushed in torrents along the sides and over the road. It seems clear that this road, which was once an Indian path, ought as soon as possible to cease to be a part of the line of communication for the mails between Halifax and Quebec.

We found Temiscouata Lake to be a fine large sheet of water, twenty miles long, which in summer could be travelled on by small craft, or in winter by sleighs. But it was of no use to us, for there was still some ice on its surface. We therefore had to continue to the Little Falls of the Madawaska River on horseback. Fortunately, I had brought a saddle with me. The baggage was put on four little carts, and brought along behind us.

The first six miles of the road were pretty good, but the last twelve were really of the worst description possible. The road was now more like the bed of a muddy river, with roots in it,

TEMISCOUATA PORTAGE IN WINTER

than anything else. And yet we could not leave it, for there were black swamps and brushwood on both sides. Some of the wooden bridges had been carried away by floods, and others had been accidentally burnt.

We plunged through streams, and occasionally got on logs which sank under the horses' feet. Sometimes we were up to the stirrups in swampy ground and mud. The drivers of the carts were wet and muddied to their waists, yet they seemed to manage to keep the baggage dry.

When we reached the Madawaska River, we found a good road for twenty-four miles. But for the next thirty-six miles, to the Grand Falls on the St. John River, strange to say there was no road at all. The river was here the road, and a canoe the means of transport.

We were now in New Brunswick, and sailing down its most important river, the St. John. We were passing the Acadian settlements, which were built here in 1783. The Acadians are the descendants of those early French settlers who were removed from Nova Scotia by the English. They live in small wooden houses scattered along the banks of the river. Those on the bank to our right now find themselves American citizens, for the settlement of the boundary dispute between New Brunswick and the State of Maine makes the St. John River the frontier at this point.

In three canoes, our party continued to glide down the deep and smooth river. The stream gradually became swifter, and then we saw the well-known signs of a cataract rising ahead—white vapour clouds stretching across the river, rising and falling, showing that we were approaching a great waterfall. The St. John River here thunders over a ledge of rocks into a deep basin seventy-five feet below, while farther downstream the river foams in rapids.

Leaving Grand Falls, I mounted a wagon drawn by three horses, and proceeded on the way towards Fredericton. At the Aroostock Ferry we took the wagon across the river in a miserable scow, but we found a comfortable inn on the other side. The roads were still not very good, as little attention had been paid to their drainage.

The smiling valley of the St. John River increased in richness and beauty as we drove down it. We arrived late at the village of Woodstock, but the charges there for gentleman travellers were high.

At Lang's Creek, the bridge had been carried away by the floods. As we crossed on a raft of loose planks resting on logs,

SAINT JOHN — 100 YEARS AGO

the water bubbled up about our feet. But at last, after a very hard day's work of "rough and tumble" travelling, we reached Fredericton, the capital city of New Brunswick.

Fredericton was chosen as the seat of government by Sir Guy Carleton in 1785. It is placed on a level site opposite the mouth of the Nashwaak, and partly enclosed by a gentle bend of the St. John River. Its situation is pleasant and cheerful, whilst an air of quiet and peace prevails. The streets are regular, and the houses are of wood or brick. The population is about four thousand. The churches are well attended, and the population, of British descent, is very loyal, orderly, and well conducted.

On May 21 I left Fredericton for Saint John, on board one of the river steamers. On our way, we could see the rich and well-cultivated banks of the lower St. John River, dotted with comfortable houses where, sixty years ago, there was not one.

The city of Saint John, the largest in New Brunswick, is well placed at the mouth of the St. John River. The river itself ends in a very large and safe harbour, abounding in herring and mackerel, in which the tide rises twenty-four feet. The city, which stands at the edge of this harbour, is built on a rocky surface. Many of its streets are steep, and when they are well paved and well lighted, the city will have a handsome appearance. It contains many public buildings, such as churches, schools, banks, and a chamber of commerce. The population is about thirty thousand.

The Falls on the St. John River, just above its mouth, are remarkable. Here the river is narrowed by great rocks to a width of a few hundred yards. At low tide, the water rushes down through this passage in a violent rapid. But at high tide, the water of the harbour is higher than the water in the basin above this rocky passage, and the water rushes with equal force *upstream*, making a rapid in the opposite direction. Between tides, boats may pass safely either up or down the passage through which the river flows.

### THE COMING CHANGE

The account we have just read helps to explain what people meant a century ago when they said that the British provinces "lie closer to England than to each other." And so long as overland journeys had to be made on horseback or in horse-drawn coaches or sleighs, what hope was there for improvement? The biggest problem of all was that loads of freight could not be moved to and from the inland provinces, except during the months when the waterways were free of ice.

Fortunately, the steam locomotive was on its way! We shall read the story of the coming of the railway later, but its importance to the people of British North America is already clear. Without the railway, the provinces had grown separately. With the railway, they could begin to grow together.

PROVINCIAL FAIR, 1852

If my cousin Seth had not been visiting us from New York, I doubt if Father would have remembered that the Agricultural Show was opening at the Fair Grounds on Tuesday. Father always said he did not believe in running off to everything that came along. But Seth wasn't backward at supper, Monday, in telling us about the progress made in the States, and it seemed pretty clear he thought Toronto in 1852 was far behind the times. Father probably made up his mind then and there to show our American cousin the exhibits from the farms and industries of Canada West. But, being Father, he didn't say anything at the time.

The Show opened Tuesday, and Seth and I were bursting with impatience. But Father always made the plans in our home and I hadn't been able to persuade Mother to ask him to let us go.

"You Americans have made considerable progress, my boy," Father said to Seth, as we finished breakfast on Wednesday. "But

we've not been exactly asleep here in the British provinces, you know!" Seth smiled in reply, for he knew how proud Father was that all the family was "pure Loyalist stock". Mother was smiling, too, when Father continued: "One can see a sample of every corner of Canada West right here in Toronto this week. H-rmph! The Provincial Agricultural Show opened yesterday at the Fair Grounds."

"I understand the exhibits are most educational, sir," answered Seth slyly (just as if we had not been talking about the Show for a whole week).

"Educational!" exclaimed Father. "H-rmph! Why, it's equal to a trip across the whole province!" He had risen from the table and was gathering his papers together in the study when he added at the top of his voice: "I'll be closing the office tomorrow. We three men must visit the Fair!"

Seth and I were both fourteen then, and I am not sure which pleased us most—going to the Agricultural Show, or Father saying "we three men".

Early Thursday morning we set out for the Fair Grounds at the head of Simcoe Street, a good half-mile from downtown Toronto. Father, who did not believe in spending money on cabs, led the way on foot. As we walked west on King Street, he began to describe the wonders of Canada West, interrupting himself from time to time to point out places of special interest.

"Think of it, Seth," he said. "Sixty years ago all this was an unsettled forest. To-day we have a city of over thirty thousand people. That's rapid growth for you!"

... WE WALKED WEST ON KING ST. ...

I was beginning to think all thirty thousand were on King Street that September morning, so heavy were the crowds moving towards the Fair Grounds. Father went on:

"Yes, Toronto can boast all the features of modern civilization, Seth—a university, a fine harbour regularly visited by lake steamers, even the magnetic telegraph. Why, I can send a message instantly from here to Quebec, or New York, or even New Orleans! And there are hundreds of miles of highways running out of Toronto into the bush and along the lake-shore, with regular coach service to carry one over them. The railroad is coming, too. Before long, we'll be served by three different lines, do you know that?"

Seth listened politely, though he had told me enough about New York to make me realize that these modern improvements were not new to him. However, we did not mind Father's descriptions of the plank roads, gravel highways, and steam railways of Canada West, when every step brought us nearer the Fair Grounds and the wonders inside.

At the south entrance there was a vast throng of people, elbowing each other as they struggled towards the narrow gateway into the grounds. A great many more must have turned out than were expected, for only two constables were posted to take tickets from thousands of visitors. As we squeezed past the barrier, Father paid the price of admission for the three of us—one York shilling apiece.

The sight inside was a real surprise. The Fair Grounds covered a huge space—over seventeen acres, Father said. Nearby was a

tremendous canvas tent, where refreshments were already being served to a crowd of customers. Around half the enclosure surrounding the grounds a carriage drive had been laid out, well marked by small pine trees that added much to the beauty of the gay scene.

From where we stood, we could count five Fair buildings, built especially for the Show and housing those displays which could not be exposed to the weather. As we walked towards them, Father told us what each one was for—the flower show here, farm produce from all across Canada West there, farm and industrial machinery in this building, and so on. Indeed, so many farmers and industries were showing their goods that there was almost as much on view outside the buildings as in, and several huge tents had been put up to help provide cover for them.

Father was chiefly interested in the Agricultural Hall, and

so that was the building we visited first. The walls inside were lined with display booths, each crowded to overflowing with samples of prize field crops.

"The Canada Company has offered a prize of one hundred dollars for the best twenty-five bushels of wheat," father explained, as we marvelled at the sacks and sacks of golden grain arranged in rows along the west side of the building. "Wheat's an important crop in Canada West, Seth," he went on. "That's spring wheat over there. And look at this, did you ever see such barley?" he added, running his fingers through the contents of a sack, almost as proudly as if he had grown it himself. "Beautiful, beautiful. Much prettier sight than the floral show, if people would only realize it."

There was another stall filled with displays of marrow-fat and common field peas. They all looked fine and plump to me but then I didn't know much about such produce. When I confessed this, Father laughed. "Indeed, the judges will be having a hard time, too, to keep from giving prizes to everyone," he remarked.

On the east side of the Agricultural Hall we found stands loaded down with various kinds of potatoes, some of them the largest I had ever seen. "Not necessarily the best, boy, not necessarily the best!" cautioned Father, who seemed to be a good judge of potatoes, too. After the potatoes came bales of flax, hops, and some very fine samples of white flour. There were other bins filled with turnips, Indian corn, cattle carrots, field beets, and broom corn. Between the booths on this side of the Hall, huge cattle squashes were neatly arranged in rows.

In the centre of the Hall, on a raised platform, stood the largest cheese I have ever laid eyes on. A placard announced that it weighed 658 lb., and was made in the dairy of Mr. Ranney, a farmer in Oxford County. This giant cheese, along with several smaller ones that stood beside it, were said to be a part of the produce of Mr. Ranney's herd of 126 milk cattle.

"Those hives came from the same farm, boy," said bather, pointing to another part of the great table which supported the cheeses. "No Canadian farmer should think he is well stocked until he has a good hive of bees!"

It was just after we entered the exhibit of farm machinery that Father introduced us to Mr. Johnson. "Mr. Johnson worked with the committee that planned this Show," we were told, "and he knows as much about this province of ours as anyone here." Mr. Johnson seemed to take such great pride in the exhibits that you would have thought they were all his own.

"These machines aren't bad, considering they were made in Canada, eh, Johnson?" said Father, with a sly wink in Seth's direction.

"They're as good as the best made in the States," Mr. Johnson assured us. "Just look at them—iron ploughs, drills, harrows, reaping machines, sowing machines, chaff and straw cutters—all made on this side of the border."

"Tell me, sir," asked Seth, "how were all these heavy exhibits brought into the city?"

Mr. Johnson began to explain. "Well, of course it will be much easier once the railways are completed. Most of the machinery comes from shops near by, and was drawn here, piece by piece. We have exhibits from all over the province, too, as you can see. At this time of year the roads in Canada West are in fair condition. I don't think we could do as well, say, in the spring of the year. It's hard enough even for a man on horseback to move about the country then."

"Now, now, Johnson," cautioned Father. "Don't let my American nephew think that we aren't making any progress up here."

Mr. Johnson laughed heartily. "Certainly we are. Why, I remember ten years ago taking a whole day to come in from Oakville on the stage. We spent most of the time pulling the

REAPER MADE IN UPPER CANADA ABOUT 1852

coach out of the mud. But as soon as the railways are finished, we'll be able to travel to Montreal in one day. And what's more, we'll be able to ship our freight by land the year round—you can't do that now by stage-coach."

"Steam will take us much farther than Montreal," Father added. "Hugh Allan's company began the ocean steamship service last year, and we'll soon be having our mail from the Old Country delivered here in as little as two weeks. Life is beginning to speed up, isn't it, Johnson?"

"Yes," Mr. Johnson answered. "They're talking about running a Canadian telegraph line all the way to the Pacific coast, now, right across the prairies and through the Rockies. And a railway, too—imagine!"

"It may come," said Father, "but it will take years. Even the Americans haven't spanned the continent with steel, yet."

All this time we were standing in the aisle between the exhibits, with people pushing past us on both sides, so it was not long before Father said we had better move along. Mr. Johnson shook hands with each of us in turn, and we followed Father out and across the grounds.

Seth remarked, "It looks as if Canada West is almost as busy a country as New York State, sir, to judge from what's on view here to-day."

"'Tis busy enough, lad," agreed Father readily, beaming his approval. "Over a million people in the province now, and nearly all of them newcomers during the past sixty years. When I was a boy in 'Muddy York', as Toronto was called then, we felt we were living in the backwoods of North America. Now look at us: we have the news by telegraph as quickly as the people who live in ocean ports; we ship our goods by lake steamer, and soon when the railway goes through we'll have steam cars as well; some of our highways may be none too good, but they do link us with the inland settlements. You're seeing things aright, lad—Canada West has really outgrown its pioneer days."

"Do you mean the colonies won't grow any more?" asked Seth, nudging me.

"Goodness, no!" exclaimed Father. "There's still plenty of land even in Canada West to be taken up by new settlers. Of

course, farming will not be as good in the north. The land is too rocky. But out west, beyond the lakes, there's British territory a dozen times as large as Canada West, and hardly a foot of it has been turned by a plough."

"Father means the lands along the Red River," I suggested.

"Yes, and all the way from there to the Rockies," added Father. "They've been doing some farming on the Red River for the past forty years, ever since Selkirk sent out his settlers. But the surface of the land in the north-west has hardly been scratched yet."

A few minutes later we found ourselves surrounded by an exhibit of ploughs, fresh from the shops where they were made. The mould-boards of some were gaily painted with coats-of-arms and Union Jacks, an idea which caused Father some annoyance. "I cannot see why any loyal citizen should want to bury the Union Jack in the mud," he declared. "I would not fancy it if I were a farmer. It is bad taste to paint them so, and I would rather bear with the rust."

"It's a fad, but it helps them sell," remarked one of the men looking after the exhibit, who had overheard us.

"Why, Billings!" shouted Father. "I didn't know you were displaying here this week!" We stopped to talk with Mr. Billings, who turned out to be an old friend of the family. He was a machine-maker, and had his shop near the waterfront in Toronto.

"Tell us," asked Father, "how well are implements selling to the farmers now? Business has been very shaky these last few years, has it not?"

"That it has," answered Mr. Billings. "We can sell things to the farmers as rapidly as they can sell their wheat and produce for export. But Canadian wheat export has been in a bad way the past half-dozen years, since Britain adopted Free Trade."

"You'd better tell the lads what you're driving at," said Father. "Well, this is the picture, boys," explained Mr. Billings. "Until 1846, six years ago, we were doing a roaring business exporting wheat, timber, and other Canadian products to the Old Country. The Americans were able to sell their produce more cheaply than we were, of course. But British ports charged a much heavier duty on shipments from foreign ports than on shipments from colonial ports, and so we had the business. Why, the Americans even sent their wheat into Canada to be milled, so that it might be sent to Britain as Canadian flour. Then the cry went up in the Old Country for cheaper bread, cheaper bread. Suddenly, in '46, we heard that Britain was going to change the law that made the Americans pay a heavy duty on their grain shipments. It looked as though the Canadian farmer would be ruined."

"But it hasn't worked out that way entirely," said Father.

"No, we're learning that we can trade without depending on Britain to protect us with duties. Some farmers say that without Britain favouring our imports we might as well join the United States. But that is all talk, just talk. Since the new canals on the St. Lawrence were completed in '49, just three years ago, the cost of shipping has begun to drop. That helps us to sell our produce cheaper. And just as soon as the Americans lower their duties on what we sell them, we shall have a new customer—and right next door, at that."

"Yes," said Father, "it isn't just trade that links the British colonies with the Old Country. Most of Canada West has been settled by British immigrants, and pretty much all of the business here has been started by British money. We have been slow in building our manufacturing industries, it's true, but you can see signs of change all about you at this exhibition to-day. Any country as rich as Canada West in timber and wheat, not to mention its other natural resources, is bound to find its place in the business life of the world."

It was late in the afternoon when Father announced that it was time to leave. We had not yet seen all the exhibits, but Seth and I were tired and satisfied. As we passed the barrier, where crowds were still coming in, Father turned to Seth.

"Well, boy, tell us what you thought of it," he said.

"It's a fine Show," my cousin answered. "I didn't know so much was going on in the Canadas. It must have taken a long while to get ready for it."

Father stopped walking, and drew Seth by the arm. Pointing back the way we had come, he said: "It *has* taken a long while to get ready for that Show, Seth. You see, this province wouldn't have had much to exhibit fifty years ago, or even twenty years ago, for that matter. These last half-dozen years we've had other fairs, of course, but none as large or as fine as this one. Yes, Seth, the people in Canada West have been getting ready for the Provincial Agricultural Show of 1852 ever since Colonel Simcoe came out as our first lieutenant-governor in 1791. I want you to remember that."

## BUILDING A DOMINION

WE have been reading in this book the stories of the British colonies in North America. Now we have come to the time when some of these colonies decided to join hands. The stories of Nova Scotia, New Brunswick, Prince Edward Island, the Canadas, the Red River, and British Columbia continue, but we begin another story, the story of the Dominion of Canada.

Why did the colonies make this great change? What were some of the difficulties which had kept them apart? How were these difficulties overcome?

### "LET US BE UNITED"

It is not surprising that the British colonies in North America should have thought about joining with one another. For years they had watched their next-door neighbour, the United States, growing in wealth and population. In comparison, the British colonies seemed poor and small. They were beginning to long for some of the advantages of union which the Americans enjoyed.

However, the colonies were widely separated. As we have read, the overland journey from the Canadas to New Brunswick and Nova Scotia was filled with hardships. The journey by water was easier, but it could only be made during the ice-free months.

Between Canada West and the Red River Colony, the best route lay through the United States. From St. Paul, Minnesota, long trains of ox-carts creaked along five hundred miles of trail to Fort Garry. Beginning in 1859, a steam-boat carried passengers and freight north down the Red River from Minnesota to the Colony.

Vancouver Island and the mainland of British Columbia, on the western side of the continent, lay months away from the Canadas. Very few people other than the fur traders attempted to make the journey across the continent.

How could colonies so cut off from one another make their dream of union come true?

The answer was: *by building railways*. The invention of the steam locomotive made it possible to cover long distances in short spaces of time. Widely separated places suddenly seemed

TORONTO STATION, 1857

closer together. By railway, a journey which had formerly taken months could be made in a few days, and heavy trainloads of goods could be moved great distances at high speed. At last the scattered colonies of British North America could be linked together.

Everyone began to catch "railway fever". However, the colonies soon found they could not afford to build all the railways that were wanted. In the 1850's, the Maritime Provinces began to build a railway to Riviere du Loup which would connect them with Canada East. But the distance was so great that, although they built parts of the line, they could not find the money to complete it. Railways were also built in the Canadas; by 1860 the Grand Trunk ran all the way from Sarnia in Canada West to Riviere du Loup. But goods for overseas still had to be shipped from American ports in the winter time. If the railway from the Maritimes were finished, Halifax and Saint John might handle this traffic instead.

There were still no railways in the western part of British North America. Travellers to the Red River could now make the journey by American railways, which by the 1850's were reaching towards the Pacific coast. Thousands of settlers were moving into the western United States on these railways. It began to look as if Rupert's Land and the North-West might some day be settled by Americans, and be taken over by the United States, as Oregon had been. Already, American miners were flocking into the gold-fields of British Columbia.

By the 1860's, most of the good farming land in Canada East and Canada West had been occupied. If more people were to come to live in Canada, they would have to settle farther west. But if the United States secured this territory, the British colonies would never be able to expand. If the colonies banded together now, they might be able to purchase the rights of the Hudson's Bay Company in the North-West.

The colonies were also driven to join forces through fear of war with the United States. What had happened to raise this fear?

The southern states had decided to withdraw from the union and form a separate nation. The northern states refused to allow the South to leave the union, and in 1860 the American Civil War broke out. After a bitter struggle, which lasted four years, the North won.

The British government had not been on good terms with the United States, and during the Civil War trouble arose which nearly led to fighting between the two nations. When the war was over, the bad feeling continued. The British colonies in North America knew that they would be the first to suffer if fighting began. They were too weak to defend themselves;

united, they would be much stronger. And if railways were built to join them together, it would be easier to move troops.

There were, then, good reasons why the British colonies of North America should come together at this time. Even so, union might still not have come about had it not been for the wisdom and foresight of leading men. One of the leaders who did as much to bring about union as anyone else was John A. Macdonald.

### JOHN A. MACDONALD AND CONFEDERATION

When a Scottish family named Macdonald came to Upper Canada in 1820, the colony was still covered with dense forests. Even in towns such as Kingston, where the Macdonalds settled, people were too busy trying to make a living in their hard surroundings to give much time to schooling. So it was that young John A. Macdonald, who was still a small boy when his family came to Canada from Scotland, went to school for only five years. Afterwards, Macdonald told his friends that if he had had more education he might have become a writer. But however successful he might have been as an author, it was very fortunate for Canada that he chose a different career.

When he was fifteen years old, Macdonald left school and went to work in a lawyer's office in Kingston. In a few years he had learned enough to open his own law-office. The people of Kingston thought so well of this young Scottish Canadian that in 1844 they elected him to be their representative in the assembly of Canada.

At first, Macdonald did not have much to say during the meetings of the assembly, where the representatives from the two Canadas met to make laws. But whenever he did rise to speak, everybody listened. They liked him, and they liked what he said. In 1847, the Tory party asked him to become a member of the

THE MACDONALD HOME, ADOLPHUSTOWN

cabinet. Shortly afterwards, Macdonald's party was defeated in the elections, and the cabinet had to resign because the opposing party now had the larger number of members in the assembly. However, seven years later the Tories were again successful. In 1857, John A. Macdonald was chosen to lead the government. Associated with him was a leading French Canadian—George Etienne Cartier.

Macdonald and Cartier found it very difficult to carry on the government. They had just a few more supporters in the assembly than the opposing party. They never knew when the voting would go against them. Several times the rival party tried to carry on the government, only to be defeated in its turn. Elections were held, but neither party could win a clear victory. Many people began to feel that the union of the two provinces was not working out, and that some other solution must be found.

Just at this time the Canadian leaders heard that Nova Scotia, New Brunswick, and Prince Edward Island were going to have a meeting to talk about a union of the Maritime colonies. When the Canadians asked if they might attend the meeting, too, they were given a friendly invitation. On September 2, 1864, delegates from the four provinces met in Charlottetown,, Prince Edward Island. The leader of the Canadian delegates was John A. Macdonald.

For a week the delegates talked together. When John A. Macdonald rose to speak he said that the British colonies had carried on separately for long enough. It was high time, he said, that they began to work together as one country. At last the delegates decided that they might be able to solve their problems by a union of all the British colonies in North America. They arranged to meet again in Quebec early in October.

Among the leaders who assembled at Quebec were outstanding men from every province. There was Charles Tupper of Nova Scotia, and Leonard Tilley of New Brunswick. George Brown, from Canada West, was a bitter political enemy of Macdonald's. Elowever, the rivals had agreed to put aside their quarrel and to work together to achieve union. George Etienne Cartier came from Canada East, as did Alexander T. Galt, and D'Arcy McGee. All these men played important parts in bringing about the union of the provinces. But it was Macdonald, with his wonderful skill in getting people to do what he wanted, who kept them working together until an understanding was reached.

GEORGE BROWN

GEORGE ÉTIENNE CARTIER

Their agreements were summed up in what were known as the "Seventy-Two Resolutions".

Months went by, and it began to look as though most of the provinces had changed their minds about union. But the government of the Canadas continued to favour the idea, and after a while the governments of New Brunswick and Nova Scotia said they were willing to go ahead, too. One of the conditions they insisted upon, however, was the completion of the Intercolonial Railway to link their provinces with the Canadas.

Delegates from these four provinces, then, met in London, England, to settle the final details with the British government. For it was the British government, of course, that had to pass any law changing the government of the colonies.

In London, John A. Macdonald took a leading part in preparing the famous law that was to bring about "confederation", which is the name given to the new union of the provinces.

### THE LAW THAT MADE A NATION

In 1867 (that was in Great-Grandfather's time), the British North America Act became law. This Act told how the people of the new Dominion were to be governed, what kinds of laws could be passed by the provinces, what kinds of laws could be passed by the new central government at Ottawa, and how the law-makers were to be chosen. It is the most important single law in Canadian history.

The Act said that the Dominion of Canada was to include the provinces of New Brunswick, Nova Scotia, Ontario, and Quebec. But the law-makers who passed it expected that the new confederation of provinces would grow, and so the Act said that other provinces could be added to the union later. One by one, other provinces did join the confederation, until the Dominion stretched unbroken from Newfoundland to British Columbia.

What did the British North America Act say about how the people of the Dominion of Canada were to govern themselves? It said that laws were to be made in the same way as in Great Britain. The people were to elect their own lawmakers, and when the king's representative signed the bills they passed, the bills were to become law.

But there was to be an important difference between the government of Canada and the government of the Old Country. In Great Britain, one parliament made laws for the whole country. In Canada, the people were to elect two different groups of law-makers. For there was to be a separate government for each province, as well as a government at Ottawa for the whole of Canada. And the king was to have his representative—called a lieutenant-governor—in each province, as well as his governor general in Ottawa. The Act ruled that the government in each province could make all the laws for its people about certain matters, and that the government in Ottawa could pass laws for Canada about other matters.

The Act then went on to say what kinds of laws the provincial governments might pass, and what kinds of laws the Dominion, or *federal* government might pass. For example, the provincial governments were to make laws about schools, about property, and the setting up of local, or *municipal*, governments. These are only a few of the matters which the British North America Act placed in the hands of the provinces.

The Act said that, for the most part, all other laws were to be passed by the Dominion government at Ottawa. This central government, for example, makes all laws about customs duties on goods brought into Canada, the armed forces of the Dominion, the Post Office, and so on.

The parliament at Ottawa has two Houses—a House or Commons and a Senate. In the House of Commons sit the lawmakers elected by the people. This is the most important part of the machinery of government. The members of the Senate are appointed by the government, and ordinarily hold office for life. For a bill to become law, it must be passed by both Houses and then signed by the governor general.

The provinces carry on the business of law-making with much the same kind of machinery as the federal government at Ottawa. However, nearly all the provinces have only one House. Like the House of Commons, this is made up of lawmakers elected by the people, and is known as a legislature. Each legislature meets in the capital city of its own province. Every boy or girl who has the opportunity should visit the provincial legislature while it is in "session".

The British North America Act became law on July 1, 1867. The Dominion of Canada had been born. And the first leader, or "prime minister", of the government of the new nation was none other than Sir John A. Macdonald. Ever since then, the first of July has been a public holiday across Canada. It is our country's national birthday.

## "DOMINION FROM SEA TO SEA"

WHY did the Fathers of Confederation call Canada a "Dominion"? It is said that the name was taken from the verse in the Bible: *He shall have dominion also from sea to sea.* One of the chief hopes of the founders of our nation was that Canada would expand westward until it stretched from sea to sea.

In 1867, the great lonely land that lay between the Great Lakes and the Rocky Mountains was still ruled by the Hudson's

Bay Company. The Company now owned even the Red River Colony, which it had bought from the heirs of Lord Selkirk. This was the only part of the North-West to which any number of settlers had come. Port Carry, which later grew into the city of Winnipeg, was the chief Hudson's Bay Company post in that part of the country.

Of the 12,000 people who lived along the banks of the Red River in 1867, the greater number were Metis—the children and grandchildren of French traders who had married Indians. A much smaller number were descended from the Selkirk pioneers, and some others were traders of the Hudson's Bay Company. A very few "Canadians" (that is, people who had been born in Canada East or Canada West) had come to live in the colony. It is important to remember that most of the people of the Red River were not Canadians, although they were British subjects. There were no roads or railways to join them to Canada. Their trade went up and down the Red River between their settlements and the United States to the south, or by way of the ports on Hudson Bay to England.

The people of the Red River were happy with their way of life—trading in furs, hunting the buffalo, and doing enough farming to feed themselves and their families. But their country was too rich and too fertile to remain thinly settled much longer.

Even before confederation, plans were being made to include this territory in Canada. Shortly after confederation, arrangements were made to buy out the Hudson's Bay Company.

The Company was to be paid a large sum of money and granted a great deal of new land in the West. The day set for Canada to take over the Red River Colony and the North-West was December 1, 1869.

But nobody had asked the people of the Red River if they wanted to become Canadians. Nobody had told them what was to happen to them now. They had, however, seen Canadian surveyors at work, measuring the land. And these surveyors were marking out the land in squares! The farms of the Metis were laid out in long, narrow strips running back from the river's edge, like those of their forefathers in French Canada. Were these farms going to be taken from them? No one had told them. The Metis decided to take matters into their own hands.

One day Canadian surveyors arrived upon the farm of a Metis, with their steel measuring chain. Suddenly a band of eighteen young Metis appeared. They had no weapons, and they did not hurt the surveyors. But they stood on the steel chain so that the surveyors could not go on with their work of measuring.

The leader of these Metis was Louis Riel.

Louis was the grandson of the first white woman who lived in western Canada. His father was a trader whose parents were French and Indian. Louis was a very clever boy, and had been sent by Bishop Tache to be educated in far-away Montreal. He might have become a priest, but decided instead to return to the West. Now the Metis felt he was just the leader they needed. But although Riel was clever, he was also hasty and rash.

The Metis soon learned that a lieutenant-governor, appointed by the Dominion of Canada, was on his way to the Red River by way of the United States. They met him at the border and refused to let him step inside their territory. Next they occupied Fort Garry and set up a government of their own, with Riel as president. Of course, they had no right to do this, even though there was no other government in the country at the time. For the Hudson's Bay Company had turned the land over to the English government, which was to pass it on to Canada. Now, when word came that trouble had broken out, Canada refused to accept the territory until the trouble was settled.

In the meantime, Riel armed his followers with the weapons in Fort Garry, and made prisoners of all who seemed likely to try to stop him. A public meeting of both English- and French-speaking settlers was then called. It was agreed at this meeting that Riel should continue as president. His government lasted for eight months.

THEY STOOD ON THE STEEL CHAIN. . . .

During this time, three men were chosen to go from the Red River to Ottawa. They were to ask the Canadian government to promise that the farms of the Metis would not be taken from them, and that they might keep their own customs and religion. Further, these agents were to urge that their country be made a new province of Canada, so that it could elect its own law-makers.

But before the three men set off on their long journey, Riel made a tragic mistake. Among the prisoners he was holding at Fort Garry was a young man from Ontario, Thomas Scott. Scott

had refused to admit that Riel had any right at all to set up a government. He annoyed his captors so much that Riel—who was a hot-tempered man, too—had him put on trial, sentenced, and shot. This led to the downfall of Louis Riel.

The news that Scott had been shot by the order of Riel made the people of Canada very angry. Plans were laid to send soldiers into the West. However, the Canadian government now did what it should have done long before. It listened to what the agents of Riel had to say, and really considered the wishes of the people of the colony. In the end, most of the demands of the colonists were met. On May 3, 1870, a law was passed making their colony a province. It was called Manitoba.

To make sure there would be no further disturbances, a force set out from Upper Canada for the North-West three days after the law was passed. The soldiers had a long and toilsome journey. First they had to travel by boats to the western end of

Lake Superior. Then they crossed overland to Fort Garry since, being British soldiers, they were not allowed to travel by way of the United States. It was nearly the end of August when the troops arrived at Fort Garry.

When Riel learned that the approaching soldiers were going to arrest him for the death of Scott, he slipped out of the fort and fled south across the American border. The fort was occupied without any fighting.

The lands beyond the western borders of the new province of Manitoba were called the North-West Territories, and a governor and council were chosen by the Canadian government to rule them. The new Dominion had reached the Rocky Mountains.

## TWO NEW PROVINCES

When the gold rush in British Columbia was over, many of the miners left the country. The number of people living in British Columbia grew much smaller, and the colony still owed a great deal of money which it had borrowed when fortunes were being found. Because the colony could not carry on by itself, it had to decide between joining the United States and joining Canada. In 1871, British Columbia made up its mind to become a province of Canada. The Canadian prime minister, Sir John A. Macdonald, promised that within ten years a railway would be built from eastern Canada to the Pacific coast.

Far to the east, the colony of Prince Edward Island was also finding it difficult to carry on. Here again, railways were a problem. The colony had built the railways it needed, but was finding the cost too heavy. Another serious problem in Prince Edward Island was that most of the land was owned by wealthy people in Great Britain, to whom it had been granted by the king more than one hundred years earlier. Settlers had never been able to buy their land outright, but always had to pay rent to the owners in England. The Dominion of Canada now promised to help the Island with its railway debts, to guarantee ferry and railway connections with the mainland, and to purchase the land from the distant owners so that it could be re-sold on fair terms to the people of the Island. Then, in 1873, Prince Edward Island became the seventh Canadian province.

The Canadian coat-of-arms carries the motto *A Mari usque ad Mare*. These Latin words mean "From Sea even to Sea". The hopes of the founders of our nation had been fulfilled.

## "SCARLET AND GOLD"

ALTHOUGH the prairies became part of Canada in 1869, it was many years before white men settled there in large numbers. In the meantime the Indians still roamed the wide plains, along with their half-white cousins, the Metis.

The Indians of the plains lived in one of the best farming countries of the world, but they did no farming themselves. Instead, they depended on the buffalo for food as well as clothing. When the early white traders arrived, the Indians traded their furs for the white man's goods—metal knives, axes, and even guns to use instead of bows and arrows while hunting.

Of course, the Indians liked best to trade with those white men who gave them what they most wanted. Now there was one thing which many of the Indians wanted very much, even though it did them a great deal of harm. That was the white man's "fire-water", or whisky. When the Indians drank whisky, they became very dangerous. Often, after they had been drinking whisky, they would begin to fight with one another, and sometimes they were badly hurt or even killed. To-day it is against the law for any of the Indians living on reservations in Canada to buy whisky. It was against the law in the early days of the Canadian North-West, too, but then there was nobody to see

that the law was obeyed. Most of the whisky was being smuggled north across the border between Canada and the United States.

In order to stop the whisky-smuggling and to take care of the Indians, the Canadian government decided to send a force of mounted police into the North-West Territories. This was done in 1873, just six years after confederation, while Sir John A. Macdonald was prime minister. At first there were only three hundred men in the new police force. This was certainly a small number of men to patrol an area as vast as the North-West Territories. But from the very beginning, the North-West Mounted Police did wonderful work. Because the Indians had so much respect for the red-coated British soldier, a bright red coat was chosen as part of the "Mountie" uniform. As one Indian said, "We know that the soldiers of our great mother [Queen Victoria] wear red coats, and are our friends."

By the next summer, 1874, the new force had finished its training in the East, and was ready to be sent into the North-West Territories. The railway had not yet been built north of the Great Lakes, so part of the little band of Mounties was moved by train through the United States to a place on the Red River about two hundred miles south of Winnipeg. Still far inside American territory, the Mounties now set out overland for Fort McLeod, almost a thousand miles away. Here, in the heart of the North-West Territories, they built a headquarters, and set about their work of keeping law and order.

The North-West Mounted Police did more than bring law and order to the Territories, however. Indians and white men alike quickly learned that the riders in the scarlet coats were their friends. One day, a lone Mountie discovered a prairie fire spreading towards the home of a settler. The settler's wife and children had fled from their home, but the flames were catching up with them. Setting spurs to his horse, the brave Mountie rode to them through the blazing prairie grass and carried them to safety.

With the coming of the white man, the buffalo began to disappear from the western plains. The Indian tribes of the prairies found it harder and harder to live. Some of them began to steal cattle from the settlers, and to break the law in other ways. The Mounties, however, quickly brought the wrongdoers to justice. They also persuaded the Indians to move into the reserves which the Canadian government now set aside for them. In the United States, the Indians refused to give up their old ways of life without a bitter struggle. But in Canada, thanks to the North-West Mounted Police, the change took place much more peacefully. However, when the Metis rose again in the West, some of the Indians did join the trouble-makers.

## THE NORTH-WEST REBELLION

On a bright June day in 1884, four men rode southward from the North-West Territories. The fringed hunting-shirts and broad-brimmed hats of the riders showed that they were plainsmen; their faces and speech showed they were Metis—fearless riders, cunning buffalo-hunters, and deadly shots with the rifles which they carried across their saddles. The tallest and strongest was Gabriel Dumont, a famous hunter. He and his comrades talked little as they rode along, for theirs was a serious errand.

They had been sent to ask Louis Riel to come back to Canada. During the ten years since the rebellion in the Red River, Riel had been living in the United States. The new government of Manitoba would not allow him to return. But his friends, the Metis, had not forgotten him. Indeed, they had twice elected him to represent them in the parliament at Ottawa, although he was, of course, unable to do so. They now begged him to come back to Canada, for they needed his help.

"You are the most popular man in the country, and you absolutely must come," read the letter Dumont carried. The four men told Riel that the Metis who had left Manitoba to take up new farms farther west were having trouble again with the Canadian government. Once again surveyors were beginning to mark out the prairies in squares, and the Metis feared they would lose their long farms along the Saskatchewan River. The buffalo were becoming scarce as the railway and settlement advanced westward. Soon the Metis would be unable to make a living by hunting, and would have only their farms to provide for their needs. They had waited and waited for papers from the government which would prove that their new farms belonged to them, but the papers had not come.

When Riel heard this story, he decided to return to Canada right away. All that summer of 1884 and the following winter he held meetings with the Metis along the Saskatchewan River, and they grew more and more excited and angry. They drew up a list of complaints and sent it to Ottawa. No attention was paid to it. In March, Riel formed a government of his own at Batoche, and made Dumont the head of his "army". He ordered the Mounted Police at the nearest post, Fort Carlton, to surrender. They refused. In a few days the second Riel Rebellion had begun.

In addition to rousing the Metis, Riel had sent runners to the Indians, who had been living peacefully on their reserves, looked after by the Mounties. Eight years earlier, Crowfoot, the great chief of the Blackfoot Indians, had signed a treaty with the white men. At that time he said, "The Mounted Police have protected us as the feathers of the bird protect it from the frosts of winter." The Blackfoot Indians now remained faithful to their treaty, but Riel was able to persuade some Crees and Assiniboines, led by Chief Poundmaker and Chief Big Bear, to rise against the whites.

Fighting first took place near Duck Lake, where the Metis defeated a force of Mounties sent from Fort Carlton. Then some

Crees, under Big Bear, attacked Frog Lake village, where they killed several people and took others prisoner. At Battleford, the white settlers fled into the stockade, frightened by the Indians under Poundmaker.

All Canada was aroused by the danger. Was our western country, which had seen no terrible Indian wars like those in the western United States, to have one at last? Troops were quickly

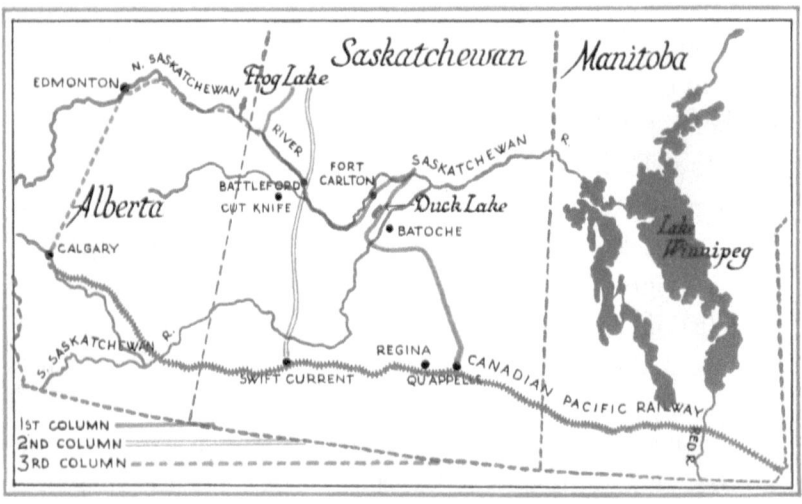

gathered together in Manitoba and the East, and were sent into the North-West on the new Canadian Pacific Railway. General Middleton commanded all the forces.

From the railway three columns were sent north. The first went through Qu'Appelle towards Batoche to fight Riel. The second set out from Swift Current to Battleford to relieve the settlers and fight Poundmaker. The third marched from Calgary to Edmonton to meet Big Bear.

At Batoche, the Metis held off the troops for a time, but at length they were defeated by General Middleton. After the battle, Riel was taken prisoner, but Dumont escaped to the United States.

The soldiers who advanced from Swift Current reached Battleford and went on to attack Poundmaker near Cut Knife. They did not succeed in driving the Indians from their position, but when General Middleton's troops came on from Batoche, Poundmaker surrendered.

The third column of soldiers reached Edmonton from Calgary, and then turned east along the North Saskatchewan River. It met Big Bear and scattered his band of Indians. The captive women and children from Frog Lake were set free, quite unhurt. Later, Big Bear himself was captured by the Mounties.

Riel was taken to Regina, and put on trial for high treason. It was argued in his defence that he had only been trying to help his people, and also that his strange behaviour showed he might be insane. On the other hand, he had twice led a revolt against the lawful government of the country. He was found guilty and sentenced to death. Several Indians who had murdered settlers were also hanged. Big Bear and Poundmaker were imprisoned for a time. However, their health broke down in the white man's jail, and they were pardoned by Queen Victoria.

### STEEL OF EMPIRE

When Sir John A. Macdonald promised the new province of British Columbia in 1871 that a railway would be built from eastern Canada within the next ten years, many people said that the promise was impossible to keep, and that the entire scheme was ridiculous. How could Canada, a poor country with only four million people, build a railway nearly two thousand miles long? Indeed, was it even possible to build a railway through the thousand miles of rocks, swamps, lakes, and rivers which lay between Ottawa and Winnipeg? Or through the six or seven hundred miles of mountains beyond the prairies?

No one really could answer these questions, not even Sir John A. Macdonald. But Sir John did fear that Canada would never become a great nation, and even that confederation might not last, unless a band of steel were built to bind the scattered territories together. The railway had to be built, and so it was built!

Macdonald was unable to keep his promise to build the railway within ten years, for in 1873 his government was defeated and he ceased to be prime minister of the Dominion. Charges were made that Sir John's party had accepted large sums of money for election expenses from the wealthy men to whom the contract for building the railway had been given. The opposition party claimed that Sir John had been "bribed" to give the contract, and although Macdonald denied this, the scandal was so great that he had to resign. After the "Pacific Scandal" had driven Macdonald from office, very little progress was made in the building of the railroad.

The people of British Columbia were much angered by the delay, and began to talk of leaving confederation and joining the United States. When the governor general, Lord Dufferin, visited their province, they built an archway on which appeared in big letters the word SEPARATION. Instead of becoming angry, the governor general cleverly suggested the word should be changed to REPARATION. By this, he meant that the government of Canada would make up for past faults by going ahead with the building of the railway.

The Tories had won the election of 1878, and Sir John A. Macdonald had become prime minister again. In 1880, he heard about a group of business men in Montreal who had made a great deal of money by building railways in the United States. One of these men was Donald Smith, who later became Lord Strathcona. Another was George Stephen, later to become Lord Mount Stephen. Sir John now persuaded these men to form a

LORD DUFFERIN IN VICTORIA, B.C.

company to build the railway. With their own money, money they borrowed, and twenty-five million dollars from the Canadian government, they began to build the Canadian Pacific Railway. In addition, the government granted them twenty-five million acres of land and turned over to them some railway lines it had already built.

Even with all this help, the company found it very hard at times to pay all its debts. Great bridges had to be thrown across rivers; vast swamps had to be filled with rocks and earth; and roadbeds had to be hacked out of the sides of mountains. This all cost a great deal of money. Sometimes Stephen and Smith did not know where to turn for another dollar to pay the labourers and to buy supplies. At last, when they could borrow no more from the banks, Macdonald persuaded parliament to vote enough money to save the railway.

The traveller who makes the railway journey to-day from Ottawa to Winnipeg can see how difficult it must have been to build this part of the railway. The ground is so swampy that it was extremely hard to make it firm enough to bear the weight of the trains. Sometimes roadbed, ties, rails and all, sank into the boggy land. New rails were laid, but they, too, sank into the marsh. At one place, underneath the line on which trains run to-day, six sets of rails are buried!

We must remember, too, that until this first railway came there were no settlements in the wilderness. Everything needed to build the railway and to supply the workers had to be brought in. The labourers carried their own "town" with them. And as the railway advanced, section hands had to be hired to inspect and keep in repair the line already built.

When the road of steel reached the prairies, the work went faster. On the flat plains very little work was needed to make a roadbed on which the ties could be laid. But there were other problems. Sometimes the Mounted Police had to protect the railway workers from angry Indians.

Once Chief Pie-a-pot and his band camped on the line marked out for the railway, and refused to move their tents. Two Mounties were sent to make them break camp. When the Mounties ordered the Chief to take away his tents, the Indians laughed heartily. What could two policemen do against so many Indians? One of the Mounties took out his watch and gave the Indians just fifteen minutes to move. Then the two policemen waited a quarter of an hour while the Indians joked and jeered. At the end of the time, one of the two Mounties strode into Pie-

a-pot's own tent and kicked down the centre pole, bringing it down on the Chief's head. Seeing that the Mounties could not be bluffed, Pie-a-pot gave in, and moved his tents out of the way.

Within five years of the time that building had been begun in earnest, the railway line was completed. This was actually only half the time that the government had told Stephen and Smith they might have in order to do the job. Different parts had been built at the same time, but the last gap was closed in 1885, when Donald Smith drove the "last spike" at Craigellachie, a village in the mountains of British Columbia.

The railway had cost so much that a good many Canadians were beginning to wonder if it had been a mistake. However, before the line north of Lake Superior had been completed, the North-West Rebellion broke out. The Dominion wanted to rush troops into western Canada. Rails were now laid over the ice and snow, and in a few days soldiers were beginning to arrive in the West. The speed with which the government troops were able to reach the scene of the rebellion brought it to an end very quickly. Many people now changed their minds about the wisdom of having spent so much money on the building of the railroad.

Sir John A. Macdonald's share in confederation was undoubtedly his greatest contribution to the building of Canada.

His part in the construction of the Canadian Pacific Railway was, however, nearly as important. It was his courage and determination, based on his dream of a great Canadian nation, which carried through this huge enterprise.

THE MOUNTED POLICE TO-DAY

In 1904, the title "Royal" was added to the name of the force, and it became known as the "Royal North-West Mounted Police". After World War I, this name was changed to the "Royal Canadian Mounted Police"—the name by which it is known to-day. At the same time, its headquarters was moved to Ottawa. Although some of the provinces have police of their own, the Mounties have now taken over the work of a provincial police in all the Prairie Provinces and the Maritimes. In each of these provinces they have the duty of seeing that laws passed by the provincial legislature are obeyed. There is a large training centre at Regina, and another at Rockcliffe, near Ottawa. New members are signed on for five years. Before going on duty they are given drill, trained in wrestling, boxing, and jiu jitsu, and given lessons on police duties.

In addition to special duties in the Prairie Provinces and the Maritimes, the R.C.M.P. must see that the laws of Canada are obeyed across the whole of the Dominion. Here are some of the Mounties' duties to-day: They enforce Canada's laws against smuggling by land, sea, and air. They protect government buildings and dockyards. They are the only police force in the Far North.

When the North-West Mounted Police was first organized, horses were the only means by which the Mounties could patrol their vast western territory. Sleds drawn by dog-teams were used

in the Far North during winter, and because northern travel conditions have not changed, dog-teams are still used by the Mounties there to-day. However, much less patrolling is done on horseback now than sixty years ago. Indeed, the force now has only a little over one hundred saddle horses altogether, although it owns more than seven hundred and fifty motorcycles and automobiles.

During World War II, the R.C.M.P. was given still more duties to perform. It sent a company of nearly two hundred men overseas to act as army police, and many other Mounties saw active service as well. Because of its many new duties during war-time, more and more men were taken on until there were over six thousand members in the force. Some of these have been discharged since the end of the war, but the force still has more than four thousand men.

The motto of the Royal Canadian Amounted Police is *Maintiens le droit*. These three French words, when translated into English, mean Maintain the right". But ever since the force was first formed in 1873, it has had such a fine record for keeping law and order that the motto we usually hear is "the Mountie always gets his man."

## THE GROWTH OF THE WEST

MOST of the towns and villages of eastern Canada had their beginnings before the first train whistle was heard in North America. But full-scale settlement of the Canadian West had to wait for the coming of the railway.

The building of the railway into western Canada made it possible for settlers to reach new homes without making long, wearisome journeys by ox-cart. More important still, the railway made it possible for them to ship their grain and cattle to distant markets. At first, the pioneers in the Canadian West had grown only enough food to support themselves and their families. Now they were able to make a "business" of farming, for they were able to offer their crops for sale to the whole world.

We must remember that the story of the settling of the Canadian West is just a part of the story of the settling of western North America. For the western United States began to fill with newcomers first, and it was not until the best lands south of the

boundary had been pretty well taken up that settlement began to spread through what are now Canada's Prairie Provinces. The Canadian Pacific Railway reached as far as Calgary by 1883, but another ten years passed before large numbers of immigrants began to flock into the lands that had been thus opened up.

Beginning in 1896, however, the Canadian government made great efforts to attract settlers to the western territories. Agents were sent across the ocean, and south into the United States as well, to tell people about the rich farming lands that were waiting for settlement. Advertisements were printed in the newspapers of these other countries, and large posters began to appear in their cities and towns, repeating over and over again the Canadian government's invitation to come and build homes in Canada. The railway, too, helped in this drive to find new Canadians. For it hoped to sell the twenty-five million acres of land which it had been given by the Canadian government. Moreover, the more people that came to Canada, the more business there would be for the railways.

Many of the newcomers bought their farms from the C.P.R., or from other railway companies which were founded later. Others bought their lands from "land companies", which bought and sold farms for profit. Many settlers, however, obtained free farming land from the government under the "'homestead" system. By paying a fee of ten dollars, a "homesteader" might be allotted 160 acres of land; he then had to live on it for two months each year and cultivate at least five acres. Three years after "filing his claim", the farm became his, to do with as he wished!

Lands in the North-West Territories were marked out into square townships, which measured six miles on each side. These townships were then divided into 36 *sections*. Each section was one square mile, and therefore contained 640 acres. The 160-acre homesteads were thus "quarter-sections".

Farmers in western Canada were faced by many problems. "Late springs" and "early autumns" meant short growing seasons, and it was necessary to develop new kinds of wheat and other crops that would ripen quickly. Seasons of drought remained a constant dread, and dry years (such as those that occurred in western Canada during the 1930's) brought ruin to many. However, there have been many good years with "bumper" crops, and besides, farmers have learned to make a science of growing grain. Drought conditions have been fought in some areas by irrigation; wheat rust and other plant diseases have been met by the invention of new crop varieties which are less likely to be attacked.

Between 1896 and 1913, three million newcomers arrived in Canada, and most of them settled in the West. Nearly one million of these new Canadians came from the United States. Almost a million more came from eastern and southern Europe, and few of this last group could speak English when they arrived. But they were hard-working folk, and many of them were experienced farmers.

The story which follows is not the story of any one pioneer, but it could be the story of many of the pioneers who came to Canada from Europe at this time.

## WESTERN PIONEER

My name is Peter Polznay, and I am twelve years old. I have lived all my life on the farm in Saskatchewan to which Grandfather came with his parents, when he was twelve years old.

Grandfather was a real western pioneer. He can remember when there were no roads—only trails winding over the fields and around the poplar bluffs. He can remember when there was no school here at all; he was a young man before he learned to read and write English.

Grandfather can remember even farther back than that. He has often told me about a city beside a river in the middle of Europe. He can remember big factories roaring all night, and his own father going out with his lunch-pail to work. He says that one day his father came home, much excited, and talked with his mother far into the night. On many nights following they talked. Then they told Grandfather it was all decided—the family was going to emigrate to Canada.

At first Grandfather was not much pleased. He did not know where Canada was, to begin with, and he did not like

to leave his friends at school. But he was told that in Canada they would live on a big farm, and if they all worked hard they would have plenty of food to eat and clothes to wear. Times had been hard in the city, and Grandfather agreed that it would be fine always to have enough to eat, and to have warm clothes for the cold weather.

"And then, you know," his parents had told him, "in Canada, everyone is free. There are the same laws for rich and poor." Grandfather says he was not much interested then in the laws. But he had become very well satisfied to go to Canada, and began to be much excited about the journey.

Poor Grandfather! He doesn't remember much about coming to Canada except that he was terribly tired and mixed up most of the time, and that he was seasick on the ship crossing the Atlantic Ocean. Father often says that is why he never went back to visit the Old Land, as some of our neighbours did.

But Grandfather only smiles at this, and says, "It is better not to go back. Besides, it was not all happiness there. And this is my country now."

It certainly is my grandfather's country now. Why, he knows just about everybody for miles around, and everybody knows him! Father says some of our neighbours wouldn't buy a cow without asking Grandfather first, or cut their grain until Grandfather Polznay said it was ready for harvesting.

Grandfather says he was very much disappointed at the first western Indian he saw. I suppose he thought, the way people do in countries where there are no Indians, that they would be dressed in paint and feathers. Until he looked at their dark faces, the stout Indian squaws in their shawls and bright head kerchiefs did not seem very different to Grandfather from the country people in the Old Land. The Indian men were tall and slim. Their long, black hair was braided in two pigtails, hanging down on each side of their faces. On their heads were bright red or green or pink silk kerchiefs like the squaws', and the "braves" generally wore an old felt hat as well. Their jackets were of buckskin, embroidered with beads—thousands of tiny little beads in different colours, sewn on by the patient squaws.

I wish Indians dressed like that now. The ones I see on the Reservation just wear overalls or blue serge suits or dresses like everybody else.

But Grandfather was looking for war-paint and feathers, and was much surprised when someone told him, shortly after he had got off the train, that the people sitting on the edge of the platform were Cree Indians. And while Grandfather stared at them, the train puffed away from the little station, and left him and his parents, and about a dozen other families from the same part of Europe, standing with their baggage around them on the platform. They knew scarcely one word of the language of their new country.

Luckily a man had been sent with them from Winnipeg who could speak their tongue and English as well. He helped

them to find farms and to buy the implements and supplies they needed. Grandfather's family had worked on a farm in Europe. When they picked out the farm they wanted now, the advisor told them they had chosen well. Our own home to-day is on that piece of land.

Of course, there was no home on it when Grandfather's family came here. It had a little creek, with willow bushes growing on each bank, and patches of woods, with slender trees with greenish-white trunks and small rounded leaves that shook in the breeze. In the West, we call these patches of woods "poplar bluffs". There were saskatoon bushes, which bore white blossoms in May and clusters of small dark fruits like blueberries in July. There were wild strawberries, chokecherries, raspberries, and gooseberries, just as there are now.

Grandfather's parents bought a team of oxen and a plough. First of all they ploughed a wide strip of land around the place where they planned to build their home. This was a fire-guard. In those days grass fires were very common, and many settlers were "burned out"—their homes and property destroyed by fires which started many miles away. At first Grandfather's family used a tent to live in. Since they had arrived in the early spring, they planted seeds right away—vegetables and some wheat and oats. They used oxen instead of horses, for the oxen were cheaper to

buy, and ate only hay, which grew wild, while horses required oats, which had to be planted and harvested.

Once the planting was done, they began to build a cabin as a shelter for the winter. All the neighbouring families worked together on each of their houses in turn. Since there were trees in this part of the country, the family built a log house, using the largest tree-trunks they could find—about eight or nine inches through—and filling in the chinks with mud. The roof was made of poles laid close together, with large pieces of sod, with the grass still on it, laid on top. The windows they had brought with them to the homestead, glass and all.

In an old picture album we still have a picture of this house. Great-Grandfather, in overalls and a wide straw hat, and Great-Grandmother, wearing her apron, are in the doorway. Grandfather, just about as tall as I am now, is standing by them, with a puppy in his arms. Some wild flowers are growing out of the roof!

I wish I had that cabin to play in now. It was used as a chicken-house when Father was a boy, but was torn down when the big barn was built.

For a long time, Grandfather's family was very poor. Some years the crops did not get enough rain, and in other years the frost came early and ruined the grain before it was ripe. And at first the farm was such a long distance from the railway that it was hard to sell the grain which they did harvest.

But Grandfather's parents gradually learned more about farming in western Canada, and began to get better crops. And at last the railway built a branch line which passed just half a mile from the farm. A station was built, with grain elevators near by. Alongside the station was built a general store, and then a blacksmith shop, and then a post-office, and then an implement shed, and then a few houses for the people who worked in the village, and then a little hotel, a school, and a church—and so in just a year or two sprang up a small town where people could visit and buy things and sell their butter and eggs.

Grandfather went to the school in that village. He was the oldest boy in the school, which made him feel shy, but he worked hard and learned very fast. My father went to that school, too. Now we have a big brick school, with over a hundred pupils, right on the highway near the farm. Grandfather teases me and says going to school is fun now. I suppose it is easier than when he was a boy.

Once when I asked in the Post Office for Grandfather's mail, a stranger beside me said, "Polznay? What kind of name is that? Polish? Hungarian? Ruthenian?"

Mr. Anderson, the Postmaster, said, "Well, friend, I don't rightly know. There've been Polznays in this district as long as there *was* a district, and probably before that. I guess it's just an old Canadian name."

## ALBERTA AND SASKATCHEWAN BECOME PROVINCES

By 1905 so many people had settled in the West that the Canadian government decided to make two new provinces in the North-West Territories. They were called Alberta and Saskatchewan. The former had its capital at Edmonton, and the latter at Regina. In 1912, the boundaries of Manitoba were extended north to the sixtieth parallel and the shores of Hudson Bay.

The three Prairie Provinces, as they were called, rapidly became world-famous for the wheat they grew. On the farms, in the towns, in the schools and universities, in the legislatures, mingled the children of people who had come to western Canada from the United States, from eastern Canada, from the British Isles, and from the continent of Europe.

And as newcomers continue to arrive from Europe to make their homes in Canada, it is the duty of those who live here to make them welcome, show them our ways, and teach them our language. For, as we read earlier in this book, we are all newcomers here. Some of us came early, and others late—that is the only difference.

CANADA'S FIRST PARLIAMENT BUILDINGS

## "GROWING UP"

AFTER his victory in the elections of 1878, Sir John A. Macdonald remained prime minister of Canada for the rest of his days. Under his leadership the young Dominion had made great progress. The Canadian Pacific Railway had been built, the North-West Mounted Police had been formed, and new provinces and new territories had been added to the confederation.

The Dominion was gaining fuller control of its own affairs, but ties with the mother country remained close. As Sir John said: "We are content; we have prospered under the flag of England. I say that it would bring ruin and misfortune, any separation from the United Kingdom."

The rallying cry of Macdonald's followers in the 1891 election was "The old man, the old flag, the old policy." The "old man" won, but it was Sir John's last election. Only a few weeks afterwards, he died "in harness". There was now no one of his political ability in the Conservative party, as the Tory party had come to be known. (The Reform party, or "Grits", were now called "Liberals".)

Among the Liberals, however, was a man who, while very different in character and personality from Sir John, also had the power to lead others, and to win the support of the people. In 1896 the Conservatives were defeated for the first time in nearly twenty years, and a great Liberal leader became prime minister of Canada.

### QUEEN VICTORIA'S DIAMOND JUBILEE

When Queen Victoria came to the throne of England in 1837, the Dominion of Canada had not yet been thought of. That was the year of the rebellions in Upper and Lower Canada. Thirty years later, Queen Victoria signed the British North America Act, which created the new nation.

Now another thirty years had rolled by. Victoria still was Queen of England. Great plans were made to celebrate the fact that she had reigned for sixty years. The celebration was known as Queen Victoria's Diamond Jubilee. Although people rejoiced all over the British Empire, the greatest merry-making of all took place in the city of London.

Leaders from all over the world were in London to take part in honouring Queen Victoria. Every British colony had sent at least one, and many had sent soldiers as well to join in a big parade through the streets of the city. That morning, the Queen sent this message to her subjects: "From my heart I thank my beloved people—may God bless them!"

The parade was a long one, and even the great leaders from other countries seemed unimportant that day because there were so many of them all together at the same time! One part of the parade was made up of Canadians. The Royal North-West Mounted Police were there in their bright scarlet coats, and the Royal Canadian Highlanders strode along in their bearskins and kilts.

But who was this tall figure at the head of the Canadians—this stately, dignified man with the fine brow and the plume of white hair? Apart from Queen Victoria herself, he caused more excitement among the crowds of onlookers than did anyone else. It was the new prime minister of the Dominion of Canada—Wilfrid Laurier. The very day before the parade, he had been made a knight by the Queen. Now people were crying, "Sir Wilfrid! Three cheers for Sir Wilfrid!"

Most of the people who were watching the parade were Londoners. Why were they giving such a rousing welcome to this leader from the Dominion of Canada? Of course, there were many reasons. Canada had been the first self-governing Dominion in the British Empire. And although Sir Wilfrid had been its prime minister for only one year, he was known to everyone as an able and clever leader. Strangely enough, what most pleased these Englishmen in the streets of London was the fact that Sir Wilfrid Laurier's ancestors were French!

Sir Wilfrid Laurier's earliest Canadian ancestor had gone out to Canada not from England, but from France. Sir Wilfrid's great-great grandparents had been living in Canada before the British had captured it from the French. Once French and English had fought each other for possession of Canada, and more than once French-speaking and English-speaking Canadians had quarrelled bitterly. But all that was now forgotten. For many years, Canada—as part of Queen Victoria's overseas empire—had been allowed to govern itself. It made those Englishmen in London in 1897 happy to think that the Canadian people had now chosen a French Canadian to be their prime minister, and that he was there to represent the Dominion at Queen Victoria's Diamond Jubilee.

The celebrations went on for many days. The leaders of Great Britain's overseas possessions were often called upon to make speeches, but none was listened to more closely than Sir

Wilfrid Laurier. One of the London newspapers said: "For the first time... a politician of our New World has been recognized as the equal of the great men of the Old Country."

Before returning to Canada, Laurier visited France, the home of his ancestors. Here again he won great popularity. Some French newspapers had not liked Sir Wilfrid's praise of Great Britain, the nation which had taken Canada from the French. Sir Wilfrid answered proudly: "We have liberty more complete than in any country in the world; liberty for our religion; liberty for our language, which is the official language as English is. What other proof of it could I give you than this? In this country, where most people are of English descent and of the Protestant religion, the last elections brought to power a man of French descent and of the Catholic religion.

"I am told that here in France there are people surprised at the attachment which I feel for the Crown of England, which I do not hide... We are faithful to the great nation (France) which gave us life; we are faithful to the great nation (Britain) which has given us liberty."

## THE "GOLDEN AGE"

The fifteen years during which the great French-Canadian leader headed the government of Canada are often called the "Golden Age of Sir Wilfrid Laurier".

Our nation was growing up. In 1891, the year that Sir John A. Macdonald died, Canada had a population of fewer than five millions. When Sir Wilfrid Laurier laid down the reins of office in 1911, over seven million people were living in Canada. Many of the newcomers settled in the young Canadian West. Industries were increasing as new inventions made it possible for men to manufacture more goods more cheaply. As the older countries turned from farming to industry, they had to buy food from overseas. And Canadian wheat was the best in the world.

With the new farm machinery, wheat could be grown on a large scale. New railways were built, and over them Canada shipped her produce to the world. Soon Canada had three lines of railways crossing the country from coast to coast, with thousands of branch lines. The building of the railways, and of the hundreds of new villages, towns, and cities, made work for many.

The farmers of the prairies needed all kinds of things, implements, building supplies, manufactured goods. Factories sprang up in southern Ontario and Quebec. People flocked to the towns and cities to work in the new industries.

In 1897 gold was discovered on the Klondike River in the Yukon, and thousands of prospectors rushed there to make their fortunes. In 1903 silver was found at Cobalt in northern Ontario. The nickel mines at Sudbury were developed. In British Columbia, the Kootenay district proved rich in minerals.

Great changes were taking place all over the world, but nowhere were the changes more rapid and striking than in Canada. Laurier proclaimed the twentieth century "Canada's century", and indeed, it seemed as if this might become true.

Although the world was busy with commerce during the "Golden Age", it did not remain at peace. The discovery of gold in South Africa had drawn many British settlers there, and trouble arose between them and the Boers, who were the descendants of the early Dutch colonists. War broke out in 1899, and the British government asked the Dominions to send soldiers. While the war did not directly concern Canada, many Canadians were anxious to take part in it. The Canadian government helped them to form regiments of volunteers that is, of men who chose to "join up" of their own free will. In the end, over seven thousand men sailed from Canada to Africa. They fought in a number of important battles and won great praise for their bravery and skill.

In 1911 the Liberal government was defeated, and Robert Borden, leader of the Conservatives, became prime minister. In 1912 and 1913 the flood of new settlers reached its peak. But the "Golden Age" was drawing to a close.

## CANADA IN WORLD WAR I

In 1914 a terrible war broke out in Europe. For years Germany had been preparing for the day when she would try to conquer the world. At last her opportunity came, and soon most of the nations of the world were drawn into the Great War, or, as it is usually called now, World War I.

The Canadian people were horrified by the actions of Germany, and decided to send soldiers to help the Allies, as the nations fighting on our side were called. Before the war ended, over four hundred thousand Canadians went overseas to fight in Europe. They fought very bravely in many battles.

In the early days of the war the Canadians took part in a famous battle near Ypres, a town in Belgium which is on a main road leading to the coast of the English Channel. The Canadians knew that if the Germans could break through here they would be able to capture seaports on the Channel, and divide the Allied armies into two. One day, strange greenish clouds swept over from the German lines towards our trenches. It was poison gas! Gas had never been used in warfare before, and none of the Allied troops had been given gas-masks. On the left of the Canadians were native troops from French Africa. When many of them were struck down from breathing in the deadly gas, the others became terrified and fled. The Germans rushed forward. The Canadians were now in a dangerous position as their left side was unprotected. Although greatly outnumbered, that night they attacked and drove the enemy back. For days the Canadians fought against heavy odds, holding the Germans until help could be sent. Afterwards, the British prime minister said that our men had "held high the honour of Canada, and saved the British army".

None of the fighting men of the Allies were more famous than Canada's airmen. They seemed to have the courage, daring, and skill needed to handle the early aircraft which were then in use. Three of Canada's brave fliers won the Victoria Cross. "Billy" Bishop shot down more enemy planes than did any other pilot on either side. Alan McLeod won the Victoria Cross when he was only eighteen years old. Colonel W. G. Barker shot down six German planes in one morning, although he was wounded in both legs and one arm.

During World War I, airplanes were very different from today. They flew much more slowly, could not climb so high in the sky, and did not have many of the instruments which help

the pilot to-day to handle his plane. Airplanes were then used mainly for flying over the enemy lines in order to observe what the ground troops were doing. Of course, the other side tried to prevent this, and air battles followed. Much depended on the skill of the pilots, as it does to-day, and each side soon had its famous "aces". Sometimes these aces had specially painted airplanes so that the enemy could recognize them. Two noted aces might fight a duel in the air, each knowing who the other was. More often, however, a group of German airmen would try to single out one Allied plane, and attack it from many directions at once.

On the day he shot down six German planes, Colonel Barker was attacked more than once by twelve or fifteen of the enemy at a time, but he was able to twist his plane about so quickly that he shot down several of the Germans instead! However, his own machine was smoking when he made a crash-landing in the Allied lines. He said afterwards: "I thought that morning I was meeting the whole of the German Air Force!" World War I lasted for four years, ending in the defeat of the Germans in 1918. More than 60,000 Canadian soldiers were killed in this war; 150,000 were wounded; and 3000 taken prisoner. More than sixty Canadians won the Victoria Cross—the highest award for valour in our Empire.

## CANADA COMES OF AGE 1919-1945

BOTH Canada and the United States were at one time part of Great Britain's colonial empire. As colonies, they were allowed to make certain kinds of laws for themselves, but the law-makers of Great Britain decided what kinds of laws they might pass. To-day, both Canada and the United States pass whatever laws they wish; they sign treaties with other countries, make their own decisions about peace and war, and run all their own affairs. We say that they are *independent* nations.

But Canada and the United States secured their independence by different means. The United States went to war with Great Britain in 1775, and not until after several years of fighting was it agreed that it should be a separate country, with the right to run all its own affairs. In Canada, on the other hand, the same important change was brought about much more slowly, and by peaceful means. No one can say exactly *when* Canada secured her independence from the mother country, but one can point to many small changes that have taken place, each of which marked another step towards nationhood.

THE LEAGUE····NEEDED THE SUPPORT OF EVERY GREAT POWER····TO SUCCEED

In 1917, during World War I, Sir Robert Borden told the British leaders that Canada should share in managing the campaign, since many thousands of Canadian soldiers were fighting in Europe side by side with the other Allies. As a result, an Imperial War Cabinet was formed, which included not only leaders of the British government, but the prime ministers of the other countries in the British Empire as well. From that moment to the end of the first world struggle, Canada and her sister Dominions shared in the control of the war. Few people questioned the right of the Dominions to have a voice in these matters, for their part in winning the war was great.

The British Dominions were not at first invited to come to the peace conference that followed World War I. But again Sir Robert Borden insisted that the Dominions had as much right as any of the other Allies to take part in it; it was not enough, he said, to let Great Britain speak for Canada, Australia, New Zealand, and South Africa. He said that each member of the empire must make its own decisions. And so it was that when the peace terms were finally settled, the representatives of the

Dominions joined the representatives of other countries of the world in signing the peace treaties.

Out of the peace conference came the League of Nations. The League was an organization of large and small world powers who believed that peace could last if problems between nations were settled by discussion in which all nations took part. Unfortunately the United States did not join the League. One of its reasons for remaining apart was that it still did not believe that it should share in the affairs of nations in other parts of the world, nor did the U.S.A. want European nations to take any greater interest in the affairs of the New World than they already did.

Canada and the other British Dominions, however, were ready to take part in the League of Nations. But at first some of the other countries of the world felt that the British Dominions should not be allowed to be separate members; they thought that this would be the same thing as giving Great Britain more votes than anyone else. But Sir Robert Borden insisted that Canada should be treated as a separate member, and in the end it was agreed. This was an important step towards nationhood for the Dominion.

It was unfortunate that the United States did not come into the League, which needed the support of every great power if it were to succeed. In the end, the League failed to keep the peace, but even the mistakes it made were useful lessons for the future. To-day we know that peace can only be kept if all the countries of the world work together, and the United States is one of the most important members in the organization that has taken the place of the League of Nations. This new body is known as the United Nations.

Canada in the early 1920's had not yet come into control of all her own affairs. Laws on certain matters still had to be passed by the British parliament, and treaties apart from agreements of the League of Nations were still handled by the British government. The Canadian leaders were anxious to see these powers given to our country, not because they resented Great Britain, but because they believed Canada had earned the right to complete self-government. Canadians were realizing, more and more strongly, that they had become a *nation*.

We must remember that the growth towards nationhood was being shared by the other members of the commonwealth, and when one Dominion changed a custom that was a sign of dependence on the mother country, it was possible for the other Dominions to ask for the same change. Canada was coming of age, and the other members of the commonwealth were coming of age, too.

It remained now for the parliament of Great Britain to put into law what was already a fact: the Dominions were still associated with one another as members of a commonwealth within the empire, but each was completely self-governing and in no way under the control of the British parliament. In 1931, the British parliament gave the Dominions complete control over their own affairs by passing an Act known as the Statute of Westminster. It is one of the important laws in the history of every Dominion in the commonwealth, for although it did not add to their freedom, it explained to the world what great freedom the nations in the commonwealth enjoyed.

Did any link remain between the Dominions? The most important bond was certainly the Crown, to whom all continued to owe allegiance, and in whose name the laws of each Dominion continued to be made. Of course, it had long before become clear that the king can govern only with the advice of his ministers, who are chosen from among elected representatives of the people. And because the king has a different set of ministers in each Dominion, each group of ministers is responsible to the people in the Dominion that elects them.

KING GEORGE VI
AND QUEEN ELIZABETH ~ SENATE CHAMBER, OTTAWA, 1939

What other links besides the Crown remain between the members of the commonwealth?

Each Dominion has copied, to some extent at least, the British machinery for making and enforcing laws. In some of the Dominions, including Canada, more than one language is spoken, but the English language is spoken in all the Dominions. Moreover, many people of each Dominion can trace their families back to the British Isles. Like members of a family, the Dominions have often met together to discuss their common problems. There is no other group of countries in the world that have as many things in common as those within our commonwealth of nations. They have acted together not only in times of peace. In the difficult days of war, too, the Dominions have taken up arms side by side.

## HOW CANADA HELPED WIN WORLD WAR II

An important announcement flashed across the Dominion from Ottawa, where the members of Canada's parliament had been hurriedly called together.

"*We do hereby declare,*" the message from Canada's lawmakers read, "*that a state of war with the German Reich... has existed in our Dominion of Canada... from the tenth day of September, 1939.*"

A tremendously important decision had been made. Most important of all, it had been made by the law-makers elected by the people of Canada.

Only a little more than a week had passed since the armies of Adolf Hitler, leader of Nazi Germany, had begun a savage attack on Poland. Since then, Great Britain and France had gone to war against Germany, because they had promised to help Poland if she were invaded.

Now our own Dominion was in the war, too. The terrible struggle which had just started was to last for six, long, bitter years.

When Canada declared war, there were less than ten thousand men in all her armed forces—army, navy, and air force. But before the victory of the Allies in 1945, more than a million Canadian men and women had gone into uniform.

Because all the land fighting took place far from Canada's shores, over half our army had to be sent overseas. At first, most of the troops sent outside the country were held in England, where they were given further training. But later they played their full part in the fighting in Sicily, Italy, and after the allied invasion of Europe in the summer of 1944—in western Europe. Indeed, some of the hardest fighting of the whole war was done by Canadians, and our losses in killed and wounded were heavy.

In addition to her splendid army, Canada sent a huge air force overseas. At the outbreak of war, the Royal Canadian Air Force was made up of only 4000 officers and men. Within four years, this figure soared to over 200,000!

Besides training Canadians, the "R.C.A.F." was given an even greater training job to do. From all parts of the British Empire, and even from many of the countries in Europe which the Germans had invaded, thousands of men were brought to Canada to be trained as fliers under what was known as the British Commonwealth Air Training Plan. So successful was this plan that the late President Roosevelt spoke of Canada as the "airdrome of democracy".

The R.C.A.E. did its full share of the fighting over Europe, and also helped to protect the convoys of ships on the Atlantic Ocean from enemy submarines and aircraft. Still other R.C.A.E. squadrons fought against the Japanese in far-off British Burma. Men of the R.C.A.F. were also to be found in every squadron of the British Royal Air Force. Thus Canadian fliers took part in air actions in every corner of the world—Europe, Africa, Asia, and Australia.

The rapid growth of Canada's navy during World War II was just as amazing as the growth of her army and air force. In little more than five years, the Royal Canadian Navy increased to fifty-two times its peace-time size!

The main duty of Canada's navy was to protect the North Atlantic convoy route from enemy submarines. The danger of such attack was so great that it was never safe for freighters to go to sea alone. Therefore they sailed together in fleets, and usually were convoyed by Canadian warships. One such convoy—the largest of the war—was made up of 167 vessels, which were loaded with over a million tons of supplies for overseas.

Besides building a strong navy of her own, Canada was able to add more than 175 ocean vessels to her little peace-time fleet of 37 merchant ships. Men from every part of Canada—many of whom had never seen salt water before—helped to man these new vessels, which were used to carry arms, food, and supplies to all parts of the world.

There were many jobs in the armed forces which women could do just as well as men. So it was that Canadian women were asked to volunteer for service in the Canadian Women's Army Corps, the Women's Division of the Royal Canadian Air Force, and the Women's Royal Canadian Naval Service. In each of these branches of Canada's armed forces, they acted as typists, clerks, messengers, cooks, and so on. In addition,

many Canadian nurses served wherever men from Canada were fighting.

While hundreds of thousands of Canadians were fighting overseas during World War II, people at home were called upon to produce more food and supplies than ever before in their history. Indeed, Canadian factories were able to turn out even more than our armed forces needed, and about two-thirds of the Dominion's wartime manufactures were sent to help her allies in the great struggle. On the farms, too, more food was grown, more cattle were raised, and more milk, butter, and cheese produced than in the years before the war.

Canada had only manufactured about 200 airplanes altogether during the five years before war broke out. But within the next five years, over 15,000 aircraft were built in the new factories across the Dominion. Besides airplanes, Canada also produced vast numbers of army trucks, tanks, rifles, guns, and shells for the troops overseas.

Because so many men and women were earning good wages in war plants across the country, Canadians had more money to spend than ever before. The Dominion government therefore passed laws to slow down or even stop the manufacture of goods people could get along without, such as pleasure automobiles, electric refrigerators, radios, washing-machines, and so on.

To make sure that what goods there were for sale would be fairly divided, many things had to be *rationed*. When goods are rationed, no one is allowed to buy more than anyone else, no matter how much he is willing to pay. The following are some of the things that were rationed to Canadians during World War II: gasoline, meat, butter, tea, coffee, sugar, preserves, and canned milk.

Of course, it cost a great deal of money to make all the arms and supplies that were needed in World War II. The government got part of this money through taxes. There were heavy taxes on wages, as well as on all goods that were sold in Canada. The rest of the money was lent to the government by the people themselves. It will take many years to pay these loans back, because although Canada received about eleven billion dollars in taxes during the war, she spent over eighteen billion dollars on the war alone.

Many new weapons of war were invented during World War II. But none was more important than the atomic bomb, which frightened Japan into surrender in the fall of 1945. The atomic bomb is the most powerful explosive ever invented, and Canadian scientists worked for years with the scientists of Great Britain and the United States in order to make it. The metal known as *uranium* is used in its manufacture. Since much of the world's uranium comes from Canada's North-West Territories, the importance of the Dominion's mineral wealth is now greater than ever.

The scientists who learned how to make a terrible weapon of warfare from uranium are now studying ways to use atomic power for peace, too. Hospitals as well as industries across Canada are already making good use of their discoveries. As these scientists add to their knowledge about atomic power, and how it may be put to work for us, it is likely that it will become even more important than hydro-electric power.

## CORNERSTONE OF EMPIRE

WE often speak of 1867 as the "year of confederation". But as we have already learned, 1867 marked only the beginning of the confederation of the provinces. It was in that year that Nova Scotia, New Brunswick, and the new provinces of Ontario and Quebec were given a single central government in addition to separate provincial governments. In 1870 Manitoba was carved out of the North-West Territories; in the following year, British Columbia joined the new Dominion; and in 1873, Prince Edward Island came into the union of the provinces as well. Alberta and Saskatchewan were added in 1905, but confederation still was not complete. For on March 31, 1949, with the entry of Newfoundland into the Dominion, Britain's oldest colony in North America became Canada's youngest province.

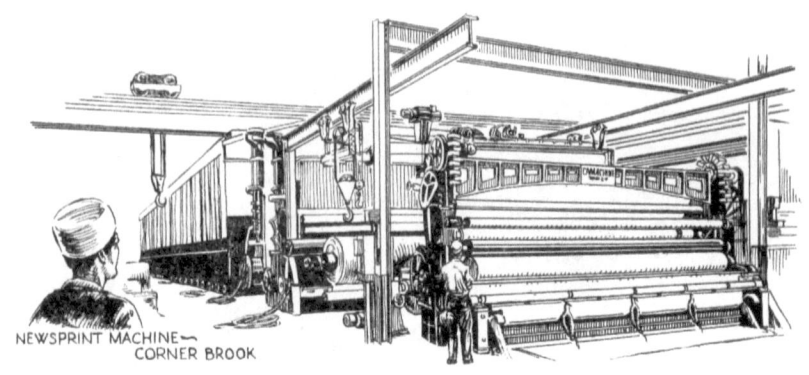

NEWSPRINT MACHINE — CORNER BROOK

## THE VOICE OF NEWFOUNDLAND

NARRATOR. Who can hear the voice of Newfoundland? Here, at the nation's gateway, there are many voices whispering to us, speaking to us, shouting at us from every side. Can you not hear the dull roar of the North Atlantic against our rugged eastern shores? Can you not hear the screaming gulls, the flapping sails of fishing schooners on the Banks? Can you not hear the barking of the seals as the hunters move into the herds? Listen! The puffing chug of the locomotive rises over the howling wind as the *Overland Limited* rams the snow drifts on the Gaff Topsail, fifteen hundred feet above sea level. Listen! The drone of a mighty air liner racing down Gander's runway to take off for Europe is being answered by the thunder of machinery in the pulp and paper mill at Corner Brook, across the island.

MILL-WORKER. Corner Brook? *I* work in the mill at Corner Brook!

NARRATOR. Who is that?

MILL-WORKER. I'm a mill-worker at the great Bowater's plant. The newsprint machine I help to run is one of the fastest in the world. It can turn out two thousand feet of paper every minute.

NARRATOR. What becomes of so much newsprint?

MILL-WORKER. It goes mostly to newspapers in the United States. Why, the forests bring this province millions of American dollars every year.

NARRATOR. How long will the forests last to keep your business going?

MILL-WORKER. My company is allowed to cut wood over eleven thousand square miles. With proper planning the forest grows back even faster than we can cut it.

NARRATOR. Pulp and paper is one of this province's most important industries.

FISHERMAN. Have you forgotten the fisheries?

NARRATOR. Where did that voice come from?

FISHERMAN. I'm setting my trawl lines five miles off Twillingate in Notre Dame Bay.

NARRATOR. That is a voice from one of the outports—the voice of a fisherman! More than half the people of this island live in the outports along the coasts. Tell us, fisherman, what is a trawl line? What is your boat like? What kind of fish will you take?

FISHERMAN. My trawl lines each carry scores of baited hooks. They're strung along the bottom between those marker buoys I've just set out. And I built this boat—twenty feet it is, with a four horse-power engine. It's cod I'll be catching, I reckon, because that's what the trawls are used for!

NARRATOR. So you're an inshore fisherman. The Banks are fished by schooners of up to a hundred and fifty tons. The men row out from them in dories to their trawls. They're the deep-sea fishermen, the ones who go out to the Banks.

FISHERMAN. But the Banks lie off the south coast.

NARRATOR. That's right. The Great Bank of Newfoundland is east of the Avalon Peninsula. Although it's all under water, of course, it covers a larger area than the island of Newfoundland itself. And there are smaller Banks as you sail west towards Nova Scotia.

FISHERMAN. That's a big business, the fisheries over the Banks.

NARRATOR. Yes, but not as big as the inshore fisheries along the coasts. Didn't you know that many more men make their living from the inshore fisheries, as you do, than from the offshore fisheries over the Banks? Why, most of the families in the outports depend on the inshore fisheries.

FISHERMAN. What else is caught along the coasts?

NARRATOR. Mostly cod, the same as here. But they catch a good deal of salmon, herring, halibut, turbot, and lobster as well. How long have you been fishing?

FISHERMAN. Since shortly after dawn this morning. But it's not—

NARRATOR. He says he's been fishing since shortly after dawn this morning! Doesn't that man realize he's been fishing all his life, and his father before him, and before that *his* father, and then *his* father. Why, this province *began* as a colony of fishermen! First fisheries, and now pulp and paper—

MINER. —and mining!

NARRATOR. What voice was that?

MINER. I'm a "Dosco" miner at Wabana, on Bell Island in Conception Bay!

NARRATOR. What is "Dosco"?

MINER. Dominion Steel and Coal Corporation. But it's iron ore, not coal, that we bring up here. Iron that can be turned into steel. As much as a million tons of iron ore a year.

NARRATOR. If you don't mine coal as well, how do you smelt the iron ore into steel?

MINER. That's done at the Company's smelters in Sydney, Nova Scotia.

NARRATOR. Why do you ship it there to be smelted?

MINER. That's where the nearest coal mines are, on Cape Breton Island. It takes tons of coal, you know, to smelt one ton of

iron ore. That's why we ship the ore to Nova Scotia, instead of bringing the coal here.

NARRATOR. Some of the coal mines on Cape Breton Island run out beneath the sea.

MINER. So do the Wabana mines on Bell Island. They run out beneath the bed of Conception Bay on the west side of the island. Even the electric power to run our cable cars comes across the strait under water.

NARRATOR. How can that be?

MINER. The power is brought over by two submarine cables from the eastern shore of the bay, three miles away. The cable cars move the iron ore from the pitheads on the western side of Bell Island to the heights along the eastern coast. There the ore is poured down into the ships that moor in the deep water beneath the cliffs.

NARRATOR. These, then, are the three chief exports of Newfoundland: the products of her forests, of her fisheries, and of her mines. What does she buy from other provinces and from other countries with the money that these exports must earn?

TRAINMAN. I can answer that. I'm a trainman on the railway that runs across the province from Port aux Basques to St. John's.

NARRATOR. Do you mean that everything that is shipped to St. John's is brought across the island on the railway?

TRAINMAN. No, St. John's is an important ocean port. But Port aux Basques lies just ninety-five miles from North Sydney in Cape Breton, Nova Scotia. Most travellers come across the strait there on the railway ferry Cabot Strait, and then take the railway overland.

NARRATOR. How long does the train journey take?

TRAINMAN. Just about twenty-four hours from Port aux Basques to the capital. Of course, much freight goes straight to St. John's by boat, and some passengers sail there direct from Halifax, too. Others come by plane, and land at Torbay, just a few miles north of the capital.

NARRATOR. You said you could tell us about Newfoundland's imports.

TRAINMAN. Out most important import is foodstuffs—things

ST JOHN'S

we do not raise or grow ourselves because Newfoundland is not one of the large agricultural provinces. Textiles, clothing, and footwear are mostly bought outside the province, too. Coal, oil, gasoline, hardware, and machinery must be brought in as well.

NARRATOR. To get money to buy all these things, Newfoundland must find markets where she can sell her own products of the sea, forests, and mines.

TRAINMAN. Yes. When markets have been good, Newfoundland has prospered But when markets have been poor, we have seen hard times.

NARRATOR. What is there to tell us about your own work?

TRAINMAN. About railroading on the island? A visitor would notice some differences, but not many. When Newfoundland joined the Canadian confederation in 1949, the railway—along with the steamship services it ran—became part of the Canadian National system.

NARRATOR. What about these steamship services that are run by the railway?

TRAINMAN. They circle the island, calling on the outports that dot the coasts. They sail to the outports on Labrador—
GOOSE BAY. This is Goose Bay calling!
NARRATOR. Where is Goose Bay?
GOOSE BAY. Here, at the head of Hamilton Inlet, in the heart of Labrador.
NARRATOR. Do any Newfoundlanders live there?
GOOSE BAY. This whole coast, from the Strait of Belle Isle in the south to Cape Chidley in the north, is part of the province of Newfoundland.
NARRATOR. But how do people earn a living there?
GOOSE BAY. Our three chief industries are the same as those of the island of Newfoundland—fishing, lumbering, and mining. Five thousand people live on Labrador the year round.
NARRATOR. How are supplies brought in to them?
GOOSE BAY. By the ships that call at the outports along the coast during the summer months. But even in winter, we in Goose Bay have visitors and mail from the rest of the world.
NARRATOR. How is that?
GOOSE BAY. The Canadian government airport here, which cost over twenty-five million dollars to build, lies on one of the important air lanes between North America and Europe. Most North Atlantic flights stop either at Goose Bay or at Gander.
NARRATOR. Yes. Newfoundland lies at the gateway to Canada, by air as well as by sea.
*(Music begins, softly at first)*
Listen! Do you hear the music?
TRAINMAN. It is a proud air, that.
MINER. Listen!... *We love thee, smiling land!*
FISHERMAN. *We love thee, windswept land!*
NARRATOR. Listen! *God guard thee, Newfoundland!*
*(All join in singing)*

"FISHING FLEETS...MADE YEARLY VISITS"

## THE STORY OF NEWFOUNDLAND

The story of Newfoundland begins before the story of any other part of Canada, because it is believed that John Cabot visited the island on his famous voyage of 1497—just five years after Columbus reached the West Indies. Although Cabot claimed "the new isle" for Henry VII, as told earlier in this book, more than eighty years went by before England made plans to found a colony upon its shores.

In the meantime, fishing fleets from western Europe made yearly visits to the fisheries off the coasts of Newfoundland. The ships' crews came ashore regularly to set up bases for their summer's work on the Banks, and to build "flakes" for the drying of the catch. The first English captain into each cove or harbour usually took command for the season, dealing out justice in rough and ready fashion and calling on all visiting-vessels—under whatever flag they sailed—to obey his orders. Little wonder, then, that these early commanders came to be known as the "fishing admirals".

In 1583, another explorer sailing under the English flag, Sir Humphrey Gilbert, landed at St. John's and claimed the country in the name of his great Queen, Elizabeth. Plans for a colony, however, died with Gilbert when he perished at sea on the homeward voyage. A little more than a quarter of a century later, another attempt was made by John Guy. This colony lasted for several years, but in the end it had to be abandoned.

Then, in 1623, Sir George Calvert (who later became Lord Baltimore) was granted lordship over the peninsula he named Avalon, and before long he was building a settlement at Ferryland. Here, forty miles north of Cape Race, he erected a majestic mansion, where he and his family lived for many years. But the English hold on Newfoundland was far from secure, and raids by the French who had settled on Placentia Bay left the colonists in a state of constant alarm. Finally, Calvert decided to abandon his colony and move to the mainland. Sir David Kirke, who had forced Champlain to surrender Quebec in 1629, now became leader of the colony at Ferryland. But although Kirke ran the settlement with a firm hand, many more years passed before England was to make good her claim to Newfoundland by making it a true colony peopled by her own emigrants.

The wars between France and England in North America led to many sharp clashes in Newfoundland. In the 1690's the French from Placentia Bay—aided by the famous Iberville—almost succeeded in driving the English from Newfoundland altogether. Twice in later years, the French overran St. John's. Peace finally was brought about by the Treaty of Paris in 1763, just four years after Quebec fell to Wolfe's army.

Even the Treaty of Paris, however, renewed an old problem for the colonists of Newfoundland and their descendants. For many years (ever since 1713), French fishermen had enjoyed the right to "catch fish and to dry them on land" along a large portion of the coastline. Now, in 1763, the Treaty of Paris not only gave France the two islands of St. Pierre and Miquelon off the south coast of Newfoundland, but it also promised French fishermen that they could go on fishing and using the shores for drying their fish as in past years! Since Newfoundland was supposed to be British, the granting of this right to French fishermen seemed a great injustice in the eyes of Newfoundlanders at the time, as it also did in later years when the grant was

BEFORE 1783          THE "FRENCH" SHORE          1783-1904

repeated with a few changes. It was not until 1904 that a final settlement of the "French Shore" question, as it was called, was reached, and France finally gave up her right to use the shores, and almost all her fishing rights.

The slow growth of settlements in Newfoundland was not blocked only by the French, however. During the island's early days, the British government itself was strongly opposed to the founding of colonies in Newfoundland! British leaders long believed that the fisheries were useful training grounds for the sailors needed by the British navy. They did not like to see the fishermen stay in Newfoundland when the fishing season was over. "Fish for England in time of peace, and fight for England in time of war," they demanded.

The merchants of western England, too, were interested in Newfoundland only because of its rich fisheries. They did not want to see colonies started in the new land. They believed that they had enough competition from the fishing fleets of the other European countries as it was, without setting up colonies in Newfoundland that might go into the fishing industry, too.

Thus, for almost a century, the settlement of Newfoundland was blocked in every way possible. People were forbidden to build within six miles of the coast; it was unlawful even to repair a house without permission; and Newfoundlanders were not allowed to fence off land for farming. Fishermen continued to come to the shores in thousands every year, but few wintered in the New World.

However, in spite of the many ways in which the British government at first tried to hinder the settlement of Newfoundland, the colonies on the island slowly grew larger and more numerous. At the time of the Treaty of Paris in 1763, when peace was made between France and England at last, about eight thousand colonists had settled in Newfoundland; in addition, there were about five thousand summer "tourists" visiting its fisheries each year. Then, during the wars in Europe with Napoleon in the early 1800's, conditions began to improve rapidly. Without competition from other European fishing fleets, the price of fish tripled, wages soared, and new settlers began to arrive in numbers. In 1814 alone, over seven thousand newcomers came to the island. The population rose to eighty thousand.

The colony was granted the right to elect representatives to its government in 1832, but it was not until 1855 that these law-makers were given full control over the government. We shall remember that the people's representatives in the other provinces won this right only a few years before this time.

Although two delegates from Newfoundland came to the

Quebec Conference in 1864 to discuss confederation, the island colony decided against joining the other provinces and many years went by before the question came up for serious thought again. In the 1890's, however, a delegation was sent to Ottawa to discuss the possibility of joining the Dominion, but no agreement was reached.

During World War I, Newfoundland's young men were quick to answer the call of their country. Adore than five thousand went overseas, where over a quarter of them gave their lives. At the same time, business improved, and for a few brief years prosperity reigned. The early 1920's, however, brought widespread unemployment; prices fell, and the government was forced to take over the railway. During the four years before the outbreak of a world-wide depression at the end of 1929, conditions improved considerably, but the country was still in no position to weather the storm that lay ahead. During the dark days of the early 1930's, hardships were many and severe. So dependent was the island Dominion on being able to sell her exports of fish, iron, and newsprint that the country was crippled when the trade of the world slowed to a mere trickle.

In 1933, Newfoundland decided to give up its right of self-government for the time being, and accepted what was known as a "commission of government", appointed by the parliament of the United Kingdom. In other words, the country agreed to become a dependent colony once again, and it continued to be governed in this way until four years after the end of World War II.

At home as much as abroad, Newfoundlanders were in the front lines during World War II. The Battle of the Atlantic raged at sea on all sides of the island, and the importance of Newfoundland as a base for defence was quickly realized. Early in the war, Canadian troops were sent to the island to help defend it against attack, which fortunately never came. In addition, Newfoundlanders began to enlist for service overseas in all branches of the armed forces—army, air force, navy, and merchant marine. At the same time, the United States was allowed to develop three important bases for its forces on the island. The rights to these bases were to last for ninety-nine years. They are located at Stephenville, Argentia, and near St. John's. The fact that Newfoundland, Canada, and the United States all saw the necessity of Allied bases in Newfoundland showed how important the island was becoming to the defence of North America.

One year after the end of World War II, the people of Newfoundland were asked to elect persons to represent them at a special meeting called to discuss how Newfoundland might be governed in the future. This meeting recommended that the people should be asked to vote to decide whether Newfoundland should remain a colony, return to governing itself as a Dominion, or join Canada as a tenth province.

It was a difficult choice. The people of Newfoundland were justly proud of their growth from colony to independent Dominion. It is not hard to understand, therefore, why many hesitated at the idea of becoming part of a much larger Dominion. But in the end, after two votes had been held in 1948, it was found that the larger number of Newfoundlanders favoured joining Canada. At long last, on March 31, 1949, Newfoundland was welcomed into confederation as the tenth Canadian province.

CAPE RACE

## THE STORY OF TRAVEL IN CANADA

THE first maps of our country showed little more than its eastern shores. Although the first explorers scoured the coastline in their sailing vessels, the interior of Canada remained unknown for many years. True, a wonderful network of inland waterways led everywhere through the heart of this continent, but the way to them was barred by rapids through which ocean-going craft could not pass. After Cartier's voyages, almost seventy years went by before any explorers broke into the lake country upstream from Montreal.

### WATERWAYS TO SETTLEMENT

If it had not been for the birch-bark canoe of the Indians, the exploration of Canada's interior might have been delayed even longer than seventy years. A man struggling on foot through the thick forests of south-eastern Canada was able to carry only a small weight on his back. But in a birch-bark canoe, a lone trader could carry hundreds of pounds of food, belongings, and trade goods for the Indians, and he was able to bring back heavy packs of furs. Because the bark canoe was light, he could easily carry it when it was necessary to make a short portage around a rapids or waterfall. Indeed, if the Indians had not already invented the birch-bark canoe, it seems likely that the white man would have had to invent it himself!

However, the bark canoe was more useful to the *coureurs de bois* and other fur traders than to the early settlers. The United Empire Loyalists, who helped to settle Upper Canada after the American Revolution, could not bring their cattle, horses, or other live-stock in such frail craft. Soon newly built sailing ships were gliding back and forth between the settlements that sprang up along the shores of Lake Ontario. The first sailing vessels on the Great Lakes were ships of the Royal Navy. But by 1800 the white sails of trading schooners were becoming a common sight.

These sailing ships could move freight anywhere on Lake Ontario, but they could not descend the St. Lawrence River below the rapids which began at Prescott. Freight cargoes and passengers bound to and from the settlements in Upper Canada had therefore to travel between Montreal and Kingston by *bateau*.

The earliest bateaus were long, flat-bottomed boats with crews of five men each, four to row and one to steer. On their open decks the passengers huddled without shelter from driving storm or summer sun. Later, larger bateaus were built that carried larger crews, and some of these could handle cargoes of as much as four tons. Even this weight was no more than could be moved in the largest bark freight canoes, which were also much faster. But the sturdy, safe bateau was more useful for the bulky cargoes carried on the upper St. Lawrence.

Still larger and safer than the bateau was the Durham boat, which came into use between Montreal and Kingston during the early 1800's. The Durham boat, named after an American ship-builder, was usually driven along close to shore by long poles, which the crew thrust against the bed of the river. The trip by Durham boat from Montreal up to Kingston took seven days or more, although the return journey could be made in three.

The larger bateaus and the Durham boats were seldom

DURHAM BOATS

taken out of the water when a rapids had to be passed. Instead, most of the crew came ashore, and dragged the vessel upstream against the swift current, the men passengers being called upon whenever help was needed. Often these barge-like craft left Montreal in fleets, so that their crews could help one another past the difficult parts of the river.

Lake schooners waited at Kingston to take on to York and Niagara the passengers, goods, and mails which had come by bateau from Montreal. Shortly after Governor Simcoe's time, a regular bateau service was also opened between Kingston and York. Now, fleets of bateaus could be seen working their way through the Bay of Quinte towards the narrow neck of land that joined the peninsula of Prince Edward to the mainland. This was the "Carrying Place"; here the bateaus were unloaded and carted on wagons to the water on the other side, where they were launched and loaded once again. For the rest of the journey to York, the bateaus hugged the north shore of Lake Ontario. If the wind was from the right direction, the weary oarsmen might hoist a sail to speed them along.

Of course, the most famous "carrying place" of all was around the falls of Niagara between Queenston and Chippewa. Dozens of wagons were kept busy during the summer months, moving goods from the wharf at Queenston to the upper Niagara River. Here they were reloaded on other lake schooners, built above the Falls to handle the trade of the upper lakes.

In the Far West, too, improvements in water transportation were being invented to suit the needs of the country. Although the bark freight canoes of the voyageurs could carry enormous loads for such frail craft, they had some drawbacks. Some kinds of machinery needed at the trading posts in the Far West could not be loaded aboard canoes. Even if that had been possible, portaging such cargoes would have been tremendously difficult. What was needed was some sturdier vessel that could be dragged overland without being unloaded. The Hudson's Bay Company traders therefore began to build what was known as the York boat.

The York boats were stoutly built of wood, and measured about forty feet long by ten feet across at their widest point. They were driven by long oars, called "sweeps", and the crew hoisted a large square sail when the wind was right. When the current was too swift, the men went ashore and pulled the boats upstream by long tow-lines. This was called "tracking". When the waterway was blocked by falls or very dangerous rapids, the York boats were dragged overland, often being rolled along on round logs, for many years, the York boat was one of the most useful vessels on such western rivers as the Nelson and the Mackenzie, where it served much the same purpose as the bateau on the St. Lawrence.

BUILDING THE LONG SAULT CANAL

## DIGGING THE CANALS

It is not surprising that little canal-building had been done in New France. Unlike Upper Canada, the settlements in Quebec and the Maritimes were never cut off from ocean shipping. Until the land about the Great Lakes became a home for the settler instead of a hunting ground for the fur trader, there was no need for an unbroken water highway into the interior.

Shortly after Canada became British, the Royal Engineers began to dig canals around the rapids on the St. Lawrence River. These first canals were narrow and shallow, but at least they made it possible for small vessels to pass upstream from Montreal.

Canals were needed, it was believed, for defence as well as for trade. It had not been forgotten that during the War of 1812 the British navy was unable to come to the aid of the little sailing fleets on the Great Lakes. Now the building of canals was speeded up, because the British government stood ready to help pay the cost.

Not only were new canals dug on the St. Lawrence, and the old ones widened, but canals were also begun in other parts of the country. In 1824, work was started on the first Welland Canal. Five years later it was carrying vessels past the greatest shipping barrier of all—the falls on the Niagara River. Work was also begun on the Chambly Canal around the rapids on the Richelieu River, and the Ridcau Canal between Kingston and Bytown (later Ottawa) was opened in 1832.

In the Maritime Provinces, most of the settlements lay close to seaports that were open the year round. Some towns, such as Fredericton, lay inland, but were on rivers that provided highways to the ocean during the ice-free months. Fewer important canals were built, therefore, in the Maritimes than in the central provinces. There still are plans, however, to connect the Gulf of St. Lawrence with the Bay of Fundy by a canal across the Isthmus of Chignecto. One of the most interesting plans was called the "Chignecto Ship Railway". This was not to have been a canal, but would have served the same purpose. If it had been completed, ships would have been carried on a specially built railway between the Bay of Fundy and the Gulf of St. Lawrence. Unfortunately, the company that began the work ran out of money, and millions of dollars were lost when the plan was finally given up.

## THE COMING OF THE STEAMBOAT

Even on wide rivers such as the lower St. Lawrence, sailing vessels were much less dependable than they were on the open sea. If the wind was not right, a river gave little room for a ship to "tack and veer". A light breeze which might keep a vessel in

motion at sea was often too weak to carry it against the current on a river journey upstream.

Then, in 1807, great news was carried to Canada in the mails from New York. An American inventor, Robert Fulton, had put one of the new steam engines on board a vessel and hooked it up to a pair of paddle-wheels. As the side-paddles churned around in the water, the boat began to move up the Hudson River! Already Fulton had announced a regular service between New York and Albany. The day of the steamboat had arrived.

Sailing vessels were to go on handling much of the worlds ocean shipping for almost a hundred years, but the advantages of steam-power over sail on river boats was admitted everywhere immediately. The new invention spread rapidly, and within two years made its first appearance on the St. Lawrence River. In 1809, the paddle-steamer *Accommodation* was launched at Montreal and put into service between that city and Quebec. Her six-horsepower engine was not always strong enough to move her against the current and at one place ox-teams were held ready on shore to help the vessel upstream. But a great step forward had been made, and new and better steamboats were being built along the St. Lawrence for the river service.

It was not until shortly after the War of 1812 that the first steamboats came into use on the Great Lakes. The earliest lake "steamers" were hardly a match for the severe storms that often sprang up on Lake Ontario and Lake Erie, but as improvements were made by the builders the new craft became just as safe as the sailing schooners. Now for the first time one could buy a

ticket for a voyage from Queenston to Kingston, and know not only the day he would arrive, but the hour as well!

It was natural that the four Atlantic provinces early came to possess many famous shipping centres. Halifax, Saint John, St. John's, Sydney, Pictou, and Yarmouth not only built up an important coastal trade among themselves, but were only a few of the Maritime ports that handled cargoes to and from the other countries of the world.

The coming of the Loyalists brought about a regular sailing-vessel service between Saint John and Digby, on the other side of the Bay of Fundy. The invention of the steamboat was welcomed by the settlers along the St. John River Valley just as heartily as by the businessmen of Montreal and Quebec. By 1816, the paddle-wheeler *General Smythe* was making a round trip each week between Fredericton and Saint John. The *General Smythe* was followed by more and better steamers, and for years the St. John River valley echoed with the shrill whistles of the new river boats.

STAGE-COACH DAYS ON THE CORDUROY ROAD

## FROM INDIAN TRAIL TO SUPER-HIGHWAY

Although we often hear frightening stories about the roads in our country a hundred years ago, some of these stories are misleading. Even if modern concrete highways *could* have existed in Canada in, say, the year 1800, how would the lives of the people have been changed? To begin with, there would not have been enough people to work on them and keep them in good condition, and of course they had neither the machinery nor the materials to do so. The people of that time could not have built even wagons that would have carried loads such as our modern transport trucks speed from town to town to-day. Without present-day machinery for snow removal, such roads would often have been impassable in winter. Even stage-coaches could not have covered long distances on them until inns and villages and towns were built where fresh teams of horses could be kept. In other words, our modern highways were built for a kind of traffic that was not dreamed of a hundred and fifty years ago. Improvements in roads and improvements in vehicles went forward hand in hand, in Canada as in other countries. As we have already seen, the first highways were the waterways. As more and more settlements grew up along the shores, each settlement found it convenient to keep in touch with the neighbouring settlement by land as well as water. First there might be only Indian trails, or footpaths, which soon grew into bridle-paths. These in turn were widened and improved with make-shift bridges. Finally, only a few sections needed to be completed to make a continuous road.

The best highways in early Canada were far worse than the poorest country roads of to-day. There were no machines for road-building. First the trees had to be cut down by hand, and the stumps rooted out. Usually the trees were cut up into logs and laid across the trail as a foundation for the road. Sometimes, but not always, earth or gravel was placed on top of the logs. What a rough ride the passengers in a stage-coach must have had on such a highway! These "wooden highways" were known as *corduroy* roads.

## NEW ROADS TO CONFEDERATION

Highways and canals alone could not solve all the problems of travel in the British North American colonies. Heavy loads of freight still could not be hauled overland, and the inland waterways were blocked by ice during much of every year. At best, travel by water was very slow. The easiest journey from the Great Lakes to British Columbia was the ocean voyage around Cape Horn—in other words, a trip half-way around the world! Little wonder, then, that people said that the "colonies lay closer to England than to each other". An entirely new kind of transportation was needed, and needed badly.

The invention of the steam locomotive in 1829 was even

more important to Canada than the invention of the steamship. In 1837, the first steam railway train in Canada was put into use between Montreal and St. Johns, on the Richelieu River. But the cost of building rail lines was tremendous. Even by 1850 there were still only fifty miles of railway in the whole of British North America.

We have already read how the people of the colonies caught the "railway fever", and what an important part the railways played in bringing the provinces together into a single Dominion, and in the opening of the West. No longer was travel brought to a standstill during the wet, muddy days of spring; no longer did the last boat down the St. Lawrence in the fall of the year end freighting for the season. A journey from Toronto to Saint John or Halifax ceased to be an adventure, such as was described earlier in this book. At last, a trip of a thousand miles could be made in greater comfort than could a trip of a hundred miles before the new age of steam.

Just before 1900, the explosions of the first "horseless carriage" were heard on the streets of Canadian cities. The day of the automobile had arrived. The rapid development of this convenient new vehicle led to a speedy improvement of Canadian roads.

When the transcontinental system of railways had been completed across Canada, men thought that travel in the Dominion had been made as fast as possible. But the invention of the airplane changed the picture once again. To-day, Trans-Canada Air Lines—owned and run by the government of Canada—has a coast-to-coast passenger plane service which is the finest and most modern in the world. Certainly the improvements in travel seem wonderful when we think that to-day we can go from St. John's to Vancouver—a distance of three thousand miles—in the same time that it took a stage-coach in pioneer days to travel forty miles.

## FOOD FOR THE WORLD

CANADA to-day has many different kinds of farms, and each farmer has to decide what he is going to grow. He must ask himself which crops will grow best in his climate and in the soil of his farm. He must also know how and where he can best sell his crops. If his community is thickly settled it may pay him better to produce vegetables, milk, butter, and eggs, which are wanted in the cities near by. On the other hand, a farmer in the more thinly populated Prairie Provinces can usually make more money by producing wheat for other parts of Canada and for shipment to distant countries.

We speak of mixed farming when a farmer produces a variety of products—some field crops, some live-stock, and so on. Mixed farming is common throughout most of the East, and more and more western farmers are going in for it as well. The dairy farmer sells milk and milk products, but he also has cattle to sell as beef from year to year. Dairy farming is common in the neighbourhood of Canadian cities, since the milk must reach the dairies without delay if it is to be pasteurized, bottled, and delivered to the customer while it is still fresh. Truck farming is the name given to the growing of vegetables for nearby markets and canneries. There are many other kinds of farming in Canada, such as wheat farming, poultry farming, fruit farming, and so on.

The farms in the Maritime Provinces are best known for apple-growing, potato-growing, and dairying. The Annapolis Valley in Nova Scotia has long been famous for its fine apples, and its orchards send large quantities of fruit to Great Britain every year. Potatoes from New Brunswick and Prince Edward Island are popular on the dinner-tables of central Canada. Most of the other field crops of the Maritimes are used to feed the dairy herds, and are not exported. Newfoundland grows potatoes and other vegetables, but not in quantities sufficient for export.

Quebec has many dairy farms, especially in districts close to the large cities of Montreal, Three Rivers, and Quebec. Tobacco and apples are also grown in important quantities, and Quebec maple syrup and maple sugar are sold in Canada and abroad.

In Ontario, the Niagara fruit-belt is famous, especially for its peaches and grapes. Some parts of the province specialize in certain crops such as tobacco, flax, and sugar-beets. Less wheat is grown in Ontario than formerly. Because of the heavy population in the cities and towns, dairy farming is very widespread. A great many Ontario farmers raise live-stock and poultry, and carry on truck farming.

A CROP IN THE CLEARING

The Prairie Provinces—Manitoba, Saskatchewan, and Alberta—produce enormous quantities of wheat, coarse grains (barley, oats, rye), and feed crops. Alberta and Saskatchewan also have many ranches which raise cattle for the market in Canada and abroad. Sheep farming, too, is carried on in Alberta. So that the western farmer will not depend entirely on the success of the wheat harvest, mixed farming is now being encouraged throughout the Prairie Provinces.

British Columbia, like Ontario, goes in for almost every type of farming. The orchards of the Okanagan and Kootenay valleys are known across the continent. Because the climate of the province varies greatly from one part to another, dairying, poultry raising, cattle ranching, and wheat-growing are all to be found within the borders of British Columbia.

The records of early times are filled with accounts of the struggles of Canadian pioneer farmers. In eastern Canada, the forests were the chief enemy of the early farmers. It is hard for us now to picture how thickly wooded most parts of Quebec and Ontario were then. Sometimes the pioneers could not wait to remove all the stumps before sowing their first crops. They cultivated the soil between the stumps with their hoes, scattered the seed by hand, harvested the grain with scythes, and threshed it with wooden flails. The early settlers on the prairies did not have the forests to clear, but they found other difficulties which often were more serious—frost, droughts, insect pests, and loneliness, because their homes were widely separated.

Farming and farm life in most parts of Canada are very different to-day. Machinery has greatly changed the farmer's job—although there is still plenty of work for him to do in order to raise his crops! But the farmer no longer must cut his grain with the scythe or cradle, nor thresh it with the flail. On some farms, the horse-drawn reaper and binder cuts the grain, while the harvesters pile the bound sheaves into stooks which are afterwards pitched into the racks and hauled in for threshing by a power-driven separator. On many farms, and especially on those in western Canada, great "combines" move down the fields, both cutting and threshing the grain as they go along. Spraying machines keep down the pests on fruit farms. Milking machines are used to milk large dairy herds. The cream separator removes the cream from the milk, whereas pans of milk used to stand in the dairy to be skimmed by hand. Indeed, farmers have had to become mechanics, in order to look after their tractors and machinery. In many parts of the country, electricity is used for lighting and power in farm buildings and homes.

Canada to-day boasts many manufacturing industries, but she still depends on her farms for her prosperity. When the farmers of the prairies cannot sell their wheat for a profit, they are unable to buy the products of the factories, no matter how many arc offered for sale. When a factory begins to sell fewer goods, it has to dismiss some of its workers and pay less money to those who stay. Soon we have hard times in the towns and cities as well as on the farms. It is important, therefore, for us to realize that our farms must do well, or Canada as a whole cannot prosper.

"OUR DAILY BREAD"

The story of wheat began in the oldest times. Grains of wheat have been found in Egyptian tombs dating back 6000 years before Christ, and the Chinese were growing wheat by 3000 B.C. The Bible tells in many places about the growing of "corn". Because our Bible was translated in England, it uses the word "corn" for wheat and other grains, as English people still do. Corn as we know it in Canada is called maize in England.

Although the early peoples of many countries planted and harvested wheat, there was no wheat in America until the white man came. The very first wheat grown in our country planted at De Monts's settlement at Port Royal (Nova Scotia) in 1605. A few years later, wheat was being harvested at Champlain's new colony at Quebec. As the Maritime Provinces and Ontario and Quebec became settled, much wheat was grown, but because western Canada later proved to be the best part of our country for growing wheat, Eastern Canada now specializes in other kinds of farming.

The Selkirk settlers at the Red River sowed the first wheat in western Canada. In the fall of 1812, soon after they made their way from York Factory to the Red River Valley, they planted the seeds they had brought with them from Britain. They had only spades and hoes to prepare the ground, and the crop was a complete failure. Their next harvest was little better. For several years the settlers were unlucky; sometimes they obtained a fair yield, but more often they suffered from floods, drought, or frosts. Sometimes grasshoppers ate the grain. No less a plague were the Nor' Westers, who trampled the crops and drove many settlers away.

By this time, some of the colonists were ready to doubt that anyone could grow wheat in Manitoba! But other settlers came and planted the fields again, and finally the farmers triumphed. The frontiers of the wheat-grower have been steadily widened, until to-day wheat has been grown successfully in Canada only 200 miles from the Arctic Circle. How science has helped the farmer to do this is an interesting story.

Most of the wheat grown in western Canada is "spring" wheat, that is, it is planted in the spring as soon as the frost is out of the ground and the fields are dry enough to be worked. The wheat grows up and ripens during the summer, and is reaped in late August or early September. (In warmer climates, "fall" wheat is frequently sown in the autumn, and harvested in the late spring or early summer.) Hours of sunlight each day are long in northern Canada, and the wheat grows rapidly. But even so, the growing season frequently proved all too short, and the first wheat-growers in the West often lost much of their crops because of early frosts. How the pioneer farmers wished that wheat could be grown in a shorter time, so that it would ripen before the frosts!

For many years, "Red Fife" wheat was grown very widely in Canada. It was named after David Fife, an Ontario farmer who sent for seed from northern Europe, which he hoped might do better in the cold Canadian climate than the seed he was using. He was not very successful with his first planting, for only one plant, with three heads, ripened. The story goes that there were five heads, but the cow ate two before Mrs. Fife saw her and drove her away. But those three heads were enough for Fife to plant and replant until he had enough seed for himself and for his neighbours. The seed did very well in Canada, and gradually it came to be used all over the country.

But although Red Fife grew well in the West and the grain was of very high quality, it was frequently caught by frost before it was ripe. The Dominion government decided to try to help the farmers. It placed William Saunders in charge of its experimental farms, and he began to try to develop an early ripening wheat. His work was continued by his son, Dr. Charles Saunders, who in 1907 finally produced the famous "Marquis" wheat. This wheat ripens earlier than Red Fife, and makes flour of the highest quality. For many years it was the most widely grown wheat in Canada, and did much to make Canadian wheat known as the best in the world.

Other types of wheat have been developed more recently—such as Thatcher, Red Bobs, Reward, Garnet, Renown, and Apex. Some of these ripen even earlier than Marquis, and others are rust-resistant. So great was the damage done by the "rust" plant disease, that scientists decided the only way to overcome it was to develop wheat that the rust could not live on. For many years they worked to produce kinds of wheat that would not "rust", and yet would be of sufficiently high quality to make fine flour; it was only about 1942 that they succeeded.

As scientists and farmers, working together, developed wheat with a shorter growing period, the wheat fields began to extend farther and farther north. Some of the best wheat has been grown in the Peace River Valley, which is two hundred miles north of Edmonton—and if you look at the map you will see that Edmonton is about as far north of the city of Quebec as Quebec itself is north of New York.

Canadians have many times won the world's championship for wheat—indeed, one Alberta farmer won the prize so often he was finally not allowed to compete any more!

At first Canada grew only enough wheat to feed her own people, but after the railways were built, western wheat began to be shipped abroad. Canada in normal times exports more wheat than any country in the world. The United States and Russia usually grow more wheat than does Canada, but do not sell so much abroad, because they need it to feed their own large populations.

"WHEAT BEGINS TO MOVE"

"George," said Mr. Brown to his young son one day at the beginning of threshing, "do you think you could drive a grain team to the elevator to-morrow? We are short-handed, and shall need to use the teams as well as the truck. You can drive Bess and Nell, and follow Dave's team."

"Sure, Dad," said George. "Bess and Nell do just what I tell them, and if I follow Dave I should be O.K." And so it was arranged. George, who was only ten, was a little scared about driving a heavy wagon-load of grain, but he was proud of his father's trust in him, and he wanted very much to see what goes on inside a tall elevator when the wheat pours in every fall in western Canada.

On George's father's farm the grain was threshed in the field, as is usual in Alberta, and as fast as the wooden grain-boxes were filled by the stream of amber wheat running out of the separator, they were driven to the elevator.

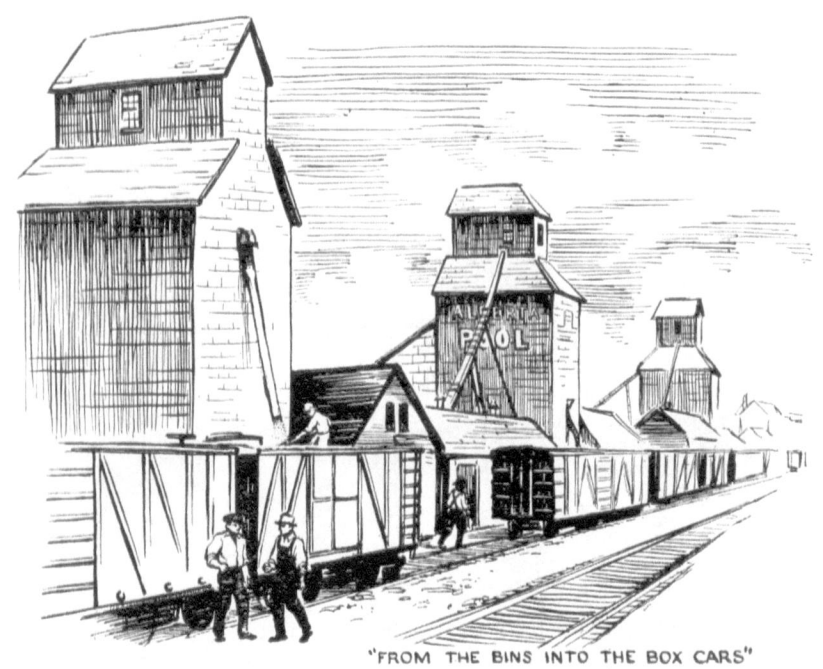

"FROM THE BINS INTO THE BOX CARS"

Several elevators stood near the railway station about four miles away. Dave and George could see them sticking up on the flat prairie as they started out. As they turned into a narrow road, the grain teams met an expensive automobile, and for a moment George wondered what would happen, for the teams could not go nearer the edge with their heavy loads. To his surprise, the big car drove into the shallow ditch and around the teams. The driver grinned and waved as he passed. Dave laughed. "Everybody makes way for wheat!" he said.

At the elevator, they drove their wagons right up on the scale. The elevator man weighed the grain-box full of grain, and "graded" the wheat. Then the grain was dropped into the receiving pit. Next the empty wagon was weighed. Then the elevator man filled out a slip of paper, which he handed to George. George passed it on to Dave, who said it was "O.K."

"O.K.?" said the elevator man. "I should think so! Even in a good season like this it is not every farmer whose wheat grades No. 1. And prices are much better than last year. Your boss will have a fine bank account when he cashes that along with his other grain checks."

"What happens to our wheat now?" asked George. It was well on in the evening and no more grain teams or trucks were coming in, so the elevator man was willing to talk for a while.

"It is carried up, or 'elevated' from the receiving hopper to the top of the elevator and then run into the bin—in this case the No. 1 bin."

"But what happens after that?" said George. "Where does it go, and how does it become flour?"

"That's a long story," said the elevator man. "But if you were here to-morrow morning you would see the grain running through pipes from the bins into the box-cars on the siding. Then the train of freight-cars starts on the long journey to the terminal elevators. Even passenger trains are often sidetracked to let wheat trains go through, for the box-cars must be emptied quickly at the terminals and brought back for more wheat."

"Everybody makes way for wheat!" laughed George.

"That's right! If we lived farther west our grain would go to the terminals at Vancouver or Prince Rupert, but this wheat will be taken to Fort William or Port Arthur. Have you seen pictures of the big terminal elevators at Port Arthur?"

"They look like rows of big round towers, I think," said George.

"Some of them hold thirty or forty million bushels of wheat; they are enormous," said the grain man, "and often they are all so jammed with wheat the grain companies and the government hardly know what to do."

"At the Great Lakes terminals the wheat is loaded into grain ships called freighters, which are specially built to carry grain. The freighters are moored beside the elevators, and big spouts lead from the towers into hatchways along the deck of the ship. These freighters carry the grain to Port Colborne, Kingston, or Prescott. There the grain is reloaded on smaller boats, as the lake freighters are too large to pass through the canals to Montreal. Many grain cargoes are also unloaded at ports on Georgian Bay and shipped across Ontario by rail to Montreal. At Montreal the wheat is loaded on steamers and so sails to Europe."

"But where is the wheat ground into flour?" asked George.

"Most of our Canadian wheat which is exported is milled in the countries which buy it, but a great deal of Canadian flour is shipped abroad too. The greater part of Canadian milling is done in the eastern provinces, but you will remember, George, that there are big flour mills too in Calgary, Edmonton, Saskatoon, Medicine Hat, Moose Jaw, St. Boniface, and Winnipeg."

"The wheat is purchased in carloads by the flour mills from the grain companies. First, each carload is carefully tested for quality. Then the wheat is cleaned and treated to remove the outermost coating. The grains are now soaked in water, to soften the bran coat, and crushed so as to break away the bran from the white centre of the grain. The broken-up grains are sifted to remove the bran, and then ground finer and sifted again. During these last siftings the finer grains of flour, those which come from nearest the centre of the white kernel, are separated from the others. Now, George, tell me who bakes the finest bread in the world, and from what wheat it is made."

George answered promptly: "My mother bakes the best bread in the world, and it is made from No. 1 Hard wheat, which my father grows."

The elevator man laughed. "Well, perhaps that is not exactly true, George, but it is near enough—near enough!"

## HARVEST OF THE WATERS

IF you have ever gone fishing, you may have learned that more fish may be found in one part of a lake than in another part of the same lake. In the same way, men who make their living by fishing in the sea know that certain parts of the ocean are better for fishing than other parts. Of four great sea-fishing regions in the world, two are owned by the Dominion of Canada. One of these is in the Pacific Ocean off the shores of British Columbia, the other in the Atlantic Ocean near the four Maritime Provinces. In addition to these two great Canadian fishing grounds, the inland fisheries in every province of the Dominion supply many tons of fresh-water fish every year. This should not surprise us when we realize that Canada's lakes and rivers contain more than half of all the fresh water in the world!

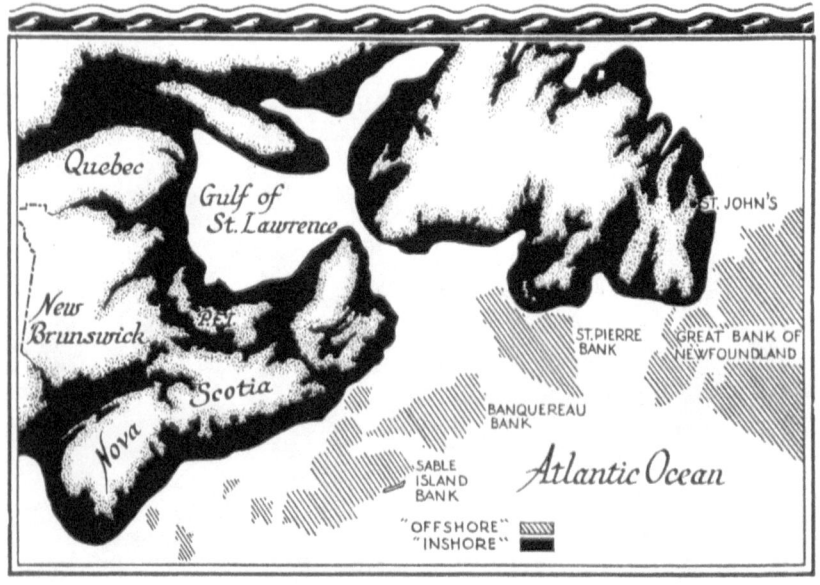

We have already read how our country was first explored by the fur trader and how it was first settled by the farmer. But we should remember that it was the fishing industry that brought Europeans into the Gulf of St. Lawrence in the first place. After John Cabot returned to England in 1497 with stories of tremendous numbers of codfish swimming off the shores of the New World, many fishermen of Europe began to cross the Atlantic every year. In those days a fishing vessel might spend as long as six months away from home. If a fisherman earned forty dollars in all that time, he was well pleased with his voyage! It is hard to believe that there were men willing to brave the dangers of the North Atlantic for so little profit.

None of these early fishermen, of course, knew why there were so many fish in the ocean off our coast. To begin with, the eastern highlands of this continent continue on below the surface of the Atlantic Ocean, and these hills under the water make shallow places in the ocean—sometimes only 200 feet deep. These arc the "banks" from which huge catches of cod, haddock, and other fish are taken every year. The largest of these fishing regions is known as the Great Bank of Newfoundland. It lies directly east of Newfoundland, where the cold Labrador Current meets the warm Gulf Stream. The Labrador Current carries countless numbers of little green water plants from the Arctic regions, and on these the codfish feed. That is why the shallow waters of the Great Bank or Newfoundland are such excellent fishing grounds. On the map you will find other banks off the coast of Nova Scotia. Although these are not so large, they change the waters over them into a "fisherman's paradise".

The fishing which is carried on over the Banks is called "offshore" fishing. These fisheries are actually carried on to-day much as they were three hundred years ago, though modern science helps in many ways. From April to October the fishing schooners set out from the little fishing villages for the Banks, on trips which may take six weeks to two months. Each schooner carries several small boats, called dories. All day long men are out in these small boats, hauling in the fish which have been caught on the lines, and baiting the hooks again. The loaded dories are rowed back to the schooner, where other men clean and salt the fish. When the schooner has a full cargo, it heads back to port. There the fish are spread on "flakes"—long racks or tables—to dry in the sun and air.

At present, more fish are caught close to the coasts of the Atlantic Provinces than over the Banks. These coastal waters make up what are known as the "inshore fisheries". The fishermen go out each morning from their homes and return each afternoon with their catches. Sometimes they use hooks and lines, baited with herring, squid, or caplin; at other times they use "codtraps"—square-shaped nets which catch large numbers of fish when the "schools" of fish are "running", that is, moving in a great mass from one place in the sea to another.

In addition to cod, the inshore fisheries produce haddock, herring, mackerel, scallops, turbot, smelts, and other varieties. Lobster is a very profitable catch. Pictou, Nova Scotia, is the chief centre of the lobster industry. Considerable quantities of salmon are caught along the north-east coast of Newfoundland and off Labrador.

## NEWFOUNDLAND SEALING

Early in March vessels leave St. John's, Newfoundland, to hunt for seals on the ice-floes off the north-east coasts of the province. As soon as seals are sighted, the hunters leave the ship and cross on the ice-floes to the herds. They kill the young seals, which are two to three weeks old, and skin them on the spot, removing a thick layer of fat with the hide. If the hunters move too far away from the ship, they may become lost. Sometimes a storm blows up, and moves the ice-floes. Many men have been lost from sealing parties, and sometimes a ship itself disappears. In 1914 a vessel with a crew of 173 men was lost on its way from the Gulf of St. Lawrence to St. John's with a cargo of sealskins.

This is not the kind of seal whose skin is prized for fur. The hides of the Newfoundland seals are used chiefly in making fine leather goods, and the fat is melted to make valuable oil.

## "SALMON IS KING"

Throughout the waters off British Columbia, from the Queen Charlotte Islands in the north to Vancouver Island in the south, "salmon is king". Large quantities of herring, pilchards, and halibut are also caught here.

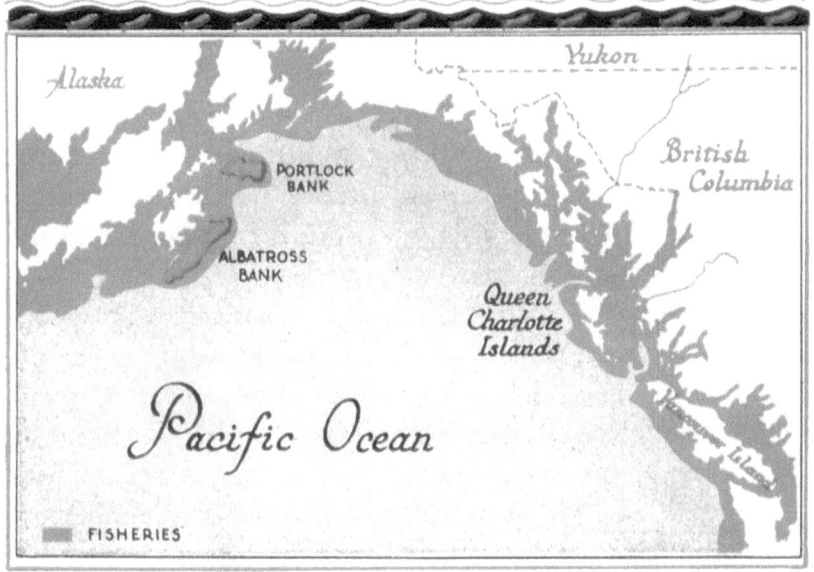

The young salmon, strange to say, are hatched inland, far up the fresh-water rivers or streams of British Columbia. The following spring they find their way out to the Pacific, where they spend the next three or four years of their lives, and grow to about twenty pounds in weight. Then, in the spring, they return up the very same rivers from which they came, leaping waterfalls and rapids, until they reach the pools in which they were born. Here they lay the eggs from which their young will soon be hatched, and then most of them die.

The fishermen make their largest catches of salmon during the spring "run" each year, by letting down their nets along the deep ocean inlets, or at the mouths of the rivers, as the salmon begin their journey upstream.

British Columbia has some of the largest fish canneries in the world. The salmon is packed raw into the cans, with salt and water; then the cans are sealed and heated until the contents are thoroughly cooked.

# FRESH-WATER FISHING

Because Canada has many thousands of fresh-water lakes and streams, every province produces a share of the Dominion's annual harvest of fish. However, less than a quarter in value of Canada's fishing harvest actually comes from these freshwater fisheries. Whitefish are the most important of those caught inland. Other important fresh-water kinds include pickerel, trout, and herring. The variety of fish products has greatly increased. In addition to dried, salted fish, Canada now sells canned fish, quick-frozen fish, and fresh fish that can be shipped in refrigerator cars all over the continent. Cod- and halibut-liver oils are among the most valuable fish products. Other kinds of fish, not suitable for eating, as well as waste products from the fish packing plants are now converted into fertilizer.

In order that the fisheries of Canada may never become "fished out", the government at Ottawa and the governments in all the provinces have taken steps to conserve the supply of fish wherever they are caught. Sometimes regulations are passed which tell just how many fish of a certain kind may be caught in any year. There are other rules which forbid the use of certain kinds of nets—nets which might catch so many fish that soon there would be none left. This kind of planning for the future is called conservation.

One important kind of fisheries conservation is carried on by our governments by building and running fish hatcheries. In these hatcheries, which can be found all across the country, fish eggs are hatched under the most favourable conditions. As the young fish grow up, they are used to "re-stock" rivers, streams, and lakes which are in danger of becoming "fished out". The money that it costs to run these hatcheries is wisely spent, since it assures us that Canada will still be famous for her fisheries many years from now.

## THE NEW FUR TRADE

THE fur trade was the most important industry of New France. Although some of Canada's later industries grew more quickly, the story of the fur trade goes on. Moreover, the value of the furs now shipped out of Canada each year is almost a hundred times as great as it was during the days of the *coureurs de bois*.

From the beginning, the exploration of Canada was tied up with the story of the fur trade. Almost every settled part of our country was first visited by a fur trader. It was the fur trade that brought De Monts to Port Royal; Radisson and Groseilliers led the English into Hudson Bay in search of furs, La Vérendrye and the other western explorers were seeking furs. Even Alexander Mackenzie, the first white man to cross the Rocky Mountains, was a fur trader.

But if furs were responsible for the exploration of our country, farming was responsible for its settlement. And as the farms of the pioneers began to spread ever deeper into the "fur traders' preserves", fewer and fewer wild animals were left in the woods near the new settlements. Yet because only the southern fringe

of our Dominion is heavily settled with people, there are hundreds of thousands of square miles in Canada still full of wild life. Indeed, Canada's North-West Territories, together with the northern parts of the Prairie Provinces, Ontario, and Quebec, remain among the world's richest fur-bearing regions.

### FUR TRAPPING IN CANADA TO-DAY

Throughout Canada's vast northland woods the trappers—Indian, white, and half-breed—roam all winter long, for this is the time of year when furs are at their best. The thick coats of fur which the animals grow to protect themselves from the cold make pelts that are much more valuable than those that can be taken in the summer months.

Each trapper lays out his trap line in the form of a great loop, often containing a hundred or more traps and reaching for as many as a hundred miles. It may take him a week or more to visit all his traps, and no sooner does he complete his round than he must start out once more. At last, with the coming of spring, his work is finished. Then the trapper sets out for the trading post with his winter's "take" of furs. During the summer he may find work on a farm or in a sawmill or factory, but before long he begins to make his traps ready, and stocks up once again with provisions for his camp in the woods. The first snows will find him prepared for another season in the wilderness.

The life of the Canadian trapper is less lonely than it used to be. Valuable minerals have been found in different parts of Canada's northland, and the mining camps often lie close to the trap lines. Airplanes may roar over the trappers' cabins, bringing in supplies to the people living at the mines. Even the trappers themselves often travel to and from their trap lines by airplane.

Of all our Canadian fur bearers, the largest is the bear—the polar bear along the Arctic Coast and Hudson Bay; the grizzly bear in the Rocky Mountains; and the black bear throughout most of our forest regions. Wolves, too, are common and widespread. The ermine—or weasel, as it is usually called—is fairly plentiful across the country. Otter, beaver, marten, fisher, and mink are other furs which may come from the country of the fur trapper. Unfortunately, the Canadian beaver is beginning to disappear, although the Canadian government is taking steps to protect this valuable animal which played such an important part in the early fur trade. A very common pelt is that of the

BEAVER  WHITE FOX

muskrat. Sometimes the muskrat pelts are plucked and dyed black; then they are sold under the name "Hudson seal".

But the most valuable part of the Canadian fur trade is made up of fox pelts. From the Arctic come the skins of the white fox, usually traded in at the fur posts by Eskimos for the food and provisions of the white man—food and provisions the Eskimos would not need if they spent their winters hunting seals and walrus as in days gone by. On the other hand, nearly all the "black and silver" fox pelts come from fur farms—an important Canadian industry.

### FUR FARMING IN CANADA TO-DAY

About one-third of the furs produced in Canada to-day do not come from the trap lines, but from "fur farms". Fur farming was first tried by the early trappers themselves. Instead of taking up their traps in the spring, when the furs became poorer in quality, they went on trapping foxes alive during the summer months. The animals caught in this way were kept in pens until the following winter, when the furs reached their

ERMINE  MUSKRAT

best with the approach of the cold weather. Before long, some of these trappers learned that it was possible to raise in pens families of the very animal they had been spending so much time and energy to trap.

Of course, not all kinds of fur bearers will live in captivity, and so trapping still accounts for most of the furs produced in Canada. But at the present time fur farms across the Dominion are producing large numbers of foxes and mink, as well as some fisher, marten, and chinchilla.

In 1894, some pure "black and silver" foxes were raised in captivity for the first time by two Prince Edward Island farmers. A few years later, twenty-five of these pelts were sold in England for more than thirty-three thousand dollars! When the news of this sale reached Canada, fox farming began to boom across the country. Of course, such high prices could only last as long as the supply of "black and silver" fox pelts remained small. As more and more farms began to raise them, prices began to drop. In one year just before World War II, over three hundred thousand such pelts were produced on Canadian fur farms. However, the average price paid for each skin that year was only a little over fifteen dollars.

Other types of pelt besides the "black and silver" have also been developed on fur farms. Some of these special types have brought extremely high prices at first, but as more and more fur farmers produce the same kind, the prices have always begun to drop. One of the best known of these special kinds of pelt has been the "platinum" fox—a lighter fur of rich appearance, one pelt of which once sold for as much as eleven thousand dollars!

Fur farming may seem to be an easy way to make money. But though new and scarce varieties of furs produced on fur farms have sometimes brought high prices, these high prices have caused more and more people to go into fur farming. As in many other industries, keen competition has turned the business of fur farming into a science, and persons entering it must learn everything about it that there is to learn if they wish to succeed.

Furs have been used for clothing since the earliest days of history. Even the barbarian found that furs kept him warm in winter. Later, when people learned to weave their clothing from wool and silk, fur became highly prized as a trimming by both men and women. We have already read about the eagerness of the French and English merchants to secure the furs of the New World for this purpose. It is said that at that time a man's wealth could be judged from the amount of fur he used to decorate his clothing!

To-day, most of the fur produced in Canada is used to make ladies' winter coats, or to trim their cloth garments. In some parts of the Dominion, especially the north, fur clothing is looked upon as a necessity by men as well as women. And because the best furs can be grown in lands with fairly cold climates, Canada remains one of the leading fur-producing countries of the world.

## BURIED TREASURE

THE great ships laden with gold and silver, which sailed to Spain from Mexico and Peru in the sixteenth century, made the Spaniards the envy of other European nations. The early explorers of France and England hoped to find such treasures in the northern part of North America, but they never did. Even when the Indians brought a little copper from the shores of Lake Superior, the French were unable to learn exactly where it had come from. Yet all the time, beneath the wilderness of rocks, forests, rivers, and lakes, lay hidden the gold and silver which they sought. Indeed, there were very many other valuable minerals, including copper, nickel, zinc, iron, lead, asbestos, and coal.

The people of New France did find deposits of iron near Three Rivers, but that was the only mining they did in the St. Lawrence valley. The coal of Cape Breton was known at this time, too, and some of it was mined. However, mining in eastern Canada did not become important until long after the country

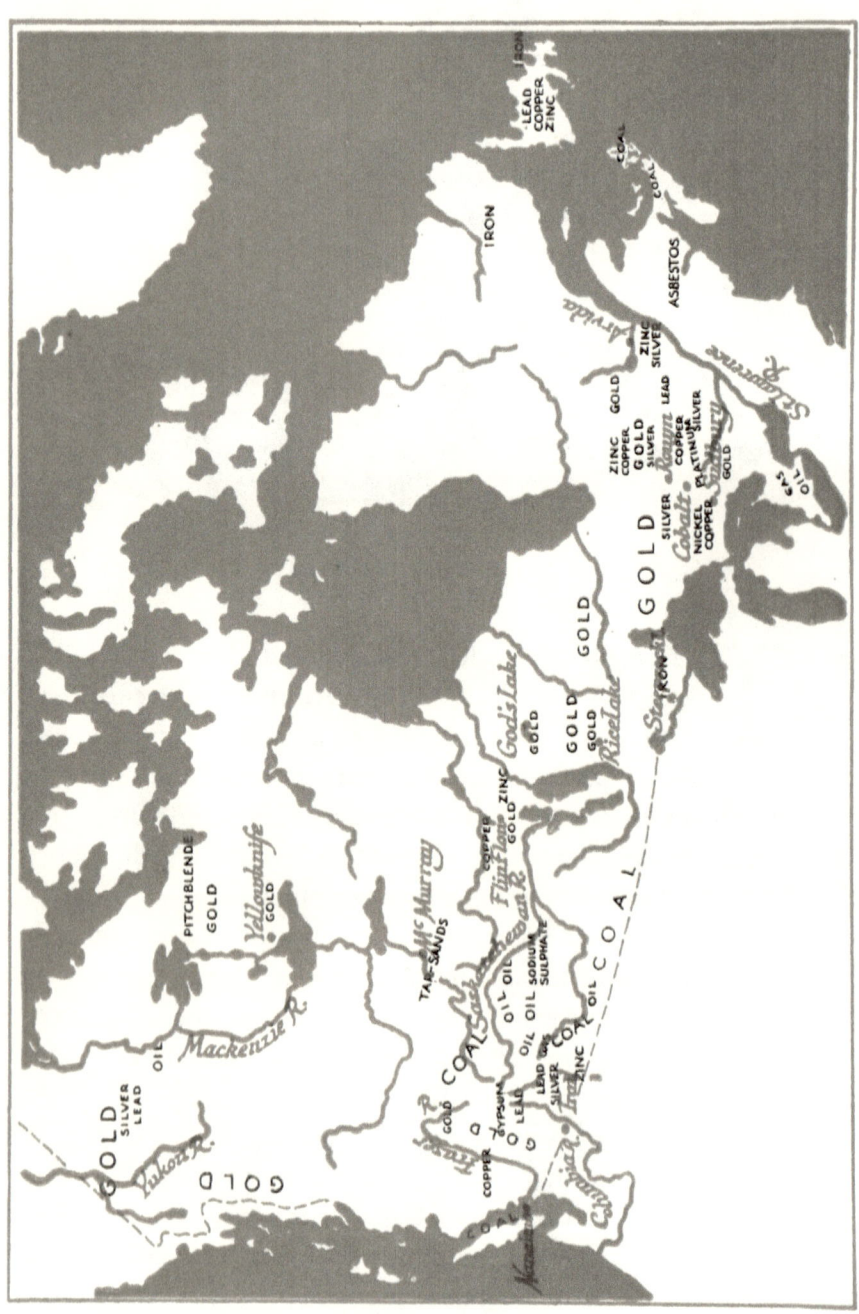

had been settled by the white man. This was not so in British Columbia, where mining came before farming.

Over a century ago, coal was discovered at Nanaimo on Vancouver Island. In 1858, a gold rush to the Fraser River began. Discoveries of other minerals were made across Canada during the next fifty years, but not until the present century did the Dominion become famous as a mining country. It is believed, moreover, that the greater part of Canada's mineral wealth has not yet been discovered.

Most of Canada's minerals have been found in the Canadian Shield, the Rocky Mountains, in Nova Scotia, Newfoundland, and Labrador. The Canadian Shield is the name given to a vast area which curves around Hudson Bay. Thousands of years ago, this part of Canada was covered with great fields of moving ice which scraped off the soil and laid bare the rocks which hold so much of our country's gold, silver, copper, and nickel. Most of this country is still rocky and barren, and makes poor farming land.

In the Rocky Mountains, gold was first discovered in the rivers. The running water had washed this gold out of the rocks. Sometimes it was found in large nuggets in the sand bars and beds of streams. At other times, the sand of the river bed was stirred up with water in a tray by the gold-seeker, and if he were lucky a few grains of gold "dust" might settle to the bottom as he poured off the muddy mixture. This method of collecting the gold was known as "panning". Gold is still found in the Rockies, but it is in the rocks themselves, as in the Canadian Shield. Modern machinery is needed to mine this rock and break it up to take out the gold and other minerals.

The men who hunt for minerals are called prospectors. Some of them search all their lives, and never succeed in finding a rich mine. Others may make a lucky "strike", and become rich overnight. When a prospector makes a "strike", he "stakes a

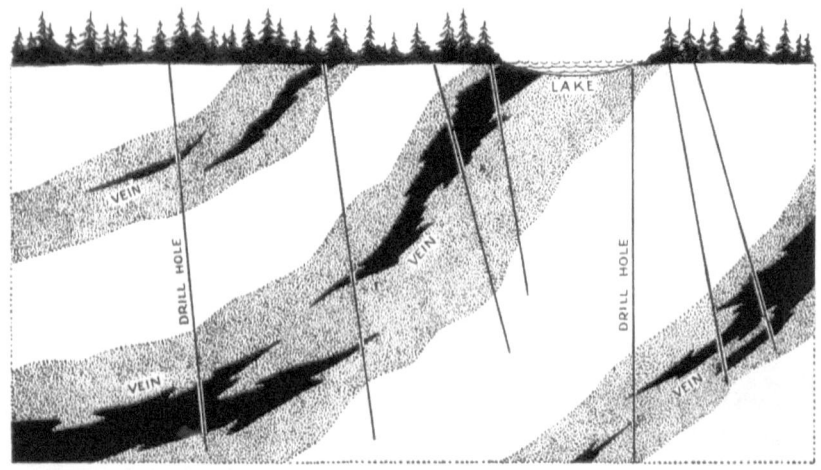

claim", that is to say, he plants stakes in the ground around his discovery and hurries to the government office to "record" his claim, so that no one else can claim that place, too. When other prospectors hear that he has found gold, they all rush to stake claims near by. This is called a "gold rush". You have heard about the gold rushes to the Fraser and the Cariboo. Another very famous rush occurred when gold was found in the Klondike River in the Yukon in 1896. The most recent discoveries have been made in Northern Ontario and Quebec, Northern Manitoba, the District of Mackenzie, and in Labrador. The nickel and copper deposits near Sudbury were found in 1883, when the Canadian Pacific Railway was being built. However, it was not until almost twenty-five years had passed that Sudbury grew into the great mining centre which it is to-day. The silver mine at Cobalt, Ontario, was found accidentally when the Timiskaming and Northern Ontario Railway was being built in 1903.

Gold, silver, and copper lie in the rocks in veins. These veins may be rich or poor in the mineral they contain, and usually stretch for some distance through the rock. Often only one end of a vein will reach the surface, and even then it may be covered with soil or moss. After a vein has been discovered, a wonderful tool called the diamond drill is used to find out how far the vein reaches, how wide it is, and in what direction it goes. The diamond drill is a hollow tube of steel which has diamonds fastened to the bottom edge. Diamonds are the hardest substance known, and they will cut through even the hard rocks which contain the ore, as the rock containing the mineral is called. By drilling deep holes into the surface of the rock near the vein, the miners can bring up long cylinders of the rock beneath and find out whether or not it is worthwhile to sink a mine, and if so, where.

Then machinery is set up and a deep hole called the shaft is blasted with dynamite down through the rock. Tunnels are bored out from it at different levels. The ore is carried up the shaft to the surface in an elevator. Next it must be crushed, ground, and sometimes melted, before the metal it contains can be taken out of it.

Often several different metals are found in the same ore. At Trail, B.C., a huge plant separates gold, silver, zinc, and lead from the ore. At Sudbury, Ontario, near which most of the world's supply of nickel is to be found, copper and platinum are also obtained. Flin Flon, in northern Manitoba, produces copper, zinc, and gold. At Rouyn, Quebec, the mines yield gold, silver, and copper. At Buchans, Newfoundland, copper, lead, and zinc are extracted from the ore.

The life of a mine is often very short. As the metal becomes scarcer, the mine ceases to pay and is closed down. But prospectors are always searching for new mines to take the place of the old.

Coal is found in beds, or seams, some of which are very thick. It is mined in large quantities in Nova Scotia, Alberta, and British Columbia. Some coal is also mined in southern

Saskatchewan and Adanitoba. At Cape Breton, Nova Scotia, the coal mines run far out under the sea. Much of the coal produced in Cape Breton is used for making steel from iron brought from Newfoundland. The Newfoundland iron mines at Bell Island run out for miles under Conception Bay. Vast quantities of iron ore have been discovered in Labrador as well. Iron is also being mined at Steep Rock, west of Port Arthur, Ontario. The search for minerals in Labrador has scarcely begun, however.

Many other kinds of minerals, besides those named above, are produced in Canada. We must not forget that oil, although it is a liquid, is really a mineral and comes from beneath the surface of the earth. Most of Canada's oil has so far been found in Alberta. Another mineral found in Canada is asbestos—the fireproof covering used on furnaces and in buildings. Almost all of the known world supply of asbestos is in the province of Quebec. Nor must we forget that even

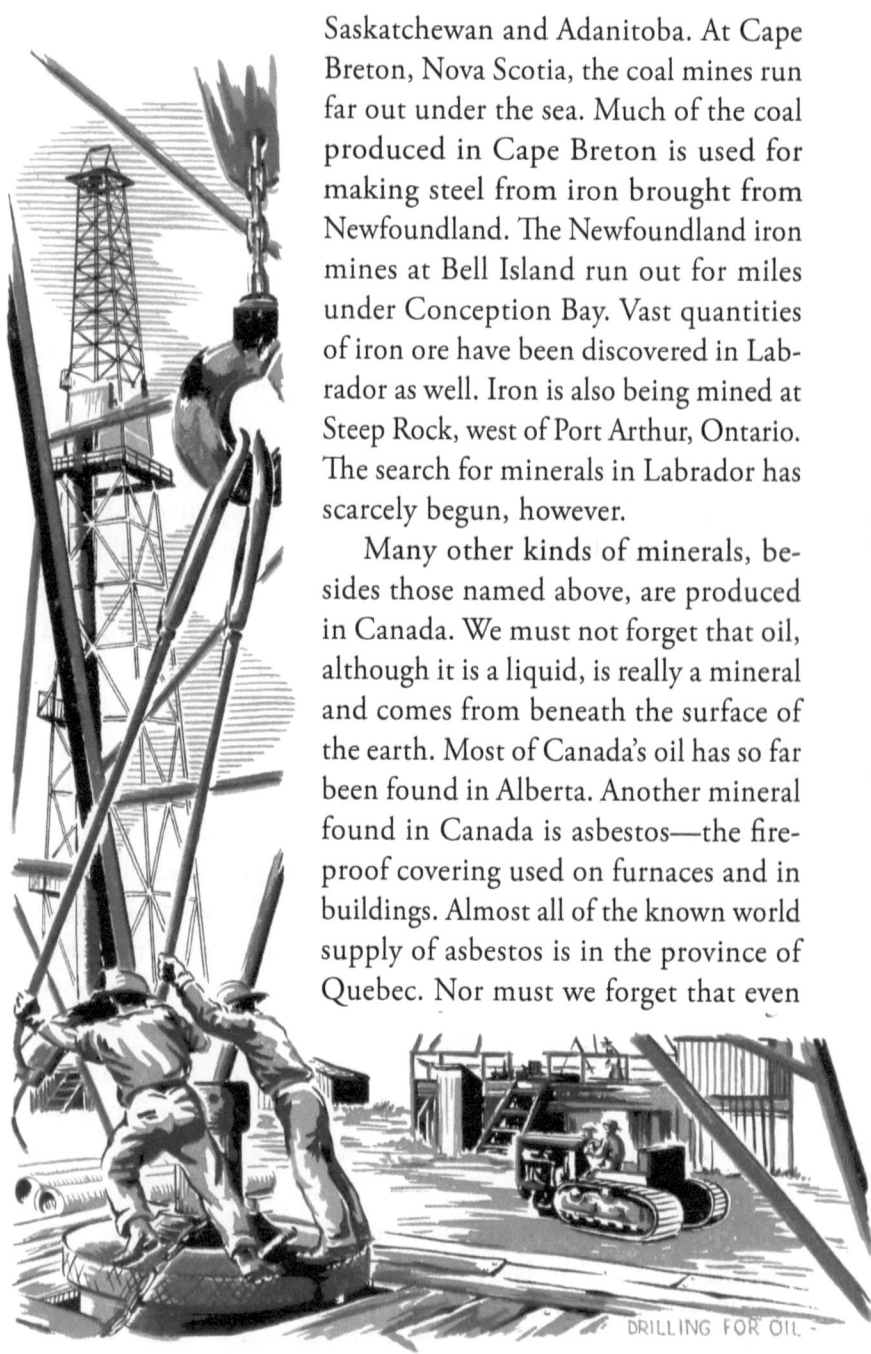

DRILLING FOR OIL

the sand, gravel, and stone, used in building are mined from the earth.

If the early explorers, who were so disappointed when they found no minerals, could only know that Canada now earns over five hundred million dollars from her mines every year, they would be startled indeed!

## THE NEW NORTH

Many of Canada's mines are in the Far North. Although boats have travelled up and down the Mackenzie River system ever since the days of Alexander Mackenzie, the minerals of the north were not found until airplanes began to fly over the wilderness of rocks, lakes, and swamps. Fitted with skis in winter, and pontoons in summer, airplanes can fly into remote areas, carrying prospectors, workers, machinery, and supplies. In just a few years, the invention of the airplane has so changed the northland, that we now often call it the "new" north.

World War II brought great changes to this part of Canada. To defend North America from the Japanese, the Canadian and American governments built a highway more than 1500 miles long through northern British Columbia and the Yukon, to connect Edmonton, Alberta, with Fairbanks, Alaska.

Oil had been found in 1919 on the east bank of the Mackenzie River, about seventy-five miles south of the Arctic Circle. Some wells were drilled, and oil supplied to steamers, trading-posts, and mines. However, during World War II great quantities of oil were needed as fuel for American army vehicles in Alaska. New wells were drilled, and a pipe-line nearly six hundred miles long was built across swamps and mountain-passes, to carry oil from Norman Wells to Whitehorse.

Along the banks of the Athabaska River near McMurray, the sand is dark, for it is held together by a black, tarry substance.

These "tar-sands", as they are called, have long been known—the Indians liked to burn the "tar" to keep off the mosquitoes, it is said, and the material could be used to mend leaky boats. Later it was discovered that gasoline and other oil products could be obtained from the tar-sands. At present, however, it costs more to obtain oil from tar-sands than from oil-wells. But one day, if the oil-fields of the world begin to run dry, we may be very glad that Canada has such huge quantities of tar-sands in the northland.

Gold is mined in northern Manitoba at Flin Flon, God's Lake, and Rice Lake. One of the richest discoveries has been at Yellowknife, on Great Slave Lake, where a good-sized mining town has grown up in the wilderness.

The most important mine, however, is the Eldorado, at Great Bear Lake, right on the edge of the Arctic Circle. Here a Canadian prospector discovered large stores of pitchblende, which is the ore containing radium and uranium. Radium is far more precious than gold, and is used in hospitals for healing. Uranium is the mineral which plays such an important part in the making of the atomic bomb, with which the Allies were able to force Japan to surrender in 1945.

Still rich in furs, and with new discoveries of mineral wealth steadily being made, the importance of the north to Canada is growing rapidly. Probably most of the people of Canada will continue to live near the southern border, but we can no longer look upon the north as a barren and unproductive wilderness. The New North will play a most important part in Canada's future.

## TURNING TREES INTO DOLLARS

MOST of us are very fond of trees; the streets of our cities are lined with them and we plant them about our homes. We often wish that there were more trees, and regret that so many of them were cut down in days gone by.

Yet it is easy to understand why early settlers in Canada looked on the trees as their enemies. The forests in those days often hid fierce savages and dangerous animals. And since almost all of eastern Canada was heavily wooded, the trees had to be cleared from the land before any crops could be planted.

The pioneers were glad, of course, to have wood to build homes and to use as fuel. But they could not sell the wood they did not use themselves—other settlers had far more than they wanted, too! The only thing they could do was to burn it. From the ashes they made potash, which they could sell for making soap and glass.

Many of the early explorers have described for us the splendour of Canada's forests. Jacques Cartier told of the "goodly trees" he saw on the banks of the St. Lawrence River as he sailed upstream towards Hochelaga. Both shores of the river were covered with hardwoods and softwoods. Among the hardwoods were the beech, maple, oak, birch, elm, ash, and basswood. The softwoods included the white pine, red pine, spruce, balsam, hemlock, cedar, and tamarack. "Hardwoods" are trees with broad leaves; all hardwoods shed their leaves in autumn. The leaves of "softwoods" are so narrow they are called "needles"; softwoods (except the tamarack) keep their needles the year round.

The first Canadian timber sold abroad was white pine. These splendid trees frequently grew to a height of 150 feet, and a thickness of three feet. They were very straight, and made fine masts for sailing-ships. As early as 1700, white pine logs were

shipped from New Brunswick to France to be made into masts. After the British won Canada, the pines which grew along the St. John River were kept for the masts of English ships. A good mast sold for $500—a very large sum in those days.

The white pines were also sold as "square timber". The trees were cut down and hewn square with axes. Then they were fastened together to form rafts, and floated downstream. Since the trip usually took a long time, the lumbermen and their families built huts on the rafts, in which they lived while on the river. When the rafts reached Quebec or Saint John, the square timber was loaded on sailing vessels and shipped to England.

After a while, the sale of square timber to England fell off, but by that time the United States was beginning to buy a great many logs from Canada. After the best trees in the Ottawa

PULPWOOD BEING CARRIED UP TO MILL

Valley had been cut, loggers began to move west to the Trent River and upper St. Lawrence. As these areas became "logged out" they moved on to Georgian Bay and Lake Huron—ever farther and farther west.

The logs were floated down the rivers, then tied into rafts and towed down the Great Lakes, usually to American sawmills. Later on, Canada began to build more sawmills of her own, and to export sawn lumber instead of logs. In New Brunswick the most important sawmills were built along the St. John, Restigouche, and Miramichi Rivers. The largest mills in Quebec are along the Gaspe Peninsula, since those on the Ottawa River no longer have as large supplies of timber to handle as in days gone by. Ontario's chief sawmills are to be found in the country between Ottawa and Sault Ste Marie.

Because the cheapest and simplest kind of power to turn the saws was waterpower, the sawmills always were built along the rivers and streams. Not only did the river furnish the power to turn the saws, but it brought the timber to the mills as well. It is easy, therefore, to understand why settlements often sprang up about a waterfall. Many of these early "mill" villages have grown into great towns or cities. Sometimes, when other industries had not taken root before the forests near by were cut down, these towns began to shrink after the closing of the sawmill. But the waterfall or dam which provided the early sawmill with waterpower can also provide hydro-electric power to-day, with the result that industries very often have been attracted to such villages.

Eastern Canada now manufactures much less sawn lumber than formerly, because the best trees for this purpose have been cut down. There is little white pine left, for example. However, vast amounts of paper are made from such woods as spruce, balsam, and poplar. The logs are floated downstream to the mills where they are ground or cooked into pulp to make the newsprint on which our daily and weekly papers are printed, as well as to make many other kinds of paper. This book is printed on paper made from pulpwood. There are mills in Newfoundland, Nova Scotia, New Brunswick, Quebec, Ontario, Manitoba, and British Columbia. Even the Prairie Provinces cut spruce logs in their northern parts to feed the paper mills. Pulp-and-paper is now Canada's leading industry in the value of goods manufactured. By far the greater part of Canada's newsprint is sold to newspapers in the United States.

Lumbering in eastern Canada has usually been carried on only during the fall, winter, and early spring. To-day, more and more camps are cutting all year round. The logs are loaded on sleds as soon as the snow comes, and then pulled to the nearest lake or river where they are piled on the ice. To-day, tractors and trucks have largely taken the place of horses and oxen for this work. With the break-up of the ice in the spring, the logs are carried downstream on the spring flood. Sometimes the logs jam at a bend or narrow place in the stream or river. Then the lumber-

men who have been "driving" the logs, jumping from one to another in their spiked boots, have to break up the jam with their peaveys—short poles with iron hooks on the ends. This is dangerous work, for when the jam is broken, the logs move away with a rush. When the logs arrive at the mills, they are often kept together in booms on the river until they are needed. These booms are made by chaining large outside logs together, end to end, so that the loose logs in the middle cannot drift away.

The forests on Canada's Pacific coast are famous for their Douglas fir, white fir, red cedar, western hemlock, and Sitka spruce. These trees, which are found on the mountains sloping towards the ocean, range from two to six feet in diameter and 150 to 250 feet in height. The logs are so huge that a dozen horses might be needed to drag one of them through the forest, although to-day steam engines and tractors are almost always used. Sometimes these logs are hauled to a nearby logging railway by means of "spar" trees. To make a "spar" tree, a skilled lumberman climbs a tree and cuts off the top. A pulley is then attached to the top of the trunk which remains, and a wire rope run through it. One end of this wire rope is then fastened to the log which is to be moved. When the other end is wound in by an engine, the log is dragged through the forest. The logging railway then carries it down to the coast near by. Here the logs are joined together to form rafts, and towed by tug-boats to the sawmills along the British Columbia sea-coast.

British Columbia's first sawmill was built near Victoria, just three years after the Hudson's Bay Company built Fort Victoria. To-day, the province has some of the largest sawmills in the world. After the building of the Panama Canal, it became possible to send lumber cheaply from British Columbia to the eastern United States and to Europe. At present, more than half of the sawn lumber which Canada exports is sent from British Columbia.

Unfortunately, Canadians have been too wasteful in their use of the forests. When trees are cut down without care, often poor "scrub" trees grow to take the place of those removed. That is what has happened to a great part of Canada's once splendid forests. Often sufficient care is not taken to avoid leaving tops and dead branches in the woods after cutting, which adds to the danger of forest fires. Those of us who holiday in the woods should be extremely careful about using matches and putting out camp fires. Many serious fires have resulted from people throwing burning matches and cigarettes from automobiles, or failing to put out their camp-fires completely. Unless Canadians pay much more attention to preserving their forests, one of the Dominion's greatest industries will some day practically disappear.

## WHEELS OF INDUSTRY

THE cheapest way to turn electric generators is by the power of falling water. Electric power generated in this way is known as "hydro-electric" power. Since one of the world's greatest waterfalls is on the Niagara River, it is only natural that we should find one of the world's largest hydro-electric plants there too. Indeed, the hydro-electric power generated at Niagara Falls is carried by wires all over Southern Ontario. One of the chief reasons why Southern Ontario and Quebec have so many manufacturing industries is the cheapness of hydro-electric power, and the amount of it that is generated at Niagara Falls, on the St. Lawrence River, and elsewhere in this part of Canada.

Other great Canadian hydro-electric power plants are to be found at Montmorency Falls, beside the rapids on the St. Lawrence River, on the Gatineau River, at Grand Falls in New Brunswick, and at Deer Lake in Newfoundland, to mention only a few. British Columbia is speedily developing hydroelectric power plants along its many rapid-flowing rivers. More industries are growing up in the Prairie Provinces as well, where at present only a part of the electric power possible is being generated. A great deal of hydro-electric power is required to run the machinery used in mines and in pulp-and-paper plants. Huge power plants have been constructed solely to meet the needs of these industries.

In many parts of Canada, where the rivers do not drop quickly in waterfalls or rapids, man has been able to make his own waterfalls by building dams. Wherever these dams have been built, hydro-electric generating plants have been made possible. One of the greatest in the world is to be found at Shipshaw in Quebec. Although Shipshaw was built on the Saguenay River hundreds of miles from the nearest big city, it has already become the centre of the world's largest aluminium industry. This has happened only because hydro-electric power at Shipshaw had been made so very cheap and plentiful by the building of the dam. The raw material from which aluminium is made is sent to Shipshaw all the way from South America.

## CANADA BUYS AND SELLS

Every nation in the world is both a buyer and a seller. In a small village, the shoemaker sells shoes, and buys his food from the grocer, the butcher, and the baker. The grocer, the butcher, and the baker buy shoes from the shoemaker. The countries of the world have to do business with each other in the same way. Canadians cannot use all the wheat, gold, newsprint, or fish they can produce. It is because other nations have been eager to buy these products that Canadians have ploughed the wide prairies, developed the fisheries, drilled mines, and built large factories. Compared with many countries, Canada has a small population, but it carries on a big business—one of the biggest in the world.

Although Canada manufactures a wide variety of goods, there are still many things Canadians need that cannot be made in their own country, or that can be produced more cheaply elsewhere. Fruits such as oranges, lemons, bananas, and pineapples cannot be grown on Canadian farms. Canada is too far north to produce tea, coffee, or spices. Cotton and rubber can be grown only in southern lands. Canada buys oil from other countries because at present Canadian oil-fields do not produce as much oil as the nation needs. People living in Ontario and Quebec buy coal from the United States because some American coal mines are much nearer to them than any Canadian mines.

Trade between nations is necessary, but every nation must be careful not to buy more than it sells. If it spends more money in buying goods abroad than it earns by selling its own products, it will soon find itself in debt, just as our village shoemaker will if he spends more money for groceries than he takes in by selling shoes. In order to make sure that Canada does not buy more than it can afford, the Canadian government controls the flow of goods. It does this chiefly by placing duties on imports. Raising or lowering the duties raises or lowers the cost of such goods. When they cost more, people naturally buy fewer of them. Sometimes, when the "balance of trade" has been very much against Canada, the government has even had to forbid buying anything abroad except bare essentials. Since Canadians everywhere are affected by the duties on imports, great care must be taken to see that they do not lead to unnecessary hardships.

Rich in minerals, rich in agriculture, rich in timber and pulp-wood, rich in hydro-electric power, rich in fisheries, and rich in furs, our Dominion can rightly be looked upon as one of the most favoured nations on the face of the earth. But she can hope to make the most of all these gifts of Nature only if the nations of the world can learn how to live together at peace with one another.

# INDEX

Acadia, 69-74, 134: Acadians in N.B., 284; de Monts, 46-48; expulsion, 139-45, 146; La Tours, 71-74; Phips, 109
*Accommodation*, 378, 379
Air force, 345-46, 353, 355
Aix-la-Chapelle, Peace of (1748), 135
Alabama River, 120
Alaska, 21, 22, 38, 42, 197, 198, 268, 270, 399 : Highway, 41 3
Albany (N.Y.), 378
Albany, Fort, 102, 104, 107
Albatross Bank, 399
Alberta, 320, 337, 385, 391-94, 411, 412
Alexander, Sir William, 70, 71
Algonkin Indians (*sometimes spelled as in French*, Algonquin), 31, 34, 36, 50-52, 5 5, 65, 67
Alleghany Mountains, 146, 147
Alleghany River, 147
Amherstburg, Fort, 211
Amundsen, Roald, 21
Annapolis Basin, 46, 48
Annapolis Royal, 134, 138, 140, 141, 177
Annapolis Valley, 384
Anticosti, 14
Appalachian Mountains, 167
Argentia, 361, 371
Arkansas River, 120
Army, 307, 344-6, 353-56
Arnold, Colonel Benedict, 169-72, 208
Aroostock Ferry, 284
Assembly, 242, 262-63, 264: in Lower Canada, 251, 252; in New Brunswick, 257; in Newfoundland, 257; in Nova Scotia, 255; in Prince Edward Island, 257; in Upper Canada, 182
Assiniboia, 223
Assiniboine Indians, 34, 125, 319
Assiniboine River, 126, 223
Astoria, 206
Athabaska, Lake, 188, 201, 202
Athabaska Pass, 206
Athabaska River, 201, 207, 413
Atomic energy, 356, 414
Avalon Peninsula, 359, 361, 367

Baie Verte, 177
Baldwin, Robert, 263
Banks, fishing, 359-60, 366, 396-97
Banquereau Bank, 396

Barker, Colonel W. G., 345, 346
Barkerville, 268, 274, 277
Bateau, 373-74
Batoche, 319, 320
Battle of the Atlantic, 370
Battleford, 320, 321
Beauport, 87, 88, 90, 91, 155
Beausejour, Fort, 139-41, 145, 146
Beaver Dams, 215
Bedford, Fort, 147
Bedford Basin, 134
Begbie, Judge Matthew, 271
Behring, Vitus, 197
Behring Strait, 22, 197, 198
Bell Island, 360-62, 412
Bella Coola Indians, 34
Bella Coola River, 200, 204
Belle Isle, Strait of, 14, 361, 364
Beothuk Indians, 34
Big Bear, 320, 321
Bishop, "Billy", 345
Black Robes, 58-61, 64, 65
Blackfoot Indians, 34, 187, 319
*Bluenose*, 13
Boer War, 343
Bona Vista, 361
Borden, Sir Robert, 343, 348, 349
Boston, 72, 109, 128, 130, 137, 139, 166
Botwood, 361
Braddock, General Edward, 147-49
Brandon House, 223
Brant, Joseph, 185
Brantford, 185
Brebeuf, Father Jean, 65
Bristol, 5, 6, 10
British Columbia, 269-77: and confederation, 322; exploration, 197-207; farming in, 385; fisheries, 398-99; forests, 419, 420-21; hydro-electric power, 422; Indians, 29; mining, 314, 409, 411
British Commonwealth Air Training Plan, 353
British Empire, 339-40, 347, 348
British North America Act, 305-7, 339
Brock, Sir Isaac, 212-14
Brockville, 279
Brown, George, 304-5
Brule, Etienne, 53, 54
Buchans, 361, 411
Buffalo, 23, 24, 25, 123, 315, 319
Buffalo (N.Y.), 215
Burin, 361

[ 425 ]

Button, Thomas, 20-21
Bytown, 237, 377

Cabinet, 262-63
Cabot, John, 5-11, 21, 93, 129, 366
Cabot, Sebastian, 10
*Cabot Strait*, 362
Calgary, 320, 329, 394
California, 197, 269
Calvert, Sir George (Lord Baltimore), 367
Canada Act, 180
Canada East, 262, 300, 302-5
Canada West, 262, 287-97, 302-5
Canadian National Railways, 363
Canadian Pacific Railway, 320, 321-26, 329, 410
Canadian Shield, 409
Canadian Women's Army Corps, 354
Canals, 237, 296, 376-77
Canoe, 24, 30-32, 36-37, 190, 191, 372-73
Cape Breton, 14, 74, 177 : coal in, 360-61, 407, 412; Louisbourg, 135, 139, 152
Cape Chidley, 364
Cape Diamond, 154
Cape Horn, 196
Cape Race, 361, 367, 371
Cape Sable, 71
Caribbean Sea, 12
Cariboo Road, 268, 271-77
Carleton, Sir Guy (Lord Dorchester), 170-72, 285
Carlton, Fort, 319, 320
*Caroline*, 259
Caron, Father Le, 54, 57
Cartier, Sir George Etienne, 303, 304, 305
Cartier, Jacques, 12-17, 21, 22, 43, 46, 48, 69
Cascade Inlet, 199
Cedar Lake, 125, 127
Chambly Canal, 377
Champlain, Samuel de, 45-55, 57, 70, 71, 88
Champlain, Lake, 51, 54, 152, 169, 174, 219, 220
Charles, Fort, 99
Charles II, King, 93, 94, 97, 99, 100
Charleston, 120
Charlottetown, 177, 276: Conference, 304
Charnisay, Charles d'Aulnay, 71-74
Chateau St. Louis, 88, 110
Chateauguay River, 219
Chatham, 177, 211
Chebucto, 133-38
*Chesapeake*, 217-18
Chignecto, Isthmus of, 377
Chignecto Ship Railway, 377

Chipewyan, Fort, 201, 202
Chipewyan Indians, 34
Chippewa, 374
Cholera, 234-35, 236, 237
Churchill, Fort, 201
Churchill River, 188, 207
Civil War, American, 301
Clergy Reserves, 246-47
Coast Salish Indians, 34
Cobalt, 343, 410
*Colonial Advocate*, 244-45, 246, 247, 250
Columbia River, 205, 206, 207, 269, 270
Columbus, Christopher, 8, 10, 12, 18
Commission of government, 370
Commonwealth, British, 261, 350-51
"Company of Adventurers", 93, 100, 107
Company of New France, 83
Conception Bay, 361-62, 412
Confederacy of the Three Fires, 161
Confederation, 298-314, 357, 371
Connecticut, 128, 132
Conservation, 400, 421
Conservative party, 338, 339, 343
Conspiracy of Pontiac, 162-64
Constitutional Act, 180
Cook, Captain James, 197-99
Coppermine River, 188
Corn Laws, 296
Corner Brook, 358, 361
Cornwallis, Colonel Edward, 133, 136
*Coureurs de bois*, 82-84, 93, 113, 401
Craigellachie, 325
Cree Indians, 34, 319, 320
Crevecoeur, Fort, 120
Crowfoot, Chief, 319
Cumberland, Fort (Acadia), 139-42
Cumberland, Fort, 147, 188
Customs duties, 307, 424
Cut Knife, 320, 321

Dairy farming, 384, 386
Daniel, Father, 65
Dartmouth, 134, 138
Daulac (Dollard des Ormeaux), 65-68
Declaration of Independence, 173
Deer Lake, 422
Delaware, 128, 132
Detroit, Fort, 161, 162, 163, 179, 211-12, 213
Detroit River, 211-12
Diamond Jubilee, 339-41
*Diary of Mrs. Simcoe*, 181-85
Digby, 177, 379
*Discovery*, 18
Dogrib Indians, 34
Dominion Day, 307

*Don de Dieu*, 55
Douglas, Sir James, 269-71, 276
Douglas, Fort, 223, 224, 225, 226
Drake, Sir Francis, 129, 196-97
Duck Lake, 319, 320
Dufferin, Lord, 322
Dumont, Gabriel, 318, 319, 320
Dundas Street, 183, 214
Duquesne, Fort, 146-49
Durham, Lord, 258-62
Durham boar, 236, 37 3-74
Dutch, 64, 93, 95, 115, 130

Edmonton, 320, 337, 390, 394
Edward, Fort, 140, 142
Eldorado, 414
Elgin, Lord, 262-67
Erie, Fort, 215
Eskimos, 22, 34, 38-42, 404
Executive Council, 242-43: in Lower Canada, 251, 252, 261; in New Brunswick, 257; in Nova Scotia, 256; in Prince Edward Island, 257; in Upper Canada, 245, 247, 248, 250, 261
Exports, 423-24

Family Compact, 261, 262, 264: in New Brunswick, 257; in Nova Scotia, 254, 255; in Upper Canada, 246, 247, 248, 249, 250
Farming, 383-94
Federal government, 306, 307
Ferryland, 361, 367
Feudal system, 75-82
"Fighting Governor" 108-12, 115
Fisheries, 395-400: Atlantic, 396-98; Cabots, 6-7, 11 ; fresh-water, 400; Newfoundland, 359-60, 366, 367-68, 369; Pacific, 398-99
"Fishing admirals", 366
Five Nations, 34
Flin Flon, 411, 414
Florida, 120, 129
Forests, 415-21
Fort William, 124, 191, 192-94, 207, 226, 393
Forts, *see names of* (Albany, Beausejour, etc.)
"Fourteenth Colony", 169
Francis the First, King, 12, 13
Fraser, Simon, 206-7
Fraser, Fort, 206
Fraser River, 200, 203, 204, 206-7, 268, 270, 273, 274, 409
Fredericton, 179, 278, 284, 285, 376, 379
French River, 54, 186
"French Shore", 367-68

Frog Lake, 320, 321
Frontenac, Count, 108-12, 115, 118
Frontenac, Fort, 102, 115, 120
Fruit Farming, 384, 385
Fulton, Robert, 378
Fundy, Bay of, 44, 46, 71, 73, 134, 140, 377
Fur-farming, 404-6
Fur trade, 186-95, 221-27, 372-73, 401-6

Gaff Topsail, 358, 361
Galt, Sir Alexander T, 304
Gander, 358, 361, 364
Garry, Fort, 299, 309, 310-13
Ga'spe, 14, 15, 418
Gatineau River, 422
*General Smythe*, 379
George, Fort, 215
George III, King, 141
George VI, King, 258, 351
George, Fort, 206
Georgia, 128, 132, 174
Georgia, Strait of, 199
Georgian Bay, 26, 52, 54, 65, 89, 186, 394
Gilbert, Sir Humphrey, 44, 367
Globe, The, 276
God's Lake, 414
Gold rush: Cariboo, 271-77, 410; Fraser River, 270-71, 409, 410; Klondike, 343, 410; Kootenay, 343
"Golden Age of Sir Wilfrid Laurier", 342-43
Golden Hind, 196
Goose Bay, 364
Governor general, 243, 251-52, 162-61, 306, 307
Grand Falls, N.B., 284, 422
Grand Falls, Nfld., 361
Grand Island, 215
Grand Pre, 134, 140, 142-45
Grand River, 185
Grand Trunk Railway, 300
"Great Admiral", 9
Great Bank of Newfoundland, 359-60, 396, 397
Great Bear Lake, 201, 414
Great Company, The, 107, 187
Great Khan, 6, 12
Great Lakes, 93, 95, 97, 373
"Great Migration", 229-41
Great Slave Lake, 188, 201, 202, 414
Great War, The, 344-46
Green Bay, 115, 119
Greenland, 3, 4, 18
Griffon, 117, 118, 119
Grits, 338
Gros Ventre Indians, 34

[ 427 ]

Groseilliers, 94-100, 113
Grosse Isle, 236
Guy, John, 367

Habitants, 76-82, 83, 159, 168, 169, 281-82
Haida, 28, 34
Halifax, 153, 177, 282: founding, 133-38, 139; Howe, 253-56; port, 138, 362, 379; railways, 301; shipping, 379
Hamilton, 184
Hamilton Inlet, 364
Harbour Grace, 361
Hayes River, 123, 224
Hearne, Samuel, 188
Henday (*sometimes spelled* Hendry), Anthony, 187
Hennepin, Father, 118
Henry, Alexander, 188
Henry IV, King, 44-45
Henry VII, King, 5-10
Hincks, Sir Francis, 263
Hitler, Adolf, 352
Hochelaga, 14, 15, 416
"Homesteading", 330
Horses, 24-25, 31, 126
House of Commons, 307
Howe, Joseph, 253-56
Howse Pass, 206
Hudson, Henry, 18-21, 97, 130
Hudson Bay, 201 discovery of, 18-21; French expedition (1672), 114; and Hudson's Bay Company, 96-107, 186, 187; Iberville, 101-7
Hudson River, 18, 64, 93, 95, 130, 174
Hudson Strait, 18, 20, 98, 103, 105, 106
Hudson's Bay Company, 93-107, 122, 123, 186-88, 221-27, 269, 270, 301, 308-9, 310, 375
Huron Indians, 26, 27, 34, 52, 54, 55, 58-61, 64-65, 67, 89
Huronia, 54, 57
Hydro-electric power, 422-24

Iberville, Sieur d', 101-7, 108, 122, 367
Iceland, 3, 6, 7, 18
Igloo, 40-41
Ile Roy ale, 134
Ile St. Jean, 74, 134, 177
Illinois River, 120
Immigration, 297: British Columbia, 271; and Confederation, 301; "Great Migration", 228-41; Western Canada, 328-37, 342-43
Imperial War Cabinet, 348
Imports, 423-24

Indians, 22-42, 333, 372: and Black Robes, 58-61, 64-65; and Daulac, 65-68; North-West Rebellion, 315-21; Pontiac conspiracy, 161-64; and the railway, 324-25; and Ville-Marie (Montreal), 62-63
Industries, 422-24
Inshore fishing, 359, 397-98
Intendant, 85
Intercolonial Railway, 305
Iroquois Indians, 34: canoes, 31, 37; and Champlain, 50-52, 54; and Daulac, 65-68; and Frontenac, 108; and fur trade, 96; and Hurons, 64-65; and Montreal, 61; villages, 26, 27, 30, 32
Isle St. John, 74, 134, 177

James Bay, 18-21, 99, 101, 103
Jesuits, 57-65, 89, 116
Jogues, Father, 61
Joliet, Louis, 115-16, 118

Kaministiquia, Fort, 124, 125
Kayak, 39-40
Kelsey, Henry, 123
Kildonan, 226, 227
"King's Girls", 86
Kingston: capital of Canadas, 262, 279; (in 1832), 237; in Mrs. Simcoe's time, 181-82; and Sir John A. Macdonald, 302; from Montreal to, 373, 374
Kirke, Sir David, 54-55, 367
Kootenay, 385
Kootenay House, 206
Kootenay River, 206

La Fontaine, Sir Louis-Hippolyte, 263
La Reine, Fort, 125, 126
La Salle, Sieur de, 114-21, 122
La Tour, Charles de, 71-74
La Tour, Madame de, 71-74
La Verendryes, 124-27, 186, 187
Labrador, 14, 38, 361, 364, 398, 409, 410, 412
Lachine, 236
Lachine Rapids, 14
Lake of the Woods, 125
Lalemant, Father Gabriel, 65
Land-granting, 239, 243, 246-47, 329-30
Langley, Fort, 278, 273
Latches, pioneer, 241
Laurentians, 91, 155
Laurier, Sir Wilfrid, 339, 340-43
Laval, Bishop, 88, 108
League of Nations, 348, 349, 350
Legislatures, provincial, 307

Lescarbot, Marc, 47
Levis, General, 157-59
Lewiston, 220
Liberal party, 338, 339, 343
Lieutenant-governor, 242-43, 245, 246, 247, 248, 250, 257, 306
Ligonier, Port, 147
Log houses, 240
Logs, squaring, 240
London (Ontario), 183
Long Sault Canal, 376
Long Sault Rapids, 67, 68
Long-houses, 26-27
Louis XIV, King, 121
Louisbourg, 134: Aix-la-Chapelle, Peace of, 135, 137; in Seven Years' War, 141, 145, 152, 153
Louisiana, 107, 121, 122
Lower Canada, 180, 242
Loyalists, 175-80, 208, 37 3
Lumber, 4, 415-21
Lundy's Lane, Battle of, 215, 220
Lunenburg, 134, 138

Macdonald, Sir John A., 302-5, 314, 321-23, 326, 338, 339
Mackenzie, Sir Alexander, 199, 200-5, 206, 222
Mackenzie, William Lyon, 243-50, 252, 259
Mackenzie, District of, 410
Mackenzie River, 201, 202-3, 375
McGee, Thomas D'Arcy, 304
McLeod, Alan, 345
McLeod, Fort, 206, 317
McLoughlin, Dr. John, 269, 270
McMurray, 413
Madawaska River, 283
Magellan, Ferdinand, 18
Maine, 45, 46, 128, 169, 170, 284
*Maintiens le droit*, 327
Maisonneuve, Sieur de, 62-63
Malecite Indians, 34, 36
Mance, Jeanne, 62
Mandan Indians, 125, 126, 127
Manitoba, 337: claimed by Button, 21; confederation, 313; farming, 385, 388; Kelsey, 123; mining, 410, 411, 412; pulpwood, 419; rebellion, 309-13; Red River Colony, 221-27, 301
Manitoba, Lake, 125, 127
Maple syrup, 384
Maritime provinces, 4, 138, 304, 377, 384, 395-98
Marquette, Father, 115-16, 118
Marquis wheat, 389-90

Maryland, 128, 132, 147
Massachusetts, 73, 109, 128, 130, 132, 141
*Mathew*, 5, 6
Maurepas, Fort, 125, 126
May-pole, 77-82
Medicine Fdat, 394
Membertou, 69, 70
Metis, 221, 224, 309-13, 315, 317-21
Mexico, 12, 118, 126
Mexico, Gulf of, 106, 116, 120, 121
Michilimackinac, Fort, 102, 116, 117, 120, 188
Micmac Indians, 34, 69, 70, 136, 178
Middleton, General, 320-21
Midland, 54, 65
Minas Basin, 377
Mining, 360-62, 407-14
Miquelon, 160, 361, 368
Miramichi River, 177, 418
Missionaries, 35, 5 3-54, 56-68, 113, 116
Mississippi River, 95, 106, 114, 115, 116, 118, 119-21, 125, 144, 167
Missouri River, 120, 125
Mistassini Indians, 34
Mixed farming, 384, 385
Mohawk Indians, 185
Moncton, 177
Monongahela River, 147
Monopoly, 45, 83
Mont Real, 15
Montagnais Indians, 34
Montcalm, Marquis de, 151-56, 157
Montgomery, General Richard, 169-72
Montgomery's Farm, Battle of, 249
Montmorency Falls, 422
Montreal, 102, 120, 128, 280-81: American invasion, 170, 171; and canals, 376; capital of Canadas, 262, 264, 265-67; Cartier at, 14, 15; Daulac saves, 65-68; founding of, 61-63; fur trade, 186; Seven Years' War, 157, 159, 160; shipping, 378, 394
Monts, Sieur de 45, 46, 48, 49, 386
Moose Factory, 102, 103
Moose Jaw, 394
Moraviantown, Battle of, 211, 213-14
Mount Royal, 14, 15
Mount Stephen, Lord, 322-23
Municipal government, 262, 306
Murray, General James, 157-60

Nanaimo, 409
Nashwaak River, 285
Naskapi Indians, 34
Navy, 353, 354-55
Necessity, Fort, 147

Nelson, Fort, 102, 103, 104, 105, 106, 123
Nelson River, 20, 123, 224, 375
Neutral Indians, 34
New Amsterdam, 130, 131, 132
New Brunswick, 14, 396: Beausejour, 139; confederation, 304-5, 306; early travel in, 280, 282-86; farming, 384; forests, 417, 418, 419; hydro-electric power, 422; La Tours, 70-74; Loyalists, 176-79; de Monts, 45, 46; responsible government, 242, 257
New England, 74, 109, 135, 141, 142, 144, 174, 176
New Hampshire, 128, 132
New Jersey, 128, 132
New Wales, 20
New York (city), 93, 102, 128, 130, 132, 166, 173, 174
New York (state), 1 32, 378
Newark, 181, 182
Newfoundland, 357-71: Cabots, 11, 14; claimed by England, 44; farming, 384; fisheries, 11, 235; hydro-electric power, 422; Iberville, 104; mining, 409, 411, 412; Peace of Paris, 160; responsible government, 257; sealing, 398
Newsprint, 358-59
Niagara: Falls, 118, 119, 182, 215, 374, 377, 422; Fort, 102, 120, 215, 374; Peninsula, 384; River, 212, 213, 214, 215, 216, 218-19, 249, 250, 374
Nipigon, Lake, 124, 125
Nipissing, Lake, 52, 54, 186
*Nonsuch*, 98-99
Nootka Indians, 29, 34
Nootka Sound, 198, 199
Norman Wells, 413
Norsemen, 3-4, 20
North Carolina, 128, 132
North West Company, 188-95, 201, 206-7, 221-27, 269
North-West Mounted Police, 315-21, 324-25, 326-27
North-West Passage, 18, 21, 198, 207
North-West Rebellion, 318-21, 325
North-West Territories, 309, 313, 315-21, 330, 337, 356, 402, 413-14
Notre Dame Bay, 359, 361
Nova Scotia, 14, 128, 396: Acadians, 139-45; confederation, 304-5, 306; farming, 384, 387-88; fisheries, 11, forests, 419; French in, 46, 55, 57, 69-74; Halifax, 1 33-38; Loyalists, 176-79; mining, 360-61, 409, 411, 412; responsible government, 242, 253-56; Seven Years' War, 146, 160

*Novascotian*, 255, 256

*Ode to Newfoundland*, 365
Offshore fishing, 359, 396-97
Ohio River, 115, 120, 146, 147, 167
Oil, 413-14
Ojibwa Indians, 34
Okanagan, 385
Ontario: Champlain, 52-54; confederation, 306; farming, 384, 385, 386; forests, 419; hydro-electric power, 422; Loyalists, 179-80; mining, 410, 411, 412; Simcoes, 181-85
Orchards, 384, 385
"Order of Good Cheer" (*or* "Order of the Good Time"), 47, 69
Oregon, 268: boundary, 269-70; Treaty, 270
Orleans, Island of, 49, 77-82, 92, 236
Oswego, Fort, 152, 163
Ottawa, 267, 305, 377
Ottawa Indians, 161
Ottawa River, 52, 54, 61, 66, 115, 186, 237, 418
Outports, 359, 364
*Overland Limited*, 358
Oxen, 87, 88, 238, 328, 334
Oxford Lake, 224

Pacific coast, 28, 29
Pacific Scandal, 322
Panama Canal, 421
Papineau, Louis-Joseph, 251, 252, 265
Paris, Peace of, 160, 367, 368, 369
Parliament, 182, 306-7, 352
Parliament buildings, 218, 266-67
Parrtown, 176, 177
Pas, The, 127
Passamoquoddy Bay, 46, 177
Peace Conference, 348^9
Peace River, 200-1, 203, 206, 390
Peace Tower, 347
Pemmican, 195
Penn, William, 131
Pennsylvania, 120, 128, 131, 132, 147
Philadelphia, 128, 167, 173
Phips, Sir William, 109-12
Picton, 179
Pictou, 379, 398
Pie-a-pot, Chief, 324-25
Pilgrim Fathers, 130, 131
Pioneers, 177-79, 184-85, 238-41, 385, 386
Pittsburg, 146
Placentia, 361
Placentia Bay, 361, 367
Plains of Abraham, 154, 156, 157-58

Plains tribes, 24-25
Plattsburg, 219, 220
Ploughs, 241
Plymouth, 130
Polo, Marco, 6, 10
Pontiac, 161-64
Port Arthur, 393, 412
Port aux Basques, 361, 362
Port Colborne, 394
Port Roseway, 176-77
Port Royal, 46-48, 57, 69-71, 386
Portage La Prairie, 126
Portlock Bank, 399
Portugal, 12, 13, 43
Post Office, 307
Potomac River, 147
Poundmaker, Chief, 320, 321
Poutrincourt, Baron de, 46, 48, 69, 70
Prairie Provinces; farming, 385; growth of, 328-37; hydro-electric power, 422
Prescott, 237, 279, 373, 394
Prime minister, 307
Prinee Albert, 127
Prince Edward county, 374
Prince Edward Island, 134, 177, 396: Cartier, 14; Charlottetown Conference, 276, 304; confederation, 304-5, 314; farming, 384; fur farming, 405; responsible government, 242, 257; Treaty of Utrecht (1713), 74
Prince Rupert, 393
Prospecting, 409-11
Providence, R.I., 128
Provincial Fair (1852), 287-97
Prudhomme, Fort, 120
Puget Sound, 199
Puritan, 130

Quakers, 131
Qu'Appelle, 223, 320
Quebec (city), 102, 128; American invasion, 170-72; Cartier at, 15; founding of, 48-49, 61; Frontenac, 109-12; Kirkes' capture of, 54-55; Peace of St. Germain, 71; seat of parliament, 267; Seven Years' War, 151, 152-56, 157-61; (in 1666), 87-92
Quebec (province), 76, 396; confederation, 306; farming, 384, 386, 388; forests, 417, 419; hydro-electric power, 422, 42 3; Loyalists, 179, 180; mining, 410, 411, 412
Quebec Act, 167, 168
Quebec Conference, 304-5, 369-70
Quebec Resolutions, 305
Queen Charlotte Islands, 200, 398, 399

Queen Charlotte Strait, 199
Queenston, 215, 216, 374, 379
Queenston Heights, Battle of, 214-16
Quinte, Bay of, 54, 374

Radisson, Pierre, 94-100, 113
Railways, 286, 289, 295, 299, 300-1, 305, 314, 319, 321-26, 328-29, 342-43, 362-64, 381-82
Rainy Lake, 124, 125, 192
Rainy River, 207
Raleigh, Sir Walter, 129
Rationing, 356
Rebellion in Lower Canada, 250-52, 260
Rebellion in Upper Canada, 248-50, 260
Rebellion Losses Bill, 264-67
Recollets, 57, 118
"Red fife", 389
Red River Colony, 221-27, 301, 309-13, 388
Reformers, 247, 248, 256, 257, 262, 263, 338
Regina, 320, 321, 326, 337
*Relations*, Jesuit, 57
Reserves, 317
Responsible government, 242-57, 258-67, 369
Restigouche River, 418
Reversing Fails, 286
Revolutionary War, American, 165-74, 175-76, 188, 208-9
Rhode Island, 128, 1 30
Rice Lake, 414
Richelieu River, 50, 51, 85-86, 152, 377, 382
Richibucto, 177
Rideau Canal, 237, 377
Riel, Louis, 310-13, 318-21
"Right of search", 209-10
Riviere du Loup, 280, 282, 300
Riviere Verte, 282
Roads, 247, 271-77, 278-86, 289, 292-93, 380-82
Roberval, Sieur de, 16-17, 43, 48
Rocky Mountains; Alexander Mackenzie, 203-7; Henday, 187; La Verendryes, 127; minerals, 409
Roman Catholic Church, 5 3-54, 56-68, 113, 116, 160, 168, 251, 252, 281, 341
Roosevelt, President Franklin D., 353
Rouge, Fort, 125, 126
Rouyn, 411
Royal Canadian Air Force, 353, 354, 355
Royal Canadian Mounted Police, 315-21, 324-25, 326-27
Royal Canadian Navy, 353, 354-55
Royal North-West Mounted Police, 326
Rupert, Prince, 94, 97, 100
Rupert River, 98

[ 431 ]

Rupert's House, 102
Rupert's Land, 268, 301
Russia, 197, 270
Rust, 330

Sable Island Bank, 396
Saguenay River, 423
St. Anne's, 177
St. Boniface, 394
St. Charles, Fort, 125
St. Charles River, 87, 155
St. Clair, Lake, 211
St. Croix, 45, 46
St. Croix River, 45, 46, 49, 177
St. Francis River, 282
St. Germain, Peace of, 71
St. Ignace, 65
St. James, Fort, 206
Saint John, 134, 140: (in 1844), 285; La Tours, 71, 72, 73; Loyalists, 176, 177; railways, 301; shipping, 379, 417
St. John River, 71, 72, 74, 176, 178, 179, 284-86, 379, 417, 418
St. John's, 361, 362, 363, 367, 371, 379, 382, 396
St. Johns, Que. 382
St. Joseph, 65
St. Joseph, Fort, 120
St. Louis, 65
St. Louis, Fort, 90, 92, 120, 154
St. Louis, Lake, 236
St. Malo, 13
St. Martin's Day, 76
St. Mary's River, 186
St. Pierre, 160, 361, 368
St. Pierre Bank, 396
St. Pierre, Fort, 124, 125
St. Stephen, 177
Ste Marie, Fort, 64, 65
Sailing ships, 377-78
Salaberry, Lieutenant-Colonel de, 219
Saratoga, 174
Sarcee Indians, 34
Saskatchewan, 320, 331-36, 337, 385, 412
Saskatchewan Rebellion, 318-21, 325
Saskatchewan River, 123, 125, 127, 188, 319, 320
Saskatoon, 37, 394
Sault-au-Matelot, 172
Sault Ste Marie, 102, 113, 120, 186, 418
Saunders, Sir Charles, 153, 389
Saunders, William, 389
Savannah, 128
Scott, Thomas, 311-12, 313
Scurvy, 15-16, 17, 20

Sea-otter, 29, 198, 203
Sealing, 29, 38, 39, 358, 398
Seattle, 199
Seigneurs, 75-82, 83, 168
Selkirk, Lord, 222-27
Semple, Governor Robert, 225, 226, 227
Senate, 307
Seven Oaks, 223, 225
Seven Years' War, 146-56, 160
Seventy-Two Resolutions, 305
Severn, 102
*Shannon*, 217-18
Shawnee Indians, 211-14
Sheaffe, General, 215-16
Shelburne, 176-77
"Shining Mountains", 127
Shipshaw, 423
Simcoe, Colonel John Graves, 181-85, 297
Sirncoe, Mrs., 181-85
Simcoe, Lake, 52, 54, 183
Simpson, Sir George, 227
Sioux Indians, 126
Sitka, 268
Skeena River, 200
Slave Indians, 34
Slave River, 201, 202, 203
Smith, Donald (Lord Strathcona), 322-23, 325
Snowshoe, 32
South African War, 343
South Carolina, 128, 132, 174
Spain, 8, 12, 13, 43, 93, 118, 126, 129, 196, 197, 198-99, 269, 407
Square timber, 417
Stadacona, 14, 15, 16
Stage-coach, 380
Statute of Westminster, 350
Steam locomotive, 381-82
Steamships, 237, 293, 377-79
Steep Rock, 412
Stephen, George (Lord Mount Stephen) 322-23
Stephenville, 361, 371
Stoney Creek, 184
Strathcona, Lord, 322-23, 325
Sudbury, 343, 410, 411
Swift Current, 320, 321
Sydney, 360, 379

Tache, Archbishop, 310
Tadoussac, 102
Talon, Jean, 84-86, 90, 91, 92
Tariffs, 424
Taxes, 165
Tecumseh, 211-14
Telegraph, 289, 294

[ 432 ]

Temiscouata Portage, 282-83
Texas, 121
Thames River, 211
The Pas, 127
Thirteen Colonies, 120, 129-32, 1 35, 146, 151, 160, 165-74, 175, 179
Thompson, David, 206, 207
Thornhill, 238
Three Rivers, 66, 95, 102, 128, 384, 407
Ticonderoga, Fort, 152
Tilley, Sir Leonard, 304
Timiskaming and Northern Ontario Railway, 410
Tipi (*sometimes spelled* tepee), 24, 25, 28
Tomahawk, 27
Fonty, 118, 120
Torbay, 361, 362
Tories, 262, 303, 338
Toronto, 37, 183, 248-49, 262, 267, 287-97, 300
Totem poles, 30-31
Tour, Charles de la, 71-74
Tour, Madame de la, 71-74
Trade, 423-24
Trafalgar, Battle of, 209
Trail, 411
Trans-Canada Air Lines, 382
Transportation, 24, 30-32, 36-37
Trapping, 402-4
Travel, 372-82; airplanes, 382, 413; automobile, 382; canoe, 24, 30-32, 35, 36-37, 186, 187, 190, 191, 372-73; Cariboo Trail, 271-77; (in 1844) 278-86; railways, 286, 289, 295, 299, 300-1, 305, 314, 319, 321-26, 328-29, 342-43, 362-64, 381-82; steamships, 237, 293, 377-79; travois, 24
Travois, 24, 25
Tsimshian Indians, 34
Tupper, Sir Charles, 304
Twillingate, 359, 361

Umiak, 39, 40
Union, Act of (1841), 262
United Empire Loyalists, 175-80, 208, 373
United Nations, 349
United States of America, 10, 131, 147, 182, 184, 208-20, 250, 258, 259, 269-70, 284, 301-2, 322, 328-29, 330, 347, 349, 359, 371, 417, 419, 421
Upper Canada, 180, 181-85, 211-20, 238-41, 242, 287-97
Uranium, 356, 414
Ursulines, 61
Utrecht, Treaty of (1713), 74

Vancouver, Captain George, 199
Vancouver, 199, 268, 269, 382, 392
Vancouver, Fort, 206, 269, 270
Vancouver Island, 29, 198-99, 268, 269, 270, 271, 276, 398, 399, 409
Verendryes, La, 124-27, 186, 187
Victoria, Queen, 267, 339-41
Victoria, 271, 421
Victoria Cross, 345, 346
Victoria, Fort, 268, 269-71, 421
Vikings, see Norsemen
Ville-Marie, 62-63
Vineland, 4
Virginia, 120, 128, 129, 130, 132, 174
Voyageurs, 113, 122, 190-1, 221, 375

Wabana, 360-62
Wampum, 164
War of 1812-1814, 208-20, 376-77, 378
War of Independence, 165-74, 175-76, 208-9
Washington, George, 147-48, 173-74
Welland Canal, 377
Welland River, 215
West Coast, 28, 29, 196-207, 269-71
Wheat, 387-94
White Bay, 361
Wigwam, 25
Williamsburg, Va., 128
Wilmot, Lemuel, 257
Winnipeg, 37, 126, 227, 309, 394
Winnipeg, Lake, 125, 188, 207, 221, 223, 224, 225, 320
Winnipeg River, 125, 207, 223
Winslow, Lieutenant-Colonel John, 140, 141, 142, 143, 144
Wolfe, General James, 151-56, 157
Wolfe's Cove, 154, 155
Woods, Lake of the, 223
Woodstock, N.B., 177, 284
World War I, 344-46
World War II, 352-56, 370-71
Yale, 268, 273
Yarmouth, 177, 379
Yellowknife, 414
Yonge Street, 183, 238, 239, 248
York, 183, 214, 218, 244, 248, 374
York boat, 375
York Factory, 224
Yorktown, 174
Ypres, 344-45
Yukon, 343, 399, 410

[433]

www.ingramcontent.com/pod-product-compliance
Lightning Source LLC
Chambersburg PA
CBHW020108240426
43661CB00002B/72